Navigating Your Future Success

Third Edition

Bruce J. Colbert
University of Pittsburgh at Johnstown

BVT Publishing
Better textbooks, better prices
www.BVTPublishing.com

BVT Publishing

Better textbooks, better prices

www.BVTPublishing.com

Publisher and Managing Director: Richard Schofield
Production and Fulfillment Manager: Janai Escobedo
Senior Designer: Tim Gerlach
Typesetter: Suzanne Schmidt
Managing Editor: Anne Schofield
Proofreader: Matt Ferguson
Permissions Coordinator: Jade Elk
Ancillary Coordinator: Tiffany Koopal

eBook Value Pack ISBN: 978-1-5178-0487-9
Textbook^Plus (Loose-Leaf Bundle) ISBN: 978-1-5178-0486-2
eBook^Plus ISBN: 978-1-5178-0485-5
Loose-Leaf ISBN: 978-1-5178-0483-1
Soft Cover ISBN: 978-1-5178-0484-8

Dedication

To the loving memories of Robert and Josephine Colbert,
who taught me how to journey through life.

To all the teachers who serve as travel guides to lifelong learning
and to all the students who embrace the journey.

About the Author

Bruce Colbert is the director of the Allied Health Department at the University of Pittsburgh at Johnstown. He has authored twelve books, written several articles, and has given over three hundred invited lectures and workshops throughout the United States and Canada. Many of his workshops provide teacher training on making learning engaging and relevant to today's students. In addition, he conducts workshops on developing effective, critical, and creative thinking, stress and time management, communication, and team building. Bruce is most proud of his volunteer work with wounded veterans for the Compass Program in helping them to successfully transition into the workplace.

To the Student

A Personal Message before Beginning Your Journey

You have an opportunity to be more successful in life—academically, professionally, and personally. But where to begin? Why not start with *you*?

How can you be successful in class or at your job when you're constantly stressed out, worrying about grades or money, and short on time?

Unfortunately, stress is a part of life for all of us. You can't always control the things that cause you stress, but you can learn to control how you *react* to stress—and even how to *use it to your advantage*. You see, not all stress is bad.

You've heard it before: Attitude is everything. It sounds easy enough, but how can you keep a good attitude when you're overwhelmed? A good attitude won't make all your problems disappear, but you'd be surprised how a few simple steps can make everything less difficult.

Life is a journey. How you navigate through life determines whether it's a smooth ride as well as how far you'll get. It all begins with how you manage stress, what kind of attitude you have, and how you manage your time, money, and other resources. Think of these personal skills as parts of a car. Stress management is like the radiator, your attitude is like the oil, and your time, money, and other resources are like fuel. You won't get too far on an empty tank—but it's also important to make sure the engine doesn't overheat and that everything is well-oiled and running smoothly.

Like maintaining a car, you need to maintain your life. We'll teach you how to run your life like a well-oiled machine in the early chapters of this book. Then we'll provide you with a road map to help you navigate whatever academic and professional paths you choose to take. This interactive guide will help you develop the skills you need to have a smooth and successful journey through school, leading you to the job you deserve.

Our goal is to keep it simple—maybe even fun—so that you can enjoy and take ownership of your unique journey through life.

Safe travels!

Bruce Colbert

To the Instructor

A Personal Message to the Teacher

You are the most vital guide your students will have during their journey to improve not only their academic skills but also, more importantly, their lives. I know it is said over and over again, but in this course, *you truly can make a difference!*

This textbook is designed to interactively engage students in the reading and even more so in assessing themselves and developing personalized action plans for improvement in each behavior and skill we discuss. The writing style is conversational and follows a "read a little, do a little, test a little" pattern to keep their attention and actively involve them in the content.

It is my genuine hope that I have given you a useful tool with this textbook that will accompany you and your students along your successful journeys. While this isn't about me, there is some background that I think will help you, especially in learning from the early mistakes I made.

Sincerely,

Bruce Colbert

The Story of This Book

When I began my teaching career in the 1980s (yes, before personal computers and cell phones), I had several older students returning to school to retrain as respiratory therapists after losing their jobs in the steel mills. They were all struggling with their science courses, and as a young, inexperienced teacher, I thought, "They just aren't working hard enough." Nothing could have been further from the truth; they were each studying for several hours each day.

The issue wasn't a lack of time or effort. After personally working with the group, I identified the problem: They weren't getting much out of their study time because worry and stress were causing their minds to "race a million miles an hour," preventing them from truly focusing on the study task at hand. These students had the work ethic and the "smarts" to succeed, but stress had formed a major roadblock.

I soon learned two very important lessons that not only helped my students to succeed but also helped me in achieving success. First, I learned that the so-called *soft skills*—like stress and time management—were critical to master *first* to lay a solid foundation for success when approaching more academic skills, like those used in math, science, and other college courses. That is why this textbook focuses on developing students' soft skills to their maximum potential from the very start.

The second lesson I learned was that if you want students to make these behavioral changes, you must keep it simple, practical, and even make it fun. You must show students *why it's important* for their success to get them to commit to the change, and then give them practical steps (and not too many) to develop and enhance the desired behavior. That's what relevant learning is all about.

You will be amazed once your students learn to manage their stress and time how it will positively affect other soft skills covered in this textbook, such as their attitude, goal setting, communication, and decision-making skills—to name but a few.

Again, my best to you on your guided journey.

Brief Contents

Contents

Part One   Traveling Toward Personal Success   1

Part Two   A Road Map for Professional Success   147

7 Communication in Action: *Presenting Yourself to Others*   149

8 Group Interaction and Team Building: *Working Together Works*   177

Preface

Why This Book?

This project grew from several years of fun, interactive workshops on academic and personal success with both students and teachers. From these interactions, two main concerns stood out. First, many students felt overwhelmed and unprepared for their transition to higher education. Second, when they took academic success courses, they again became overwhelmed with all the exercises, programs with numerous steps, and information. They found it hard to sift through it all to find the most positive and immediate strategies for their new and, yes, sometimes chaotic lives. This book was written to show students how to be successful in a very tangible, interactive, and practical way—in other words, to get back to basics that work. The 3rd edition builds and improves upon the original project vision.

What Are the Goals and Guiding Principles?

The main goal is to encourage students to assess their current skills and to develop specific action plans for improvement. A secondary, though still very important, goal is for readers to *enjoy* a journey toward self-improvement. *Navigating Your Future Success* is readable and relevant to engage students in assessing their academic and workplace skills and developing a plan for success, starting with the critical foundation of stress management.

Logical Learning Outcomes

How will students do well if they are stressed out? Stress impacts all aspects of our lives and is a major barrier to success academically, professionally, and personally. In this book, students will learn to harness stress in a *positive* way and set goals intrapersonally to improve those aspects of themselves that will contribute to their external success.

This program provides:

Personal Success Skills—Internal (or intrapersonal) success skills focus on how to do well "within yourself." Stress management is followed by positive attitude, time management, goal setting, learning styles, critical and creative thinking, improving memory, and test taking.

Professional Success Skills—These skills focus on succeeding in your program and beyond. Communication, group interaction, team building, job seeking, and leadership development are all covered.

Proven Affective Teaching Techniques—This book includes exercises to facilitate positive behavioral changes. Affective teaching differs from cognitive (theory) teaching, so behavioral changes are presented succinctly to show quick, positive results that last.

In summary, this book strives to personalize the material, making it easier for students to internalize and actually use these concepts and skills during—and long after—their postsecondary education.

Why This Ordering of Chapter Topics?

Most academic success books place stress management in the middle or end; however, this text emphasizes it from the start. Many college surveys indicate that stress is the main barrier to academic success. If new students cannot manage stress and their minds race a million miles per hour, how can they go on to develop higher-level critical and creative thinking skills, set proper goals, manage their time, and study effectively? The skills presented follow a progressive, logical learning sequence.

The first six chapters focus on the student's internal success skills to "get them grounded" in the basics before moving on to higher-level skills or tasks.

- **Chapter 1**   Stress management lays the foundation for students to harness their stress in a positive manner.

- **Chapter 2**   Now they are able to set personal goals.

- **Chapter 3**   With motivating goals in mind, students begin to develop effective time management techniques.

- **Chapter 4**   To "free up" valuable study time in the midst of their busy schedules, students will sharpen their study strategies.

- **Chapter 5**   Material on learning styles, improving memory, and test taking is now added.

- **Chapter 6**   Then we "fine tune" students' higher-level skills in critical and creative thinking.

With these *intra*personal skills mastered, students are now prepared to move on to *inter*personal skills. The last four chapters deal with succeeding within the academic program and beyond.

- **Chapters 7 and 8**   Communication, group interaction, team building, and leadership development are covered.

- **Chapter 9**   A full chapter is devoted to job-seeking skills and methods to thrive in a career after graduation.

- **Chapter 10**   This chapter explores enhancing personal health and wellness as a way to ensure success academically and professionally.

While the rationale for this ordering might seem obvious, it bears repeating. You must begin to work on yourself and the foundational skills first before you can truly enhance your skills in working with others.

What's New to This Edition?

All topics are updated with the latest research while maintaining the "get to the heart of the matter" approach. The following information expands upon on the logical learning sequence of the revision and highlights the new and revised features to support the goals and guiding principles of *Navigating Your Future Success*, 3rd edition.

Effective Teaching Techniques

REVISED! Use of Effective Behavioral Change Techniques. Short, simple, and effective techniques are used so students can actually make these behavioral changes. This book does not offer the "ten steps to stress management," crowded with copious amounts of information, losing students in numerous steps and long lists. The stress management system is a simple yet highly effective two-step method.

REVISED! Personalized Assessment and Interactive Techniques. Allows students to assess their strengths and identify areas that need improvement. Each chapter begins with a behavioral assessment of their current skill level and ends with the development of personalized action plans.

REVISED! Readability and Relevant Learning. With an emphasis on approachability and practical application, this book uses a simple, conversational writing style to help students learn and personalize their strategies for skill development. The content is academically rigorous, but explanations are grounded in relatable examples and written to be easily understood by students of all levels. Each chapter explores *why* these skills are needed and *how* to develop them fully. Peppered with humor and "gee whiz" facts, this material is designed to be less theoretical and more personal.

REVISED! Managing Technology and Media. Technology trends can be a distraction or a blessing for students. This book acknowledges tools like social media and smart phones and addresses how to utilize (or limit) them effectively for academic and personal success.

Supplements & Resources

Instructor Supplements

A complete teaching package is available for instructors who adopt this book. This package includes an **online lab, instructor's manual, test bank, course management software,** and **PowerPoint™ slides.**

BVT*Lab*	An online lab is available for this textbook at www.BVTLab.com, as described in the BVT*Lab* section below.
Instructor's Manual	The instructor's manual helps first-time instructors develop the course, while offering seasoned instructors a new perspective on the material. Each section of the instructor's manual coincides with a chapter in the textbook. The user-friendly format begins by providing learning objectives and detailed outlines for each chapter. The manual then presents lecture discussions, class activities, and critical thinking questions for further discussion. Lastly, additional resources—videos, articles, websites—are listed to help instructors review the materials covered in each chapter.
Test Bank	An extensive test bank is available to instructors in both hard copy and electronic form. Each chapter has approximately 25 multiple choice, 10 true/false, 5 short answer, and 3 essay questions ranked by difficulty and style. Each question is referenced to the appropriate section of the text to make test creation quick and easy.
Course Management Software	BVT's course management software, Respondus, allows for the creation of tests and quizzes that can be downloaded directly into a wide variety of course management environments, such as Blackboard®, Web CT™, Desire2Learn®, Canvas™, and others.
PowerPoint Slides	A set of PowerPoint slides for each chapter comprised of slides covering all key topics, learning objectives, key figures and charts, and summary and conclusion slides.

Student Resources

Student resources are available for this textbook at www.BVTLab.com. These resources are geared toward students needing additional assistance, as well as those seeking complete mastery of the content. The following resources are available:

Practice Questions	Students can work through hundreds of practice questions online. Questions are multiple choice or true/false in format and are graded instantly for immediate feedback.
Flashcards	BVTLab includes sets of flashcards that reinforce the key terms and concepts from each chapter.
PowerPoint Slides	All instructor PowerPoints are available for convenient lecture preparation and for students to view online for a study recap.

BVTLab

BVTLab is an affordable online lab for instructors and their students. It includes an online classroom with a grade book and class forum, a homework grading system, extensive test banks for quizzes and exams, and a host of student study resources.

Course Setup	BVTLab has an easy-to-use, intuitive interface that allows instructors to quickly set up their courses and grade books and to replicate them from section to section and semester to semester.
Grade Book	Using an assigned passcode, students register for the grade book, which automatically grades and records all homework, quizzes, and tests.
Class Forum	Instructors can post discussion threads to a class forum and then monitor and moderate student replies.
Student Resources	All student resources for this textbook are available in digital form at BVTLab.
eBook	Students who have purchased a product that includes an eBook can download the eBook from a link in the lab. A web-based eBook is also available within the lab for easy reference during online classes, homework, and study sessions.

Customization

BVT's Custom Publishing Division can help you modify this book's content to satisfy your specific instructional needs. The following are examples of customization:

- Rearrangement of chapters to follow the order of your syllabus
- Deletion of chapters not covered in your course
- Addition of paragraphs, sections, or chapters you or your colleagues have written for this course
- Editing of the existing content, down to the word level
- Customization of the accompanying student resources and online lab
- Addition of handouts, lecture notes, syllabus, and so on
- Incorporation of student worksheets into the textbook

All of these customizations will be professionally typeset to produce a seamless textbook of the highest quality, with an updated table of contents and index to reflect the customized content.

Acknowledgments

There are so many people to acknowledge for a book of this scope. First and foremost, I want to thank Anne Schofield for her phenomenal editing skills, which enhanced the readability and, most importantly, the relatability of this book. I have worked with many editors and she is top notch. Richard Schofield deserves special thanks for believing in this project and putting together such a talented production team. My thanks to all the production staff at BVT who worked hard to produce the book, including Janai Escobedo (Production and Fulfillment Manager), Tim Gerlach (Senior Designer), Suzanne Schmidt (Typesetter), Matt Ferguson (Proofreader), Tiffany Koopal (Ancillary Coordinator), and Jade Elk (Permissions Coordinator). Finally, my special thanks to my son Jeremy, who contributed to content development, updating the "look" and especially the language and technology to reach today's students.

Note: Every effort has been made to provide accurate and current internet information in this book. However, the internet and information on it are constantly changing, so it is inevitable that some of the internet addresses listed in this textbook will change.

Contributing Author

Jeremy Colbert is a graduate with high honors of Shenandoah University with a degree in music education. He currently teaches at the Pittsburgh Music Academy, serving as chair of the Guitar Department. He has directed the Music Alive! program within the Pittsburgh Public School's award-winning "Summer Dreamers" academic camp, cofounded the Pittsburgh Summer Rock Academy, and regularly performs as a professional musician. He is a certified instructor in the Suzuki method and has taught music theory, choir, voice, piano, and guitar lessons.

Reviewers

First and foremost, a special thank you to Darin Baskin of Houston Community College for his help enhancing the 3rd edition.

Continued thanks to all the reviewers involved with the 2nd edition:

Michael Culligan, St. Petersburg College

Lisa B. Davis, Hinds Community College

Amy Johns, Moberly Area Community College

Your guidance, wisdom, and experiences honed this book into a more focused and relevant learning text. I also appreciated the encouragement along the way and the recognition of the different approach with the focus on emotional and social development.

And thanks to the reviewers who helped lay a solid foundation for this book in the 1st edition:

Glenda A. Belote, Florida International University

Michelle Buchman, Everest College

James Cebulski, University of South Florida

Philip Corbett, South University

Gigi Derballa, Asheville-Buncombe Technical Community College

Goldean Gibbs, Ohio Institute of Health Careers

Shirley Jelmo, Pima Medical Institute

Marilyn Joseph, Florida Metropolitan University

Margaret G. Kennedy, Lansing Community College

Sharon Occhipinti, Florida Metropolitan University–Tampa

Kate Sawyer, Lincoln Educational

Allison Schmaeling, Capps College

Kimber Shaw, Boise State University

Mary Silva, Modesto Junior College/ YDDC

Jill Strand, University of Minnesota–Duluth

William E. Thompson, Texas A & M–Commerce

Theresa Tuttle, ECPI College of Technology

Dr. Dale Weinbach, Miami International University of Art and Design

Katie Winkler, Blue Ridge Community College

Part One

Traveling Toward Personal Success

Stress Management

The Skill that Affects All Others

Objectives

By the end of this chapter, you will be able to:

- Explain stress
- Identify types of stress
- Analyze the causes and effects of stress
- Identify your current stress levels
- Differentiate "good stress" from "bad stress"
- Develop your own personal two-step stress management system
- Build awareness of your stress management abilities

Why Learn This Skill?

Stress management is the one foundational skill that will increase your chance of having a healthy, happy, and successful journey through life. If your stress is out of control, so are your physical and mental health, academic and job performance, decision-making, and personal relationships. Let's first look at how stress affects your academic performance. A recent Associated Press and MTV poll found that 85 percent of college students reported feeling stress *daily*. Of the students polled, 60 percent reported feeling so stressed out that on one or more occasions they could not complete their assignments. Therefore, mastery of this skill is critical to your future academic success.

Many stress management systems are complicated and difficult to use. Have you ever read an article claiming to contain twenty steps to a stress-free life? First, there is no such thing as a stress-free life. Second, if you're already overwhelmed, just the idea of a twenty-step process is stressful! This text was created to provide a simpler, more realistic two-step system.

Another problem with stress management systems is that they're supposed to work for everyone even though each of us is unique. Just because a particular method worked for the professional speaker who developed the program does not mean it will work for a student who is juggling multiple roles, such as being an employee, a student, and a single parent. By reading this chapter and completing the exercises within, you will develop a simple and effective stress management system that will work for *you* in your academic, personal, and professional life.

1.1   Introduction

Going to school and learning should be a positive and uplifting experience, but a lack of good stress management skills can make you feel like the panda in the "after" picture in Figure 1-1 below. If you can relate, think about the following questions: Is the "after" picture how you really want to feel for a substantial portion of your life? Do you think you will make good decisions, perform well academically, or even feel well if you spend most of your time feeling like the "after" picture? Also consider the effect of consistently going home to your loved ones looking like the "after" picture. What might that do to your personal relationships? Keep this picture in your mind as you travel through this book.

1.2   Relax—Stress Is Manageable

This book starts with stress management for one very important reason: Whether you are a recent high school graduate or someone going back to school later in life, whether you are attending a four-year university or a community college, whether you are a young adult experiencing independence from your parents for the first time or a parent yourself, we all deal with stress. Many college surveys indicate that stress is the main barrier to academic success. If you are overwhelmed by stress, you won't be able to think critically and creatively, set goals, manage your time, or study effectively. You may mistakenly believe you simply need to work on your time management or study skills when really the first thing you must do is get your stress levels under control. Once you have learned how to manage your stress, you can begin to develop the other skills necessary for success in college and beyond.

Figure 1-1   Can you relate?

Before Work/School

After Work/School

1.3   What Is Stress?

We all deal with stress, but it doesn't have to rule your life. Stress management is both possible and necessary for success, and this book is designed to help you. In fact, beyond simply *managing* your stress, it's also possible to *turn your stress to your advantage*. You may not realize it now, but stress isn't always a bad thing. That said, before you can learn to use stress for success, you first need to understand what stress is all about. This chapter provides an understanding of stress that will serve as the foundation for your personalized stress management system. Instead of letting stress work against you, you will learn to make it to work for you.

What is stress? One of the common misconceptions about stress is that we need to wipe it out of our lives, and our goal should be to become "stress free." Nothing could be further from the truth. Stress is needed for our very existence, and there are several examples of good stress. A physiological example of good stress is the "fight-or-flight" response that kicks in when emergencies occur. Your body senses the stress brought on by danger and prepares you for action. You feel your heart begin to race and your body undergoes several physical changes to prepare to face the perceived threat. This kind of stress is an important survival response—one we can't, and shouldn't, get rid of.

Mental stress can also be good. Riding a rollercoaster or watching a horror film can be a stressful experience, but these are activities we do for fun. Similarly, engaging in challenging coursework can be stressful, but it's how we learn and grow and, ultimately, the experience should be rewarding. The stress of a deadline can motivate you to work instead of procrastinating, and the stress of a new experience, like going to college, doesn't diminish its value. But if stress isn't all bad, then what should the goal of stress management be? Stress management, we will soon discover, is about walking the fine line between good stress for optimal performance and bad stress, where your performance is greatly impaired. In other words, good stress is when you hype yourself up for the game and bad stress is when you take yourself out of the game.

Before you begin to develop your stress management system, it is important to get a baseline assessment of your current stress levels. In Exercise 1-1, let's find out where you are now to see how much you can improve in the coming months and years once you begin to use this simple system in your day-to-day life.

1.4   A Working Definition

So, what *is* the best definition of stress? If you read books on stress, you will find many different definitions. According to the American Institute of Stress, Hans Selye, the father of stress theory, defined stress as "the nonspecific response of the body to a demand made upon it." Let's try to define stress in a more user-friendly way. We have already established that some stress is needed, both physically and mentally. However, at times, we let this stress get out of control. When that happens, instead of helping us, stress causes serious harm. Based on this, the best way to define stress is in terms of how our bodies and minds *react* to stress. Here's our working definition of the **stress reaction**: how our minds and bodies react to events, people, and situations in our lives, largely shaped by our perceptions.

Stress reaction

How our minds and bodies react to events, people, and situations in our lives, largely shaped by our perceptions

Exercise 1-1   Baseline Assessment: *Your Stress Number*

Rate the following statements with numbers
1 through 4 as follows:

1 = Rarely   3 = Frequently
2 = Sometimes   4 = Always

_____ 1.   I have low energy and feel tired.

_____ 2.   I worry a lot about problems or how
               things are going to turn out.

_____ 3.   I can spot all the things others are
               doing wrong.

_____ 4.   I feel the need to be perfect at what I do.

_____ 5.   I skip my workout/exercise sessions.

_____ 6.   I feel sad.

_____ 7.   My mind goes a million miles per hour.

_____ 8.   I take on everyone else's problems.

_____ 9.   I try to control other people.

_____ 10.   I feel like I can't do anything right.

_____ 11.   I avoid risks for fear of failure.

_____ 12.   I let my work pile up.

_____ 13.   I feel like I'm being pulled in all directions.

_____ 14.   I have a pessimistic attitude.

_____ 15.   I get tension headaches.

_____ 16.   I have a difficult time sleeping.

_____ 17.   I overreact to situations.

_____ 18.   I feel guilty if I relax and do nothing.

_____ 19.   I lose my sense of humor.

_____ 20.   I get angry easily over little things.

Now add up your answers and see where you
stand: _____

60–80:   This chapter could be a life-changing
            experience.

50–59:   Your stress is out of control, and you
            desperately need this material.

40–49:   Your stress is causing problems for you,
            and you would gain moderate benefit
            from this chapter.

30–39:   Stress is affecting you, and this chapter will
            help with the stress in your life.

20–29:   You are doing pretty well, but this chapter
            can help you do better.

Mind–Body Connection   Let's take a closer look at this definition. Notice how it begins with "how our minds and bodies react…" This shows the close relationship is between the body (physiologic responses) and the mind (psychological responses). You may have read elsewhere that heart and lung disease are among the top illnesses affecting people in the United States. However, think about *why* many individuals develop heart or lung disease. Much of lung disease is caused by smoking, which is an unhealthy response to stress. Likewise, heart disease is often caused by poor diet, smoking, and lack of exercise. These are all the unhealthy habits of someone who doesn't properly handle stress in his or her life. Just think about the following common statements as they relate to stress and the mind–body connection:

- I couldn't catch my breath.

- My heart was racing.

- My brain was fried.

- My stomach was twisted in knots.

Our Perceptions Define Our Stress Now let's continue on with the rest of the definition: "… react to events, people, and situations in our lives, largely shaped by our perceptions." Notice the words *our perceptions*. We can drive this point home using the example of donating blood. Take a look at the pictures of the two first-time volunteer blood donors in Figure 1-2.

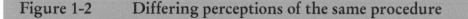

| Figure 1-2 | Differing perceptions of the same procedure |

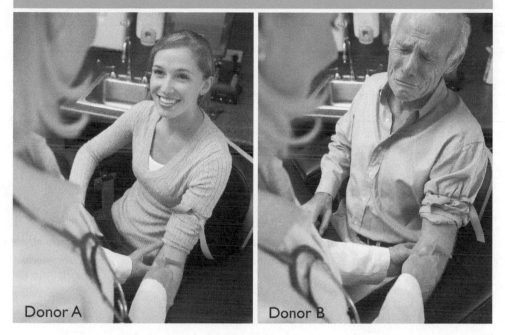

Donor A

Donor B

Donor A is calm and relaxed throughout the whole procedure and even smiles and jokes with the technician. Donor B is highly stressed, sweaty, and in general a "nervous wreck" throughout the whole procedure. However, both patients had the *same* procedure with the *same* technician in the *same* environment. You would think their reactions would be exactly the same. Why is there a difference in their reactions?

The answer is that their perceptions were different. Obviously, the perception of the first donor was more positive, whereas the second donor was full of dread. The way you look at a situation has a big effect on how you feel about it. If you look at giving blood as a positive experience ("I get to help people!"), you will feel better about doing it. If you look at it as a negative experience ("They're going to stick me with a needle!"), you won't feel as good.

Keep in mind that most stress occurs as a result of how we *interpret* and *react* to a situation, person, or event—not solely because of the situation, person, or event itself. It is sometimes hard to admit that we cause most of our stress, but the good news is that if we do cause it, then we can actually control it.

Hans Selye developed many of the terms associated with stress. He referred to anything that causes stress as a "stressor" or "trigger." It's important to become aware of the stressors in your life in order to learn to manage them. Give Exercise 1-2 a try.

List and describe the top three stressors or triggers in your life.

1. _____
   _____

2. _____
   _____

3. _____
   _____

1.5   Types of Stress

We've established that stress is a physical and emotional reaction based on our perceptions. Let's further define stress to include two broad categories: *external stress* and *internal stress.* Keep in mind, the more we learn about stress, the better we can manage it.

1.5a   External Stressors

External stressors are things *outside* of you, and they include your environment, social interactions, major life events, and daily hassles. Sometimes these things are beyond our control, but we can control how we react to them. Please see Table 1-1 for examples of some external stressors in our lives.

1.5b   Internal Stressors

Internal stressors are things *inside* of us—like our thoughts—and they include things like being pessimistic or too self-critical as well as our habits and personality traits. These thinking styles are examples of the internal "mind talk" we engage in. You'll read more about mind talk elsewhere in the book, including information on just how powerful this internal dialogue can be and how it can either help you grow or hurt you. For example, someone who is a perfectionist might have unrealistic expectations for him- or herself. Any time perfectionists make mistakes, they tend to engage in self-critical mind talk. Instead of helping them grow, this can cause a great deal of negative stress as the perfectionist dreads the next mistake. Please see Table 1-2 for some more examples of internal stressors.

Table 1-1   Examples of External Stressors

External Stressors	Examples
Environment	Noise, heat, bright lights, confined spaces
Social interaction	Bad relationships, aggressive interactions, new social situations
Major life event	Starting school, moving, getting married, getting divorced, job loss or change, family sickness or death
Daily hassle	Commuting to work or school, car repairs, paying bills

Table 1-2   Examples of Internal Stressors

Internal Stressors	Examples
Habits	Lack of restful sleep and exercise, smoking, drug abuse
Personality traits	Workaholic, perfectionist, people-pleaser
Negative thinking styles	Pessimistic, self-critical, rigid thinking, racing mind

1.6   Harmful Effects of Stress

It is a fact of life that we all have temporary stressors that are both external and internal in nature. Currently, you may be studying for that big exam, deciding on your career path, going on a job interview, or having a major issue impact your life. The question is, will you handle your temporary stressors and turn them into a positive experience? Let's first explore what happens if you cannot—the harmful effects of stress. We will then finish this chapter by learning how to face stress in a positive way, giving you the tools to properly manage stress.

1.6a   Chronic Stress

No matter what the change or challenge may be, it is important that you do not let stress adversely affect your performance and health. It is especially dangerous when you remain in a chronic (long-term) state of stress. *Chronic stress* equals poor performance, poor decisions, and poor health. It can affect you physically, mentally, emotionally, and behaviorally.

Physical symptoms of chronic stress can include sweating, muscle aches, digestive problems, loss of appetite, headache, and dizziness, to name just a few. *Mentally,* chronic stress manifests itself as anxiousness, forgetfulness, confusion, panic attacks, and loss of humor. *Emotional changes* include anxiety, nervousness, fear, irritability, impatience, and even depression. *Behavioral changes* may include increased alcohol intake, appetite changes, smoking and drug abuse, restlessness, nail-biting, and increased aggressiveness. Do any of these sound familiar?

Chronic stress has been related to conditions such as heart disease, depression, ulcers, and migraine headaches. Some say it is the leading cause of health problems in our hectic, high-paced society. Look at some of these facts concerning stress:

- Chronic stress has been shown to weaken the immune system.
- It is estimated that heart disease causes over a third of all deaths in the United States. Stress can play a major role in this disease.
- The majority of heart attacks occur on Monday mornings.
- The stress-related disorder of hypertension (high blood pressure) is estimated to affect as many as sixty-five million Americans.
- Research shows that stress plays a role in osteoporosis in women.
- Chronic high levels of stress can contribute to weight gain

1.6b   Stress and the Workplace

Stress also has major effects in the workplace. According to the National Institute for Occupational Safety and Health (NIOSH), job-related stress generates more health complaints than other life stressors. Studies cited on the American Institute of Stress website indicate 80 percent of workers feel stress on the job and nearly half say they need help in managing their stress.

1.6c   Stress and Academic Performance

One of the reasons why stress management should be the first behavior addressed for students adjusting to college is its relationship to academic performance. A groundbreaking research study conducted by the University of Minnesota's Boynton Health Service surveyed 9,931 students at fourteen different two- and four-year schools. They compared academic performance (as measured by GPA) to health problems such as stress and poor habits such as smoking, drinking, and gambling. It is not surprising they discovered students with unhealthy behaviors had significantly lower GPAs.

Furthermore, the study showed stress to be one of the *biggest* factors related to a lower GPA. Of the 69.9 percent of students who reported they were stressed, 32.9 percent said that stress was hurting their academic performance. The good news in the study was that students who said they were able to handle their stress effectively performed much better than those who said they couldn't. The main researcher in the study, Dr. Ehlinger, said, "If students can manage their stress, then their stress level will not matter."

Food for Thought

It is estimated that $300 billion is spent annually in the United States on stress-related compensation such as workers' compensation claims, reduced productivity, absenteeism, accidents, and medical/insurance costs (American Institute of Stress)

1.7   Good Stress versus Bad Stress

Hans Selye was once quoted as saying "stress is the spice of life." His quote was meant to show that without stress, progress is rarely achieved, and additionally that boredom itself can become stressful due to a lack of progress. Selye used the term *eustress* to describe positive stress. "Eu" means easy or normal. Conversely, Selye used the term *distress* for negative stress. We are going to simplify things and use the terms **good stress** and **bad stress** instead. *Good stress* refers to the stress necessary to progress and succeed through life. *Bad stress* is the overwhelming and counterproductive stress that weighs us down.

Good stress

Stress that is necessary to progress and succeed; also known as *eustress*

Bad stress

Stress that is overwhelming and counterproductive; also known as *distress*

1.7a   Stay in *Your* Zone

The main goal of this chapter is to help you develop a personalized system to keep you in your "good stress zone" so you can perform at your best in school, at your job, and in life. First, it's important to recognize your personal stressors and the way it feels when your stress is out of balance or, in other words, when you have entered your "bad stress zone." How do you, individually, react to too much stress? If you can recognize these warning signs in yourself, it's easier to identify when your stress levels are too high, making it possible to manage them. Notice we are not focusing as much on the triggers. That's because life circumstances and the stress they cause will always come and go. It's more practical to focus on how stress makes you feel physically and mentally. Seeing these feelings for what they are—signs that you're too stressed—is valuable for your health and can keep you maintain a positive attitude even when life gets hard. Your reaction to stress is a wake-up call that says you need to cope with what's going on in your life before it overtakes you.

Let's revisit the notion that not all stress is bad for you. Survival stress is an important and necessary stress. If confronted by a life-threatening event, your fight-or-flight response will kick in. In other words, your body gets ready to either fight or flee the dangerous situation. In a true emergency, this response can maximize your chance for survival.

In your everyday life, stress can motivate you to get things done. It can be difficult to work on large assignments well before the deadline (even if you know you should), but once that due date starts approaching, you probably find your motivation to work is much higher. A little bit of stress is good for you while performing important tasks. The key is finding a balance.

Food for Thought

There are many stories of people performing herculean feats when their fight-or-flight response, or adrenaline rush, kicked in. Stories include people of average strength lifting cars to save someone trapped underneath or carrying items such as refrigerators while running from a fire.

1.7b   Good Stress

Stress is often unavoidable when it comes to everyday events such as a big exam, a job interview, or giving a speech in front of the class. But can it also be helpful for succeeding in these tasks? Studies show that you actually perform better if you have moderate stress and are not totally "cool as a cucumber." If you are not under enough stress, your performance may suffer because you are bored or unmotivated. However, if you let stress get out of hand and you panic, you have entered into the bad stress zone. In the bad stress zone, your anxiety rises to the point where you perform poorly or worse, not at all.

1.7c   Bad Stress

As already stated, a certain amount of stress is normal. We need it to develop and grow. However, going beyond your good stress zone and entering your bad stress zone can be harmful. You need to be able to identify when this is happening. The best way is to look for physical and emotional signs that the stress is getting to be too much for you. From our previous discussion on the harmful effects of stress, it should be clear what high levels of bad stress can cause. It's no wonder that individuals who don't know how to manage their stress have more accidents, poorer attendance, and difficulty studying and learning. If bad stress persists and becomes long-term (or chronic), it can become destructive. The American Institute of Stress lists several effects of stress in the *bad zone*, including:

- High blood pressure, heart attack, or stroke
- Stomach pain
- Lack of sleep or insomnia
- Decreased immune system functioning
- Depression and personality changes
- Problems with learning
- Frequent headaches

Real-Life Application
Preventive Medicine and Early Intervention

For a long time, doctors waited until people got sick to treat them. However, recently, *preventive medicine*—treating people in a way that stops them getting sick in the first place—has gained a lot of attention. Tension headaches indicate you have been in your bad stress zone for some time. But what if you could identify that you were in your bad stress zone before the headaches became a problem? If you could identify earlier signals that precede a headache, you could take steps to prevent many headaches from ever happening. One thing to look for is nervous habits such as biting fingernails, pulling your hair, shaking your leg, or clicking your pen. These are usually early signs that you have just entered your bad stress zone. If you intervene right away, you can prevent yourself from developing more serious problems like headaches. This self-awareness is often difficult because many of these habits are so automatic that we just ignore them. Try to be more aware of these habits. If you can catch yourself shaking your leg, it's possible to prevent the subsequent muscle tightness, upset stomach, and headache that may follow.

1.8   Your Two-Step Stress Management System

Now that you have some background information about stress, you can develop your personalized stress management system. Take your time with each step, and remember that this system will evolve over time and with continued use.

1.8a   Step 1: Become Aware of Your Good and Bad Stress Zones

It's time to take the first step in our two-step process for creating a personal stress management system. Here you will learn to become aware of your individual good and bad stress zones. Exercise 1-3 will help you recognize your good stress zone.

Exercise 1-3   Determining Your Good Stress Zone

Write at least three adjectives or phrases that describe you when you are in "your good stress zone." Write more if you can think of them because the better you describe and know your good stress zone, the more likely you are to spend more time there. In other words, select words that describe you when you are functioning well, running on all cylinders, hitting your peak, and so on. To get you thinking, some adjectives may include *happy, focused,* and a *sense of humor.* Phrases may include "I'm more productive when I feel…" or "I feel more motivated when I'm…" Remember, choose words that best describe you when you are doing well in *your* life.

_____

_____

_____

_____

_____

_____

Keep these words and phrases in mind because we will soon use them to develop your personalized stress management system.

You defined your good stress zone in Exercise 1-3. Now, in Exercise 1-4, let's go on to develop awareness of your bad stress zone. Then we can discuss how to stay in the good zone and avoid the bad.

List several (as many as you can) mental *and* physical changes that occur when you are in your bad stress zone. In other words, come up with a list of things that happen to your body and mind when you are "losing it," not running on all cylinders, and not functioning well. To jog your memory, some possible examples could include stomachaches, forgetfulness, nervous habits, eye twitching, making mistakes, irritability, headaches, or muscular tension. Remember to list your own responses. Some may be the same as the examples given, but they must relate to *your* life.

_____

_____

_____

_____

_____

_____

You have now developed a contrasting picture of your good and bad stress zones from Exercises 1-3 and 1-4, but we need to take it just a little further. In Exercise 1-5, you will develop your personal stress chart. This will give you a complete picture of both your good and bad stress zones. In addition, it will allow you to see how your reaction to stress goes from bad to worse so you can intervene early to return to your good stress zone. See Figure 1-3 for an example of one of the author's stress charts.

Figure 1-3   Example of completed stress chart

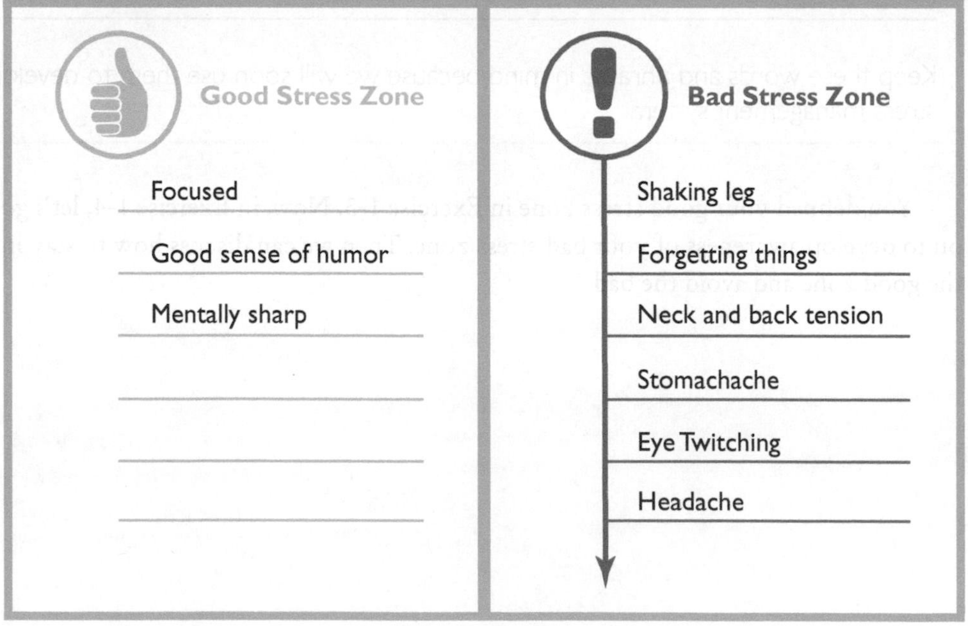

Good Stress Zone	Bad Stress Zone
Focused	Shaking leg
Good sense of humor	Forgetting things
Mentally sharp	Neck and back tension
	Stomachache
	Eye Twitching
	Headache

Exercise 1-5   Making Your Personal Stress Chart

Using Figure 1-4, place your descriptions from Exercise 1-3 in the Good Stress Zone. Now look at your list from your bad stress zone (Exercise 1-4) and place the items in *chronological* order starting with what occurs first when you just begin to enter your bad stress zone. You can also compare your chart to Figure 1-3, which shows a completed stress chart as an example.

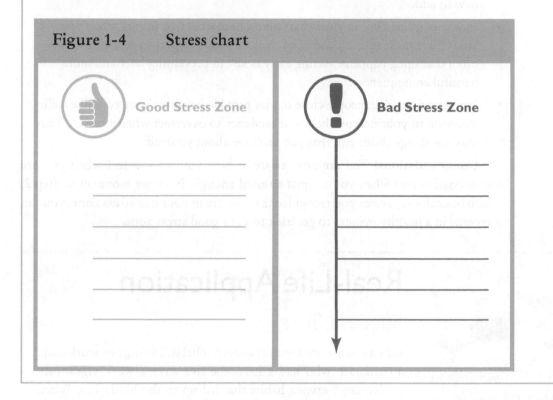

Figure 1-4   Stress chart

Good Stress Zone

Bad Stress Zone

You have now completed Step 1 of the process. Your personalized stress management system can help you recognize when you are in your good stress zone. Most importantly, it will show you how to recognize when you are beginning to enter your bad stress zone so you can quickly intervene to prevent further bad things from happening.

For example, look at Figure 1-3. If the author intervenes as soon as his leg starts shaking, he can quickly go back into the good stress zone. If he doesn't intervene, he will move further down the line to more serious consequences like forgetting things and getting a stiff neck. If he still doesn't intervene, he might wind up with a stomach- or headache.

People who get frequent tension headaches (four or five a week) have used this system to reduce their headaches down to one or even *none* a week. By recognizing the early warning signals—such as shaking their leg or rolling their neck because of tension—and doing something about their stress, they are able to get things under control before their stress results in a headache.

Please note that your stress chart will continue to develop over time. Here are some helpful hints:

- As stated previously, a nervous habit such as tapping a pen, shaking a leg, or biting your nails is an early warning sign you are entering your bad stress zone.

- Make sure your list contains both mental and physical signs of stress.

- Review your stress chart every few months to see if you discovered something new to add.

- Pick something later in your chart (like a headache) that occurs when you are at your most stressed and keep track of your progress in reducing how often that thing happens. Acting early is key to preventing later and more harmful consequences.

- Pay attention when people close to you provide insights about you, like calling attention to your nervous habits or tendency to overreact when stressed. They may see things about you that you can't see about yourself.

Congratulations! You are now aware of how you act and feel when you are too stressed versus when you are just stressed enough. Now we move on to Step 2, which basically says once you recognize that you are in your bad stress zone, you can intervene in a healthy manner to get back to your good stress zone.

Real-Life Application
Success Story

Often you are not aware of a nervous habit. During one workshop, an attendee who had a headache five days a week vigorously denied any nervous habits that led up to the headaches. When pressed, she began to click her pen very quickly. Even as she was doing so, she continued to deny any nervous habits. That is, until the pen clicking was brought to her attention. She said, "I didn't even know I was doing that." Then a friend said, "Yes, and you always chew on your hair when you're stressed out," and a coworker said, "You drive me crazy when you tap your pencil and grind your jaw." In fifteen minutes, she had a fully developed stress chart with many early indicators that could signal an alarm to intervene before her headache began. Within six months, she indicated she was down to one to two tension headaches per week! What a positive change in her quality of life!

1.8b   Step 2: Perform a Healthy Intervention

Notice the word *healthy*. If every time you enter your bad stress zone, you drink alcohol, take other drugs, or reach for something to eat, you can develop addictions. That is an unhealthy way to cope with stress. So, what are the healthy options? There are many, and they depend on your particular situation. This chapter ends with some ideas for what to do when you know you're in your bad stress zone. Please note that not all of these will work for any given situation; they are presented here to give you options to think about as a starting point.

Exercise   Physical exercise relieves stress. The type of exercise is up to you and can be as simple as taking a brisk walk. If you are more physically fit, you may want to include jogging, bicycling, or lifting weights. Finding a good workout partner or participating in team sports increases the likelihood that you'll work out regularly because socializing makes exercising more fun.

Aerobic exercise also releases *endorphins*, which are the body's natural pain killers and mood-elevating chemicals. Exercise can be used on a regular basis to help *prevent* you from entering your bad stress zone. It can also be used when you find yourself crossing into the bad stress zone and just need to take a brisk walk to clear your mind.

Of course, you can't always drop everything while at work or taking a test and just begin exercising when things get stressful. This is why it is important to have a variety of options to choose from for any particular situation. People who have office jobs and spend a lot of time sitting at the computer can do certain office exercises, such as periodically stretching to help relieve their tension. Some workplaces even have office aerobics and exercise sessions built into the workday.

Nutrition and Sleep   Good health practices such as getting enough sleep and eating healthy food increase the probability that you will remain in your good stress zone even when stressors do come your way. It's like hydrating yourself before physical exercise instead of waiting until you are dying of thirst. Sleep is a must for us to function and handle stress. Research has shown that lack of sleep makes you more susceptible to illness, more irritable, and less able to focus. Health experts recommend that most adults get between seven and nine hours of sleep a night.

When you get run down because of sleep deprivation or poor nutrition, every little stressor will send you into your bad stress zone, and it may be difficult to escape. Remember what happens when people stay in their bad stress zone for extended periods of time? It can create chronic stress, which can lead to high blood pressure, diabetes, and heart attacks, to name just a few possible outcomes.

Good nutrition is a must for our growth and development. It also helps to fight bad stress and disease. One part of practicing good nutrition is to drink plenty of water. Water makes up the majority of our body, and it aids in digestion, absorption of nutrients, and removal of waste products. Although water is found in most foods, drink at least six to eight glasses each day for good health.

Caffeine, found in coffee, tea, and many sodas, is a potent stimulant—it makes you feel energized. However, large amounts can make you anxious and nervous and can prevent you from getting a good night's sleep. Maintaining a well-balanced diet, and ingesting caffeine in moderation, is important for your long-term health.

Time Off   Taking time off from work or school helps you deal with stress in a positive way. Both the body and mind need to get away and recharge their batteries. Getting lost in a hobby or listening to your favorite music can slow down your mind. Slowing down your mind can help you take a calmer look at what's causing your stress and move you back into your good stress zone.

Did you ever have a major problem come into your life and the more you focused on it, the more stressed and emotional you became with no solution in sight? It is hard to come up with ideas and use good decision-making skills in this frame of mind. Even taking fifteen minutes for yourself can help greatly. When life gets busy, you might find it hard to make time for yourself. If you are responsible for taking care of others, this can make it even harder. Reach out to people in your life who support you and remember that if you are in your good stress zone, you won't just be a better student—you'll be a better parent, spouse, sibling, friend, or coworker too.

When a problem is causing unrelenting stress, take a break and get away from the problem by doing something else. In many cases, the solution will then come to you as if by magic. It's not magic, just your subconscious mind working for you. You'll read more about this later. Basically, by stepping away from the problem and distracting yourself with a hobby or music, you are calming your mind, and a calmer mind may be better able to come up with the solution.

Humor Therapy   It has been estimated that children laugh a hundred times a day. Maybe there is a lot to be learned from children. How often do you think adults laugh each day? How often do *you* laugh?

Humor also has psychological effects, such as helping to resolve problems and to reduce stress and anxiety. You have probably been in a stressful situation with other people when a joke broke the ice. Humor therapy is even used to enhance some medical treatments. It is often said that "laughter is the best medicine."

There are several techniques you can use to add humor to your life. One of the most effective tools is to simply *smile* and laugh out loud more often. Look for humor in every situation you can, and don't be afraid to laugh at yourself. At the same time, always remember to take your study and work responsibilities seriously.

The next time you are on hold, or dealing with one of those frustrating automated telephone menus, or in a traffic jam and beginning to tense up and stress out—put a big smile on your face. You will find it is nearly impossible to feel bad when you are smiling. This will prevent something that is out of your control from ruining the rest of your day. Try it now with Exercise 1-6 to demonstrate its effectiveness.

Exercise 1-6   A Simple Method That Works Wonders

You can either do this alone or with a partner. Place a big smile on your face and try to be angry or think a bad thought. Write a description of how it worked for you.

_____

_____

Try this next time you feel yourself getting tense or worked up about something. Simply sit back and place a huge smile on your face. Sometimes the simple techniques are the most effective.

Social Support   Social support in the form of friends, family, loved ones, or clubs and organizations can all help with stress relief. Be careful because interactions with people can also cause bad stress. However, all you need to do is remain *aware* of your early stress signals, and if you notice any, do *something positive* to get you back to your good stress zone.

Although social support can be very positive, it is always good to keep in good touch with *yourself*. Do Exercise 1-7, which helps you vent safely about whatever may be causing you stress.

Exercise 1-7   Venting

Is there something happening that you perceive as unfair? Do you have a friend with a personality trait that drives you crazy? Is an upcoming event stressing you out? Using a recording device, talk to yourself about it. Make a recording of yourself talking about this problem as if you were venting to a trusted friend. Be honest, be brutal, but be yourself. Get it all out. Then let a few hours or a day go by, and *listen* to yourself. How does the problem sound to you now? Does it seem as important or "vent-worthy" as it did before? And how do *you* sound to yourself? Would you sympathize with yourself? Major leap of faith: Would you let someone you trust listen to this recording? Talking with a close friend and journal writing can be two additional and very effective ways to vent.

Relaxation Techniques   Practicing relaxation techniques will help to clear your mind and make you sharper. Many people will find a million excuses why they can't take the time to relax. Do you see the problem this sets up? If someone is that busy, then they especially need to take the time to relax and restore their body and mind or life will continue to be crazy. Just remember, if you use your cell phone a lot, you must take the time to recharge it in order for it to work. You need to recharge yourself as well. The time you take to do so allows you to listen to your body. Two types of effective relaxation techniques include breathing relaxation and meditation techniques.

Slow and deep breathing serves several purposes. First, it increases oxygen to your brain and your body, helping them work properly. It also slows your thinking to help clear your head and relax your muscles. Here is a breathing relaxation technique to try:

First, find an area with few or no distractions (noise, interruptions, etc.). You can sit in a favorite chair (recliners work best) or even lie on your bed and use this technique before going to sleep if you can't find the time during the day. Sometimes, this may even make you fall asleep, which is good because you will get a much more restful and restorative sleep. Now that you have your area, get comfortable and do the following:

1. Close your eyes and have your palms face upward.

2. Take a *slow* and *deep* breath in through your nose and out through your mouth. When you breathe in, your stomach should slowly rise (not your chest) and it should then slowly sink when you breathe out. You can put one hand over your stomach to make sure you are doing this correctly until you get used to it.

3. Continue breathing slowly and deeply, concentrating on your breathing and nothing else (thoughts might enter your mind, but simply acknowledge them and go back to concentrating on your breathing).

4. Once you are comfortable doing this, add some visual imagery. For example, as you slowly breathe *out,* visualize all the tension in your body leaving with your exhaled breath.

This is a basic relaxation technique, and with practice, you can eventually do one or two deep cleansing breaths when tension rises and feel immediate relief within only a minute. Breathing becomes important when your demanding schedule is causing stress and you need to take a quick refreshing pause. In addition, you'll see in the upcoming chapter on Learning Styles, Memory, and Test Taking how this one-minute technique can help when you begin to "stress" while taking that big exam. However, try to do at least ten slow deep breaths in the beginning until you get comfortable with the technique.

Meditation   Meditation basically means slowing your mind down and clearing it of thoughts. Techniques can vary greatly, but they all center around attempting to focus your mind on one thing and ignoring everything else. This one thing can be your breathing, as you just learned. It can also be an object, phrase, or even a positive thought.

Yoga deals with the study of meditation and has been around for centuries. Although many people think of yoga as all those bent and stretched postures, the main focus of all yoga practices revolves around breathing and clearing your mind. The physical benefits achieved through the postures paired with the relaxation of the mind's internal chatter can be quite powerful and, more importantly, peaceful. It may be an interesting and relaxing experience to take part in yoga or tai chi (meditation in movement) classes. Many schools or local community centers such as the YMCA offer these classes either free or at low cost. Remember, consistency is key in any practice.

Now that you have developed *your* stress chart and can recognize when you are entering your bad stress zone, use the upcoming Chapter Summation (Exercise 1-8) to list a few things you can do to get you back into your good stress zone. It may be something from this chapter or it may be something unique to you. Pick what works for you. It is also a good idea to pick interventions for different environments and have a "pocketful" ready for any situation. For example, you may have a "walk in the woods" as a healthy way to deal with stress. However, when the stress is mounting during an exam, this isn't something you can do. Instead, focusing on your breathing might help.

Examples of healthy ways to deal with stress.

Healthy Decision-Making

Mary has been out of school for several years and is a single parent. She has decided to go back to school to better her life and has been accepted for the fall semester, which is three months away. She has been reading about how much her program stresses critical and creative thinking skills, and she is concerned that she gets too stressed out to think clearly at times. In addition, she has attempted several study schedules but gets overwhelmed and very anxious and is unable to stick to them. What would you recommend Mary do prior to the start of school to give her a more hopeful outlook and maximize her chance of succeeding in school?

_____

_____

_____

_____

_____

_____

_____

_____

_____

Explain how using an effective stress management system can change your life.

_____

_____

_____

_____

_____

_____

_____

Describe your good stress zone.

_____

_____

_____

_____

_____

List three early indicators you have entered your bad stress zone.

_____

_____

_____

_____

_____

_____

List and describe several interventions (ways of dealing with stress), so you can have them ready in any given situation or environment.

An exercise choice:

_____

A step you will take toward better nutrition:

_____

A way to improve your sleep habits:

_____

A hobby:

_____

Your favorite relaxing music:

_____

Your favorite type of humor or favorite comedian:

_____

Your social and family supports:

_____

A favorite relaxation technique:

_____

At least one intervention for work or school:

_____

At least one intervention at home:

_____

NOTE: You may want to keep this list handy so you can pick out something that would help you at that "stressful" moment. Eventually you won't need the list because you will automatically respond with a healthy and effective intervention when your stress alarm goes off.

Know Your School

Your school will have support services to help you in many areas. Research and find what school resources can help you with stress management. One example would be counseling services. Others include student health services, resident advisers, and clergy. Check out school or community offerings of classes on yoga and meditation. List the information here, and for quick reference, place the information in a prominent place such as on your refrigerator.

Resource Name: _____

Office Location: _____

Phone Number: _____

Email Address: _____

Resource Name: _____

Office Location: _____

Phone Number: _____

Email Address: _____

Resource Name: _____

Office Location: _____

Phone Number: _____

Email Address: _____

Resource Name: _____

Office Location: _____

Phone Number: _____

Email Address: _____

Resource Name: _____

Office Location: _____

Phone Number: _____

Email Address: _____

Positive Attitudes and Goals

Preparing Your Mind for Success

Objectives

By the end of this chapter, you will be able to:

- Appreciate the power of your mind
- Determine your *locus of control*
- Reframe your thinking
- Identify and prioritize your values
- Maintain a positive attitude
- Set SMART goals
- Demonstrate the relationship between your values and goals
- Create goals to support your academic and personal success

Why Learn This Skill?

Why does attitude matter? Simply put, *attitude and self-motivation directly determine your academic and professional success*. If you have a positive attitude and are motivated to learn, you have a head start on a productive career. One characteristic that successful people share is a positive attitude. In addition, people with positive attitudes have been shown to have a more responsive immune system.

Keeping a positive outlook can sometimes be tough because we are constantly bombarded by negative messages and thoughts (just watch the news!). As you journey through life, outside messages and internal thoughts can begin, like seeds, to grow and thrive in our minds. Our minds are like gardens where, if we care for them properly, we can grow healthy fruit. If weeds take root, however, the garden can quickly become overgrown. This chapter will show you how to cultivate your mind-garden and develop a *successful* attitude. In addition, this chapter will help you set goals for personal and professional success.

> *"Most people are about as happy as they make up their mind to be."*
>
> Abraham Lincoln

2.1   Introduction

This chapter will help you examine and improve your attitudes and create effective goals. As you work through the exercises in this chapter, one goal will be to slow down your "mind talk" and make it positive and supportive. Let's begin with Exercise 2-1.

Exercise 2-1   Describe Your Thoughts

You have a way to go before we try specific techniques, so for now, choose the statement that most closely describes your current mind talk:

_____ Frantic and gloomy   _____ Distracted and rambling
_____ Fast and furious   _____ Positive and supportive

Or make up your own description: _____

Now, describe a specific internal dialogue that supports your choice. For example, if you chose "frantic and gloomy," your description may be something like, "I'm never going to pass this test—there just aren't enough hours in the day." (Hopefully this isn't yours, but if it is, we will work together to change it.)

_____

_____

_____

> *"There are no limitations to the mind except those we acknowledge."*
>
> Napolean Hill

People often stress the importance of a positive attitude. You have probably heard sayings such as "You are what you think" and "Your attitude determines your life." If this sounds like pop psychology, you may be skeptical. So, let's discuss exactly why a positive attitude is so important and actually prove just how powerful it can be. To understand this, we must begin with a basic understanding of that wonderful and mysterious thing we call the mind.

2.2   The Conscious versus the Subconscious Mind

Conscious mind

The part of the mind we are most aware of and that involves day-to-day thoughts

Subconscious mind

The part of the mind we are mostly unaware of and that is involved with survival

We can begin to understand the mind by considering it in two parts: the **conscious mind** and the **subconscious mind**. The *conscious mind* is what we are most familiar with. This involves our day-to-day thoughts about what to wear, how to pay the bills, and what the future holds. We spend most of our waking lives immersed in this part of the mind. In the stress management chapter, we began a journey to control the conscious mind so that we can manage our stress and maximize our success. In this chapter, we take that journey a bit further.

Operating just under the conscious mind is the *subconscious,* much like a submarine operates unseen under the surface of the water. This part of our mind is concerned with survival. Imagine if we had to consciously think about each heartbeat or breath! We would be unable to think about anything else. We are less aware of the subconscious because it functions more in our sleep. During our waking hours, it also functions, but often at such a level we are not even aware of it.

2.2a   The Power of the Subconscious Mind

The subconscious can be a powerful ally in developing and maintaining a positive attitude and creativity. Let's learn more about the subconscious and illustrate its power.

Important Fact 1   The thoughts or ideas you plant in your subconscious will grow there.

Proof   Have you ever had a problem weigh on your conscious mind? You think and worry about it all day. Then you go to sleep at night, and you dream about your concerns. This happens because the subconscious takes over while the conscious mind is asleep. Remember, the subconscious is the survival part of your mind. It will consider something you perceive as a threat as something it must deal with. Even if you consciously think you cannot deal with your problem, your subconscious is always on the job. While sleeping, you might have some crazy dream about the problem while the subconscious mind tries to sort it all out. This shows that the conscious thoughts that we plant in the subconscious grow there, which is why it is so important to plant positive thoughts.

Important Fact 2   The subconscious mind can be a powerful ally in creative thinking and problem-solving.

Proof   Have you ever had a problem that you consciously pondered for hours? Then, with no solution in sight, you did something you enjoyed and got your mind off the problem. Maybe you were taking a walk in the woods, listening to some of your favorite music, or taking a refreshing and relaxing shower when the answer magically came to you. It's not magic: It's your subconscious mind working on the problem at a level you are not aware of, even during your waking hours.

Hopefully, we proved that the thoughts and messages you encounter over the course of a day are planted in both your conscious and subconscious mind. If you let negative thoughts grow there, they will soon overtake you. However, you can instead plant positive thoughts, making it more likely that you'll experience positive outcomes.

This suggests that we have a certain level of control over what happens to us. It turns out there is a whole school of thought behind the question, "Do I have control over my own life?"

Food for Thought

In cave-dwelling days, people were more immersed in the subconscious because simply maintaining survival was a dominant concern. Mainly, people worried about how to get their next meal—and not become the next meal! They had to be in tune with their environment and feel danger when it was lurking behind a rock. In other words, they had a highly developed intuition, which many experts believe resides in the subconscious realm.

2.3　Determining Your *Locus of Control*

Locus of control

Your belief about who or what controls your life

Internal locus of control

The belief that you control your own life

External locus of control

The belief that someone or something else controls your life

When you run into a problem in your life, do you automatically look for something or someone else to blame? Or are you more likely to follow the old adage, "When life gives you lemons, make lemonade," and somehow find a way to turn your *problem* into an *opportunity*? Maybe your reaction lies somewhere in between. Some people feel they have little or no control over events in their lives and that things are a result of fate, luck, or other *outside* influences. Some believe their destiny lies directly *within* their control. Others may feel what happens in their lives is a combination of both *internal* (inside themselves) and *external* (outside themselves) factors. This belief about what (or who) controls your life is called your **locus of control**. *Locus* is a Latin word meaning place or location. *Locus of control* literally means location of control, the location of who (or what) is in charge of your life. If you have an **internal locus of control**, you believe you control your own life. If you have an **external locus of control**, you believe your life is controlled by something or someone else. Let's use the example of a graded paper in Table 2-1.

Table 2-1 Locus of Control for Graded Paper		
	Internal Locus of Control	**External Locus of Control**
Got an A on the paper	I did well because I... ...planned my time well. ...worked hard. ...paid attention in class.	I did well because... ...the teacher likes me. ...I got lucky. ...this class is easy.
Got an F on the paper	I did poorly because I... ...didn't pay attention in class. ...procrastinated too much. ...didn't try hard enough.	I did poorly because... ...the teacher doesn't like me. ...this topic is impossible to learn. ...I didn't have enough time.

Figure 2-1　　What locus of control is being presented?

In the table, you see the extremes of locus of control. On one end, some people might think everything *but* themselves is responsible for their grades. On the other end, some people might take complete responsibility for their grades, ignoring outside factors entirely. Most people will fall somewhere in between, taking some responsibility and acknowledging some outside circumstances. Like most things, balance is key. Some parts of your life may make it more difficult to do well in school, and those things aren't always within your control. If you work or are responsible for taking care of other people, you may have to work harder to do well in school than someone who doesn't have those added responsibilities. However, it is much better to take control of your life than to leave things up to chance. Don't hope you get lucky on your midterm, make time to study. If you do poorly, don't blame the teacher—try to figure out what you can do next time to earn a better grade. Remember, you are the captain of your ship, and although the wind helps push you along, you choose which direction to steer.

Developing a more internal locus of control ties in directly with what we will be discussing next as we take a look at four methods to create a positive and self-motivating attitude:

- Reframe your thinking
- Get rid of destructive or irrational beliefs
- Meditate
- Try humor therapy

2.4   Method 1: Reframe Your Thinking

2.4a   What Attitude Do You Present?

Your attitude will influence not only what you think about yourself but also what others think about you. You really have two simple choices: You can assume a positive or a negative attitude in any situation.

Did you ever hear a weather forecaster describe the conditions as partly sunny or partly cloudy? Aren't these the same conditions stated from a different perspective? Is this going to be a good day or a bad day for you? Which would you pick? Your answer depends on your attitude. You decide whether the glass is half empty or half full. People with *positive attitudes* would say the glass is half full or that it's a partly sunny day and it is going to be a good one. However, people with *negative attitudes* see a half-empty glass and complain about the partly cloudy weather and the lousy day they are sure they will have. In addition, they might try to blame it all on someone else. Which person is more enjoyable to work with? See Figure 2-2, which shows how just a look can convey an attitude.

Figure 2-2   What attitudes are being presented?

Let's look at the common situation of meeting someone for the first time. There is a saying, "You never get a second chance to make a good first impression." In less than thirty seconds, an impression is made that determines how people feel about each other. Do Exercise 2-2 to explore first impressions. A positive first impression will make others want to know you.

Exercise 2-2   First Impressions

What impression will you give? List three things you can say or do to give a positive first impression.

Positive things I can say: Positive things I can do:

_____   _____

_____   _____

_____   _____

Who is making the better first impression?

2.4b   Reframing Your Thinking

Reframing your attitude simply means looking at things in a more positive way. It's best to start off believing you are going to have a good day but, in reality, things may happen to make your day go differently than planned. That's life. Positive thinkers will make the best of it and *reframe* their thinking. Let's say you waited over an hour for your appointment at the doctor's office. Look at how people with two different attitudes would approach the situation:

Negative Attitude   As you might expect, a person with a negative attitude would become very upset in this situation. Their blood pressure would rise, and the experience would be a bad one for both doctor and patient. In their anger, the person might forget to tell the doctor something that could affect their treatment. After they leave, things could snowball: The rest of their interactions that day might be somewhat hostile; they might have a bad day at work or school, develop a tension headache, and have a difficult time sleeping at night. Because of a lack of restful sleep, the next day will already start off on a bad note, and so the cycle would continue.

Positive Attitude   A person with a positive attitude may initially feel upset, but will regain their composure and reframe their thinking from anger to acceptance. This person realizes they have *no control* over the situation and must simply wait to see their doctor. There is no sense ruining the rest of their day. Positive people may sit back and take a few deep breaths and then do something constructive. They may have taken some work with them to the doctor's office just in case something like this happened, as you will read about in the time management section. By getting their work done while waiting, they have turned a potentially negative experience into a positive one and can later go out to that movie they wanted to see. The following poem was written over a hundred years ago, and it may sound old and hard to understand. Dig a little deeper, however, and it still rings true today. It's about how our thoughts determine much of our lives. What does it mean to you?

> **Piece of Wisdom**
>
> *"Mind is the Master power that moulds and makes,*
> *And Man is Mind, and evermore he takes*
> *The tool of Thought, and, shaping what he wills,*
> *Brings forth a thousand joys, a thousand ills: —*
> *He thinks in secret, and it comes to pass:*
> *Environment is but his looking-glass."*
>
> —James Allen,
> Author of *As a Man Thinketh*

In Exercise 2-3, you'll read a concrete example of reframing before trying it yourself.

Reframe the following situations to create more positive outcomes. Example:

My date stood me up.

Instead of getting upset and taking it personally, I can reframe my thinking: If nothing serious happened to this person and he or she simply did not show up for the date, then I know what kind of person he or she is, and we would not be suited for one another. Instead of getting upset and ruining my night, I will either call some good friends to do something else or get some work done tonight so tomorrow I can go out with my friends and my grades won't suffer.

Now your turn:

I got a lower grade than expected on a paper or exam.

_____

_____

_____

I did not get a job that I applied for.

_____

_____

_____

While driving to an important event, I ended up lost in a new section of town.

_____

_____

_____

2.5   Method 2: Get Rid of Destructive or Irrational Beliefs

Self-fulfilling prophecy

When you make something true by acting like it's true

So far, we've stressed the importance of planting positive thoughts in the garden of the mind. However, for a garden to thrive, it also requires regular weeding to get rid of the bad plants. Have you ever heard of a **self-fulfilling prophecy**? It means if you believe something strongly enough and plant it firmly in your mind, it can come true. For example, if you tell yourself you will never get organized, you won't—because that is the seed you are planting. In addition, you are wasting a lot of time telling yourself all the reasons why you can't get organized, time you could have spent actually getting organized!

2.5a Positive Self-Talk

You can use this same principle to your advantage by using *positive self-talk*. Talking to yourself does not mean you are crazy. In fact, talking is slower than thinking and can slow your racing mind, which helps you focus. Self-talk can boost self-esteem if it is optimistic and positive. For example, replace negative thoughts such as "I'm not smart enough to pass this course" with a spoken statement like "If I study hard and plan well, I *will* do well in this course."

In addition to positive self-talk, other strategies can get rid of the weeds that may grow in your mind. Avoid dwelling on past negative or unpleasant experiences, and never carry grudges. Those thoughts only serve to waste your energy and destroy your motivation.

Test Yourself

Do You See the Glass as Half Empty or Half Full?

The following table contrasts characteristics of positive and negative attitudes. Put checkmarks by the statements that best describe you.

Contrasting Attitudes

Characteristics of Positive Attitudes	Characteristics of Negative Attitudes
_____ Think mostly positive thoughts	_____ Think mostly negative thoughts
_____ Willing to learn	_____ Resistant to learning
_____ Accepting of change	_____ Not accepting of change
_____ Upbeat	_____ Gloomy
_____ Calm and in control	_____ Out of control
_____ Open to other people and views	_____ Not open to other views
_____ Nonjudgmental	_____ Judgmental
_____ Accepts responsibility	_____ Blames others
_____ Shows sense of humor	_____ Shows little sense of humor

For each checkmark on the negative side, develop a specific action plan to move it over to the positive column.

Characteristic: _____

Action plan: _____

_____

_____

(continues)

Characteristic: _____

Action plan: _____

_____

_____

Characteristic: _____

Action plan: _____

_____

_____

It may be interesting to have someone you trust check the list, so you can learn how others see you.

2.5b   Balance Your Attitude

We should all strive for balance in our lives, including in our attitudes and emotions. Many people view anger as a negative emotion, but just like stress, a little anger can be good. It can lead us on to do better or to right a wrong. However, prolonged anger can lead to destructive behavior and illness.

We all become sad when something tragic happens; this makes us human. But it's important to know the difference between depression and sadness. If someone is sad following a painful disappointment or the loss of a loved one, it is a normal part of the grieving process. However, if the sadness remains for a long time and gets in the way of living your life, it might not be just sadness or grief anymore—it could be depression. Balance, again, is the key factor.

Look at Table 2-2, which contrasts a constructive versus destructive approach to life. Where do you fit in?

Now complete Exercise 2-4.

Table 2-2 Constructive versus Destructive Approach	
Someone who is constructive...	**Someone who is destructive...**
Confronts problems (appropriately)	Thinks problems will resolve themselves
Discusses problems in a calm manner	Fights or yells
Accepts responsibility	Blames others
Uses relaxation techniques	Uses alcohol or drugs
Accepts and learns from mistakes	Is a perfectionist
Eats healthy	Eats too much, too little, or junk food
Focuses on the present	Stresses out about the past or future
Helps others	Avoids people

Exercise 2-4   Change Destructive Beliefs

Assess yourself and check any of the negative and irrational self-beliefs you have:

_____ The place where I work owes me a job. (irrational)
_____ I must be perfect in all the things I do and say. (irrational)
_____ I never have enough time. (negative)
_____ I am responsible for other people's happiness. (irrational)
_____ I should be happy all the time. (irrational)
_____ Change is bad. (negative and irrational)
_____ Someone is out to get me. (negative and hopefully irrational!)

For any statements you checked, develop an action plan to change those beliefs to positive and rational ones. In one or two sentences, state actions you can take to turn your attitude around. For example, if you checked "Change is bad," you can state an action plan that says to reframe your thinking to embrace change as an opportunity to learn new things, have new experiences, meet new people, etc.

_____

_____

_____

_____

2.5c   Change Worry into Concern

Mark Twain's quote is cleverly telling us that most of what we worry about never happens. We waste all that energy by worrying, and nothing good comes from it. You may think we are telling you not to worry about your grades this semester, and you are right. The difference is that, rather than worrying, you should be *concerned* about your grades this semester.

When you are *worried*, you clench your jaw and your mind goes a million miles per hour with messages such as "I'm never going to understand this," "I'm never going to pass this course," and "What if I fail?"

When you are *concerned*, you do something to make sure things go the way you want them to. For example, students should be concerned about how well they will do in a difficult course. This means coming up with a plan for how to approach the course to maximize your chances for success. A student who is concerned might think, "I know this is a tough course, but if I *do* the following, I *will* pass it." This student's plan could involve:

- Studying for an hour each day

- Keeping up with all the assignments

- Talking to the teacher at least once a week

> *"I'm an old man and have known a great many problems, but most of them never happened."*
>
> Mark Twain

Food for Thought

People do not get you upset—you do! You are the only person who can make you angry or upset or feel bad. You feel the way you think. Realize you have control over your reactions and remember, it only takes a second for a second thought.

Notice the difference? *Worry* is wasted energy and no action; *concern* involves creating a plan for how to succeed. In Exercise 2-5, you can try out this strategy. Remember this old saying: "Worrying is like sitting in a rocking chair; it gives you something to do, but it doesn't get you anywhere."

Exercise 2-5   Changing Worry into Concern

A. Write down something you worry about.

_____

_____

B. Now create a plan for how to address this problem. What can you do to make the situation better?

_____

_____

C. Now write down when you will put your plan into action. (Hint: It should be a three-letter answer that rhymes with "cow"!)

_____

_____

2.6   Method 3: Meditation—Getting in Touch with Your Subconscious

Albert Einstein asked, "Why is it I get my best ideas in the morning while I'm shaving?" He came to realize that he did not have to think about shaving because he did it so often. The routine act of shaving allowed him to slow his mind down and let his subconscious bubble up toward the surface with ideas. Speaking of bubbles, have you ever had a sudden realization or a great idea while in the bath or shower? Your mind becomes relaxed and open during these familiar and comfortable activities. This tends to happen naturally, but we can also choose to slow down and redirect our thoughts using meditation, as discussed briefly in the stress management chapter. Simply put, meditation is focusing on *one thing*. Now we can build on that idea by making that *one thing* a positive thought to plant in our minds. Exercise 2-6 gets you started on meditating.

Meditation can be used to relax and recharge your mind.

Exercise 2-6   Meditating on Positive Thoughts

1. Get rid of any noises and other distractions.

2. Get comfortable in a chair or lie down with your palms facing upward.

3. Slowly breathe in through your nose and out through your mouth. As you breathe in, your stomach—not your chest—should rise. The key is slow and steady breathing. It may take a while to get comfortable with this step.

4. After you feel yourself relaxing into a slow and steady rhythm, focus on your feet and relaxing those muscles. Progressively work upward with all your muscles until you reach your forehead and your entire body is relaxed.

5. As you exhale, picture in your mind all the tension flowing out of the area you are focusing on.

This activity was discussed in the stress management chapter. You can now take it a step further by planting a positive thought in your mind after you are relaxed. As you exhale, concentrate on one simple, positive thought, such as, "I will take good care of myself," "I can do this," or "I will succeed." With practice, you will plant the thought firmly in your mind.

This activity usually takes five to ten minutes. However, if you feel you can't fit it into your hectic schedule, try doing it before going to sleep. Do this for one week, and describe any observations or results you may have seen. Did you take better care of yourself that week? Did you have a more positive attitude? Did you feel calmer, less stressed, and happier?

_____

_____

_____

2.7　Method 4: Humor Therapy

Humor was briefly covered as a way to deal with stress, but we can expand on this topic. Many scientists are researching the effects of humor on our bodies and our minds. Some research suggests that laughter improves our body's ability to fight off illness. Of course, laughter isn't *really* medicine—but it can help make medical treatments more effective. Let's look at laughter a little more closely.

2.7a　Positive Effects of Humor

Humor can have many positive effects on your physical and mental health. Laughing improves circulation, releases some hormones that act as natural painkillers and ones that improve your mood. Not to mention, a good belly laugh can even provide exercise! What about the effect of laughing on the mind?

Humor relieves stress and lessens anxiety. In addition, it can help combat depression. When appropriately used, humor can also improve your self-image and increase your creativity. In the study skills chapter, you will be encouraged to use humor in making up silly stories to help you learn. Use humor when you can, appreciate the benefits when someone makes you laugh, and remember that what is learned with humor is not easily forgotten.

So, what are some techniques we can use to add humor to our lives? Here are some suggestions. Feel free to come up with some more.

- **Tell (appropriate) jokes.** Remember, humor shouldn't be used to hurt others. Tell good jokes or stories, and avoid those that will make others uncomfortable.

- **Collect things that you find funny.** Keep track of things that make you laugh (good jokes, funny pictures, gifs, memes) by saving them on your phone, tablet, or computer (or in a desk drawer). Also, surrounding your work area with funny posters or sayings is a great way to lighten your mood. What would be someone's first impression of your work area?

  - *Smile* and laugh out loud more often. This is one of the simplest and most effective techniques. The average four-year-old laughs many times every hour. How often do you laugh each day? Laughter helps put things in perspective, and besides, it feels good. Don't forget to have a good laugh at least once a day.

  - **Look for humor in every situation you can.** It really is all around you. For example, when your social media feed is full of frustrating or dramatic posts, look for a video or meme that will remind you to stay light-hearted.

  - **Finally, remember to laugh at yourself.** People are more comfortable around those who can make fun of themselves instead of finding fault in others. Have fun at both work and school, but make sure you take your academic and professional responsibilities seriously.

Exercise 2-7 ties in with healthy habits, positive thinking, and a form of goal setting to get you ready for the next section.

Humor is all around us.

Real-Life Application

Success Story

During a workshop, a participant stated that he worked in a customer complaint department, so 100 percent of his interactions with customers were negative. He went on to say that many times, when a caller would ruin his whole workday, his bad mood would carry over when he went home. He would then treat his family horribly all because of that one bad call. He was advised that the next time a caller was "getting to him," he should simply put a big smile on his face and continue the conversation. This would help prevent him from saying something that would get him fired. Also, it would be impossible for him to get worked up while he was smiling. The participant later stated that this simple technique had a dramatic impact on the way he reacted to bad calls at work. It especially helped him to leave work in a positive frame of mind, which translated to more positive interactions when he got home.

Exercise 2-7   "Your Day"

Think ahead about a week or two to a day that will be fairly normal for you: no unusual events, just your regular schedule. Take this day and plan it as one completely healthy day for yourself. Do not take any extraordinary measures. From what you know about proper nutrition, and using what you might normally have in the house, plan three healthy meals and a few healthy snacks. Have a lot of fresh water on hand. Without interrupting your routine schedule, make time for a half hour of exercise or more: walking, biking, whatever you like. Remember to hug someone close to you in a genuine way and express your feelings to that person. If you have one, spend some unhurried time enjoying your pet. Turn off the TV, tablet, and computer, put down your phone, and read a book or listen to relaxing music. Give yourself at least eight hours of sleep and try meditating on a positive thought before you fall asleep.

Describe how you felt the next morning, physically and mentally:

_____

_____

_____

2.8   Goal Setting

2.8a   What Do You Value?

Before we take a look at goals and how to achieve them, it may be a good idea to first ask yourself what do you value in your life? What is truly important to you? Is money your ultimate goal? If so, are you looking to support and raise a family with it or would you rather work toward owning an expensive car? Maybe both! Hopefully the career path you choose will be able to not only provide you with financial security but also a sense of happiness and fulfillment.

Values and priorities are closely related. The things that matter most to you should come first when it comes to how you spend your time and resources. When this happens, you are more likely to be successful. *Values, priorities,* and *success*—these words will likely have different meanings from one person to the next, so let's think about what they mean to *you*. Your values are the things that are most important to you. Things like education, family, financial security, and so on. Some of these are things that most people value; what differentiates us is how we prioritize our values. *Prioritizing* means putting things in order from most to least important to *you*. Let's say family is your top priority, just before education. This might make it hard for you to make time for your schoolwork because you feel you must always put your family's needs above your own. Just remember, getting an education can provide you *and* your family with opportunities and financial security you wouldn't otherwise have. Prioritizing your schoolwork doesn't mean you don't value your family—in fact, sometimes our top priorities go hand-in-hand.

Keep in mind that values and priorities may shift and change over time, so it is good to make a list every so often to keep yourself in check. Try to make decisions and set goals that line up with your values; this will ultimately lead to your success, however you define it. Exercise 2-8 helps you focus on priorities.

Exercise 2-8   What do you value?

List the six things you value most. You may want to brainstorm on a separate piece of paper first and then write in your top values below. When you are done, read over your list and place a number before each value to give it a certain priority, with 1 being most important.

_____ _____

_____ _____

_____ _____

_____ _____

_____ _____

_____ _____

Now that you have your core values in mind and your priorities in order, let's think about how you can succeed through goal setting.

2.8b   Why Set Goals?

Setting goals helps you map out your personal and professional path to success. Having a well-charted map makes it more likely that you'll arrive at your chosen destination. The conclusion of this chapter will show you how to set achievable goals to map your path to academic, personal, and professional success. Research shows that people who effectively set goals:

- Concentrate better

- Show more self-confidence

- Feel more motivated

- Focus on tasks better

Can you see how concepts such as stress management, positive attitude, and goal setting are all connected? Goals will help you turn your dreams into reality by giving you an action plan with specific deadlines.

2.8c   What Are Goals?

Goals are what we aim for, the things we want to achieve in our lives. Goals motivate us and help us navigate our journey to success. You may have already chosen your educational goal, and you can further use goal setting to help you achieve it. If you haven't yet chosen your educational program, you can use goal setting in the upcoming exercises to help you determine your career path.

Developing goals will help you decide where you want to go and how to actually get there. In the academic skill chapters, you'll learn about using memory aids, such as *acronyms,* to understand concepts. An acronym is a way to shorten many words into one term by using their first letters. For example, NASA stands for the **N**ational **A**eronautics and **S**pace **A**dministration. We will introduce an acronym here to teach you how to set goals. Because this is a key factor on your journey to success and it would be "dumb" to ignore goal setting, remember to set *SMART* goals:

S = specific

M = measurable

A = achievable

R = realistic

T = time-bound

Let's look at each of these characteristics in a little more depth.

Specific   The more general the goal ("I want to get a job that pays me a lot of money!"), the harder it is to achieve. Instead, try to set goals that are detailed and specific ("I want to get a job as an architect"). To give another example, let's say your goal is to do well in your first semester. This is too vague. What do you mean by well? Instead, your goal should be something like, "I want to get a B average or better in my first semester." Now you have a specific outcome to aim for. Specific goals also make it easy to tell when you've achieved them. You will know for sure if you achieved your B-average goal when you receive your semester grades. The more specific your goal, the easier it is to reach.

Measurable   As we mentioned previously, you should be able to tell when you've reached your goal. This means you need to set goals you can measure. If your goal is too abstract ("I want to succeed"), it can be impossible to tell if you've achieved it. Instead, set goals that can be measured ("I want to pass this course"). Measuring means asking yourself *how*: How will I achieve this goal? How will I keep track of my progress? How will I know when I'm done? Finding ways to measure your progress toward your goal every step along the way will keep you on track.

Achievable   Don't set goals you can't hope to achieve ("I want to run a marathon next week even though I'm out of shape"). Instead, chart a path toward making your goals achievable ("Tomorrow I'll start training for a marathon next spring by running a mile"). However, this doesn't mean setting easy goals. Every goal you set should be a challenge—otherwise, how will you grow? For example, in sports, it is easy to play against weak competition and look really good. To improve, you need to play against people who are actually better than you. Many coaches say, "You're only as good as your competition." Become your own competition by choosing a goal that will challenge you, and then enjoy the payoff in a big way once you achieve it. Just remember to find a balance between setting goals that are challenging and achievable.

Realistic   On a similar note, setting unrealistic goals ("I want to start and finish this twenty-page paper by tomorrow") is a surefire way to set yourself up for failure. You should set goals that are within your reach ("I want to create an outline for my paper today so that I can start writing a rough draft tomorrow.") Remember, each time you accomplish a new goal, you are setting the bar a little higher. If you got a C on the last test, you should aim for a B on the next one, and so on. As you expand what is achievable and realistic for you, don't be afraid to set more challenging goals. You have to determine where you are going to set the bar for yourself. If you do try to jump too high and end up on the ground, simply get back up and try again!

Time-Bound   Many of us need deadlines in order to accomplish a task. Goals are no different. When you set a time frame for your goal, you make it much more likely that you'll achieve it. Ask yourself when, realistically, you can complete your goal. Which of the following categories does it fall under?

- Short-term goal: tomorrow, next week, next month
- Medium-term goal: one month to six months or so
- Long-term goal: a year or more

Although the time frame of *completion* is key, for medium and long-term goals, you will also want to set checkpoints along the way. This is a form of *measuring* your progress. For instance, if you have a medium-term goal of being able to run a half-marathon six months from now, you must certainly check in with your progress at least every month to make sure you are on track. Creating a schedule of minideadlines within your ultimate time frame can combat procrastination by keeping you motivated along the way.

Consider the Following When Setting Goals Always use *positive language* when stating a goal. For example, stating, "I will earn a B average or better in my first semester," is much better than stating, "I will not get any D's or F's this semester." It is better to say what you *will* do than what you *won't* do. Along with being positive, have confidence in your goals: "I *will* earn a B average or better" rather than "I will *try* to earn a B average or better."

Be sure the goals you set are *self-chosen*. Do you think you are more likely to achieve a goal someone else has set for you or one you create that is in line with your own *values*? Well-meaning people in your life may have your best interests at heart and attempt to set goals for you. Although you should consider their thoughts, your ultimate goals must be chosen by you. This gives you ownership and responsibility for your goals. Your goals should be something *you* desire and really want to accomplish.

Often, we forget to use our past successes as motivation as we continue our journey through life. When coming up with new goals, take a minute to think about what you have already accomplished. Remember that feeling of success and use it as inspiration.

It is also important to have goals that balance your personal and professional lives. If you have all professional goals and no personal development goals, you may soon burn out by not taking care of yourself. Your professional goals will then suffer. So, develop a balance of goals that complement each other. Now try Exercise 2-9.

Exercise 2-9 You Can Run, but You Cannot Hide

Think of a short-term goal, one that your friends may think is uncharacteristic of you—like getting on stage for karaoke, volunteering at the local animal shelter, or writing a letter to the editor. It doesn't have to be something that causes a large amount of anxiety, and make sure to pick something you can do within a week. Tell someone that you trust about your goal. Ask that person to give you a realistic deadline for completing it. Be prepared to prove that you have achieved your short-term goal. If you don't, you must do something for that person, like treating him or her to a nice lunch! Revisit this exercise after you have attempted your short-term goal. Did you have to buy lunch?

Your short-term goal:

_____

_____

_____

How did you do?

_____

_____

_____

Test Yourself

Which Is a Better Goal?

Circle a or b for each statement below indicating which goal you think is SMARTer.

1a. I will do better in my classes this semester and will try to participate more in class discussion.

1b. I will assess my study skills and class participation, and I will develop three specific action plans to improve them for the upcoming semester.

2a. I will exercise for thirty minutes a day at least three times a week.

2b. I will get in better shape so that I look good at the beach.

3a. I will pass a course on cardiopulmonary resuscitation (CPR) this term.

3b. I may take a CPR course to improve my résumé if it is not too hard.

4a. I will volunteer at least five hours per week for a local nonprofit organization that can help me improve my business skills and make potential contacts for the future.

4b. I will try to find some volunteer work to do. Hopefully, I will meet some people who can help me find a job later.

2.8d   Setting Successful Goals

One problem with goal setting is that people set too many small goals, get overwhelmed, and then fail. Therefore, this text focuses on goals that are medium- to long-term. This will give you a clear vision of where you want to be in the next six months to a year and will help you develop a successful plan to get there. Once you experience that initial success and see the power of goal setting, it will motivate you to go even further.

One of the first rules is to *write down* your goals and keep them where you can refer to them. Exercise 2-10 will get you started.

Exercise 2-10　Setting Your Goals

Pick one personal and one educational goal you want to achieve within the next six months to a year, and write them below. Be sure to use each of the characteristics in the SMART system. Examples are given in Figure 2-3 as a guide. Remember, these must be *your* goals. If you haven't chosen a career path, develop a goal that will help you as you explore academic programs and/or careers.

Educational goal:

_____

_____

_____

Personal goal:

_____

_____

_____

Figure 2-3 lists some examples of educational and personal goals.

Figure 2-3　Examples of educational and personal goals

Educational goal: *I will maintain a B average or above and make a positive impression on the faculty at my school in my first year.*

Personal goal: *I will develop and begin an exercise program and commit to following it at least three times a week for my first semester in school.*

2.8e　Objectives

Now that you have a clear picture of where you want to be in six months to a year, how do you plan on getting there? Next, you need to plan a course by creating *objectives*. Objectives are actions you need to take to achieve your stated goal. You can also think about your objectives as the specific steps on your path to completing your long-term goal. Developing *specific* objectives, or action plans, will help you succeed.

For example, your goal may be to graduate and start your own business. That's a wonderful goal, but you have to chart a plan of action with specific steps. Some of the objectives may include figuring out what academic program to enroll in, researching the requirements for graduating from that program, talking to other business people, obtaining an internship to gain experience and contacts, and so on. Let's continue with the goal-setting process by completing Exercise 2-11.

Exercise 2-11   Refining Your Educational Goal

Now that you have written down your long-term goals, you have your vision. Naturally you are not going to achieve all your goals overnight. You must take small steps, in the form of short- and medium-term objectives, in your journey. For your long-term educational goal, write at least three specific objectives that will move you forward. Figure 2-4 gives an example.

Rewrite your educational goal from Exercise 2-10.

_____

_____

_____

Describe why you chose this goal:

_____

_____

_____

Now develop a specific action plan.

Action plan (your specific objectives):

1. _____

_____

2. _____

_____

3. _____

_____

4. _____

_____

5. _____

_____

List some resources that can help with your action plan:

_____

_____

_____

Figure 2-4   The fully developed goal plan

Educational goal/professional goal:
I will maintain a B average or above and make a positive impression on the faculty at my school in my first year.

The reason I chose this goal:
By maintaining a B average or better, I will demonstrate that I'm learning enough to succeed in my future career. Making a positive impression on the faculty will give me good future references to secure a good job. This will all lead to a good career and the financial security to do the things I want in my life and the chance to give back to my community.

Action plan (specific objectives):
Use the methods in my student success course to manage stress and develop successful study habits and time management skills.
Use the learning resource center or group study sessions available to me on campus.
Come to class on time and get to know my teacher by being prepared and asking questions on the material.
Reevaluate my progress after the first semester.
Volunteer for special projects at school or in the community.

Some resources that can help me:
My teachers
Study Skills Center
Materials and exercises
Positive fellow students
Family and community resources

Notice in Figure 2-4 that both the action plan and resources mention *community*. We are all part of a community. This includes the community where you live and the community of your school. Getting involved in your community can help improve neighborhood conditions as well as give you valuable skills and experiences for the future. This is definitely a win/win situation. There are many ways to perform community service, including volunteer work with the homeless or senior citizens, coaching children in your community, or teaching illiterate adults to read.

Now in Exercise 2-12, you'll use the same goal-setting system to work through the *personal* goal you named in Exercise 2-10. Remember that a personal goal can be anything important in your personal life—for example, learning to play a musical instrument, learning to paint, learning sign language, or improving a personal relationship.

Exercise 2-12   Refining Your Personal Goal

Rewrite your personal goal from Exercise 2-10.

_____

_____

_____

Describe why you chose this goal:

_____

_____

_____

Now create a specific action plan.

Action plan (your specific objectives):

1. _____

_____

2. _____

_____

3. _____

_____

4. _____

_____

5. _____

_____

List some resources that can help with your action plan:

_____

_____

_____

Useful Hints for Goal Setting:

- When obstacles arise, be prepared to revise your objectives (or even your goals) to address changing conditions because *change* is a natural part of life.

- Don't get frustrated if your progress seems slow. Many people work furiously toward a goal for a while and then trail off. This is also natural. At first, you may make progress quickly. Seeing your progress slow down can be frustrating, but don't give up. When progress is fast at first and then stalls, it's called a *plateau period,* and it's common. Realize that it will pass and that you will eventually reach your goal if you keep going.

- Don't set too many goals at one time and become overwhelmed. Just as you can prioritize your values, you can prioritize your goals. Figure out what academic, professional, and personal goals matter most to you and focus on those.

- Describe and imagine what it will be like when you achieve your goal. This is called *visualization* and it can help you reach your goal. Imagine your success and feel all the good feelings. This will help you maintain your commitment.

- Learn from your past and from others. Remember that failure is not a bad thing and reframe your thinking to view failure as a positive learning experience. Michael Jordan failed to make his high school basketball team and learned from this failure. Of course, he went on to become one of the greatest basketball players in history. List the things that prevented you from reaching your goal in the past. Make a note of anyone else who has achieved your goal and learn from what they did. Also learn from their mistakes. If you can get in touch with this person directly, they may also prove to be a valuable contact in the future.

- Consider keeping a goal journal and writing notes about your progress. This activity will help you stay focused.

- Be creative and have fun with this process. Most importantly, reward yourself when you complete each objective. Even small rewards will motivate you to go to the next step in your plan. Each reward will lead you ever closer to your goal. The reward can be as simple as time with a friend, exercise, going out to eat, seeing a movie, or staying at home and watching your favorite TV show.

In reading this text and doing the exercises, you will see how each element of your journey relates to the others. Try Exercise 2-13, which connects stress management to goal setting.

Food for Thought

The U.S. Olympic Committee developed a training program to have their athletes "think like winners." It includes these four components:

- Visualize yourself in the successful performance of your event.
- Set short- and long-term goals to achieve "the gold."
- Practice physical and mental relaxation techniques.
- Concentrate on positive thoughts.

From what you have learned so far, can you apply this strategy to your plans for academic success? How does it apply to your life and your future career?

Evaluate the following goal-setting strategies from your point of view as either "very stressful," "somewhat stressful," or "not very stressful." Compare your results with the class.

3 = Very stressful   2 = Somewhat stressful   1 = Not very stressful

____ Deciding on a goal
____ Writing down your goal
____ Setting a deadline
____ Planning the steps necessary to achieving the goal

____ Taking action on the first step toward the goal
____ Following your plan through to completion

A little bit of stress can be good, so a rating of "somewhat stressful" is acceptable because it might simply indicate a need to practice that strategy until you are comfortable with it. However, you might want to explore any "very stressful" strategies and consider ways to improve those elements of goal setting, including identifying resources to help you with your goal(s) or, possibly, even modifying your goal(s).

Healthy Decision-Making

Juan knows that his education is going to prepare him to do well in his chosen profession. However, Juan has a burning desire to start his own business within two years of graduation. He is concerned that he has no business courses or background in his current academic courses. He is a year from graduation. What decisions can Juan make now that can help him to realize his dream?

_____

_____

_____

_____

Explain how the concepts from this chapter can help him succeed.

_____

_____

_____

_____

Know Your School

Your school has support services in many areas. Identify school resources that can help you with positive attitudes and goal setting. Examples could include personal and career counseling services. List the information here and add it to the information about your school from the stress management chapter. Remember, for quick reference, place the information in a prominent place, such as on your refrigerator.

Resource Name: _____

Office Location: _____

Phone Number: _____

Email Address: _____

Resource Name: _____

Office Location: _____

Phone Number: _____

Email Address: _____

Resource Name: _____

Office Location: _____

Phone Number: _____

Email Address: _____

Resource Name: _____

Office Location: _____

Phone Number: _____

Email Address: _____

Resource Name: _____

Office Location: _____

Phone Number: _____

Email Address: _____

3

Managing Your Resources

Time and Money

Objectives

By the end of this chapter, you will be able to:

- Identify effective organization and time management techniques

- Prioritize tasks to improve time management

- Evaluate and enhance your time management skills

- Utilize strategic planning in large projects such as writing a research paper

- Evaluate and maintain balance in your life

- Understand financial literacy concepts, including budgeting, taxes, and credit issues

- Build awareness of spending, borrowing, and saving patterns

- Develop a personal budget

- Develop strategies to improve your financial health, finance your education, and maintain a good credit record

Why Learn This Skill?

When you realize that time is a not a renewable resource, you begin to see how valuable it is. Once a moment goes by, it is gone forever. Time truly is our most precious asset. Like any resource, you need to use it wisely. Effective time management skills will help you get the most out of your life personally and professionally.

Managing your time well has many benefits. It allows you to complete your schoolwork and meet your other obligations, often with time to spare for the personal activities that are important to you. Time management and stress management, when used together, can help you maintain a positive "can-do" attitude in life.

This chapter also addresses the importance of managing your financial resources. Like time, for most of us, money is limited. Money can be used for many wonderful things, such as financing your education and providing for you and your family, but keep in mind that many people place too much value on material possessions. Your self-worth should not be based on how much money you make or the stuff you have.

There is a Latin saying, *carpe diem,* that means "seize the day"—basically, *live life to the fullest.* We're going to take that one step further and "seize each moment" by managing these two valuable resources in the best way possible.

3.1   Introduction

This chapter isn't the only place where we'll discuss time management. Like stress management, time management is a *foundational* skill—meaning it is important in just about every area of your life. However, here we will focus on time management in the broadest sense—how do you spend your time each day?

Wasting time is the same as wasting your life. This doesn't mean you can't take time to relax—some people might see taking a walk in the woods as a waste of time, but it might help you clear your mind or recharge your batteries, or maybe you just enjoy the beauty of nature. That would still be a good use of your time (assuming it didn't interfere with your responsibilities). No, a true waste of time is allowing minutes or hours of your day to be eaten up by things that are unnecessary, unplanned, or unimportant. Have you ever had the experience of getting to the end of the day and thinking, "Where did the time go?" Maybe you started the day wanting to do something to advance your goals, or maybe all you wanted was to do something fun, but somehow the time just "slipped away," and now you can't figure out where it went. It isn't possible to get that lost time back, but it is possible to stop any more time from slipping mysteriously through your fingers. The first step, as you'll see, is becoming aware of how you spend your time—and identifying any time wasters that might be eating it up without you even realizing.

The good news is that you have already begun to manage your time by reading this book. The steps you've already taken on your journey to success—learning to manage your day-to-day stress, having a more focused and positive attitude, setting goals and objectives—all of these things will help you better manage your time. Stress can be a major time waster, and getting it out of your way was the first step to effective time management. Having a good attitude will allow you to get more done with the time you have. Your goals will tell you where to focus your energy, and the objectives or action plans you create will give you the specific steps you need to take to accomplish those goals. This chapter will show you how to put all these things into action in your already busy day-to-day life. Let's begin with Exercise 3-1.

Do you feel like you are barely holding on to time?

Exercise 3-1   Assess Yourself: *How Good a Time Manager Are You?*

Make each statement with the number that best describes your experience.

3 = Often   2 = Sometimes   1 = Rarely

_____ I feel or say there isn't enough time in the day.	_____ I jump from one task to another and never seem to fully complete any.
_____ I put things off until the last minute.	
_____ Deadlines stress me out.	_____ I feel like I haven't accomplished very much.
_____ I am late for my appointments.	_____ I stress out over tests.
_____ I turn in my assignments late.	_____ I pull all-nighters studying for an exam or writing a paper that is due.
_____ I get overwhelmed by large tasks and don't know where to start.	_____ Total

Evaluation

21–25: You need to work on improving your time management strategies and you will greatly benefit from this chapter.

16–20: This chapter will definitely help you.

10–15: You're a pretty good time manager and can just work on those areas rated 2 or above.

If you scored 26–30, well, let's put it this way: If you follow through with the suggestions in this chapter, it will be a positive life-changing experience. Let's work on improving your number and improving your life!

3.2   Using Time Management Techniques

To become an effective time manager, you must first identify the time wasters in *your* life. Then you can use effective time management techniques to overcome them. In addition, you will learn to use time management as a powerful tool in strategic planning for large projects or assignments.

3.2a   Identifying Time Wasters

Have you ever heard someone say that there aren't enough hours in the day? Of course, the truth is that every day has the same number of hours. We all have the same amount of time; it's how we use our given time that makes the difference. One of the first steps to managing your time well is to identify and eliminate common time wasters. This can free up valuable time for other tasks or activities. Following is a list of common time wasters followed by techniques to combat them.

Food for Thought

Time is a fixed commodity. Time is the one resource equally available to every person regardless of education, sex, or social status. The best possible investment you can make is using your time wisely.

Time Waster 1: Lack of Organization   How much time do you waste looking for your keys, books, or other items? When you sit down to study, does it take you more than five minutes to actually begin? Do you forget important dates, such as birthdays and anniversaries? Exercise 3-2 will help you evaluate your organizational skills. A lack of organization may only be stealing ten minutes here and fifteen minutes there, but at the end of the day this could add up to hours of wasted time. Not only do you lose precious time but bad stress enters your life and makes it harder to maintain a positive attitude.

Exercise 3-2   How Organized Are You?

Answer each question with either "yes" or "no."

_____ Do you often misplace your keys, glasses, or other important personal items?

_____ Do you forget birthdays, anniversaries, or other important dates?

_____ Do you find yourself in trouble because you forgot to do or get something?

_____ Do you spend more than ten minutes trying to locate an assignment, a bill, or study tools that you know "had to be right here"?

_____ Have you ever lost something only to have it reappear after several months?

_____ Do you have stacks of unanswered messages, unpaid bills, and unread magazines or books?

_____ Are you frequently late for appointments, commitments, or other activities?

_____ Do you have piles of items around the house or in your room waiting to be put away?

_____ Do you feel that having more space is all that you really need to solve all your storage problems?

_____ Do you want to organize things, but when you realize how much there is, you don't know where to start?

_____ Do you usually feel that you haven't accomplished as much as you had hoped to each day?

_____ Do you have to clear things out of the way before you can sit down to relax, visit, or work?

Each "yes" answer is worth 1 point.
Add up all your "yes" answers.
My total score _____

10–12 You need to take immediate action to get organized.
6–9   Disorganization is greatly interfering with your life.
3–5   Disorganization is causing bad stress and low productivity in your life.
1–2   You are in good shape and only have a few areas to work on.

Now that you have an idea of how disorganization can affect your life, what will you do? The best way to combat organization problems is to create your own specific action plan. One hint is to tackle only one issue at a time, moving to another when you've taken care of the first. If you try to tackle several issues at once, you may become overwhelmed and fail at all of them. Tackling one problem successfully will motivate you to take on the next one, and so on. To get started, complete Exercise 3-3.

Exercise 3-3   Getting Organized

Pick one of your "yes" answers from Exercise 3-2. Write it down and think about it for a while. Develop strategies and a specific action plan that will turn that "yes" into a "no." Review goal setting and the basic components of an action plan. Don't be afraid to ask trusted family and friends for help. Two examples are given in Figure 3-1.

_____

_____

_____

_____

_____

_____

When you feel this is no longer an issue in your life, choose another "yes" answer to change.

Figure 3-1   Action plans for getting organized

Yes   Do you often misplace your keys, glasses, or other important personal items?

Action Plan: _I will now put my keys in the cabinet by the door as soon as I get home. If I have to remember to take anything to school the next day, I will put a note under my keys. That way, when I grab them in the morning, the note will remind me of what I need to take._

Yes   Do you forget birthdays, anniversaries, or other important dates?

Action Plan: _I will buy a calendar and fill in all the important dates in my life. I will keep this calendar somewhere I will see it every day, so it will remind me of upcoming important dates or events._

Time Waster 2: Lack of Strategic Planning Do you dread major tasks like writing a research paper or preparing a presentation? These special projects usually require several steps to complete. A poor strategic planner is overwhelmed by these tasks and spends more time dreading the task than getting it done. Often, poor planners do not even know where to begin. However, just by using a simple tool such as a large desk calendar strategically placed in your study area, you can become a highly effective strategic planner.

You can certainly use the calendar on your phone to do strategic planning. However, a large desk calendar in your study area usually works better for a number of reasons. First, it is in a place you (hopefully) frequently visit. The calendar allows you to write all your important

Food for Thought

Your misplaced keys or other misplaced items will always be in the _last_ place you look!

upcoming events and deadlines in one place, and at a glance, you can see what your future holds. In addition, physically writing something often helps people remember.

This type of planning gives you an overview of the entire picture even if an event takes place over several months. It may be helpful to carry a portable calendar such as the one on your phone to note things as they come up during the day and then transfer them to your desk calendar later.

Dry-erase single-month calendars have become popular and you may choose to use one, but be cautious as you cannot visually plan for more than one month in advance. You must write in each month and number the days yourself. If using this method, consider erasing the first two weeks of the month once they pass. Immediately write in the first two weeks of the following month in its place, preferably in a different color. Then, when the next month begins, you'll already have the first two weeks visible and will only have to update the second half of the month. This will give you at least a constant three to four weeks of scheduling at a glance. To keep track of your long-term schedule, we recommend also using a phone calendar or another twelve-month physical calendar along with the dry-erase method.

Now you have the important events and deadlines in your life all written in one place. But how does that help you in the strategic planning process? Let's say you have a large paper due toward the end of the semester. A poor strategic planner waits until a few days (or even the night before) and quickly throws together a poorly written project. Part of this student's issue is procrastination, but most of it is poor planning—and that's something we can fix.

Let's use the example of a smaller paper (three to five pages), assigned on the first of the month, that is due at the end of the month. If you use the following steps, not only will the project be much easier to complete, but the quality and resulting grade will be higher.

1. Place the due date on your calendar in bright red or highlight in yellow.

2. Break the paper down into specific steps that need to be done with approximate times for each step:

    a. Choosing a topic (one hour)

    b. Researching and gathering information (three hours)

    c. Developing an outline (two hours)

    d. Writing a rough draft (four hours)

    e. Getting feedback (two hours)

    f. Rewriting and rechecking final paper (four hours)

Now you know it will take around sixteen hours to finish this paper. That would be a lot to do all in one night! But, luckily, you have a whole month to get it done. Next, take a look at your calendar to see where you have the time for each of these tasks. Make sure you give yourself plenty of time before the deadline to complete your paper. This way, you will have some extra time in case something takes longer than you thought it would or if something unexpected comes up (like your printer breaking down).

You can write these tasks on your desk calendar in blocks of time. For example, you might break your research time into two days of one and a half hours each (see Figure 3-2). Remember, your first few attempts are learning experiences. Keep notes on areas that did not go as planned so you can improve in the future. Now that you have your major tasks planned, you can continue to update your calendar and repeat this process for each assignment. Exercise 3-4 gives you a chance to try this out.

Figure 3-2   Strategic plan for writing a paper

August   **Year 2014**

Sun	Mon	Tue	Wed	Thu	Fri	Sat
					1 Choose term paper topic and title (1 hour)	**2** Jill's birthday
3	**4** Research and gather info for term paper 1½ hours	**5** Continue to research and gather info for term paper (1½ hours)	**6** Movies with Joe	**7** Mom and Dad's anniversary	**8** Football camp 8 a.m.–3 p.m.	**9** Football camp 8 a.m.–3 p.m. Develop outline for term paper (1 hour)
10 Football camp 8 a.m.–3 p.m. Continue to develop outline for term paper (1 hour)	**11** Football camp 8 a.m.–3 p.m. Phone bill due!	**12** Football camp 8 a.m.–3 p.m.	**13** Begin to write rough draft for term paper (1½ hours)	**14** Continue to rough draft for term paper (1½ hours)	**15** Football practice 1–3 p.m.	**16** Football practice 1–3 p.m. Finish rough draft for term paper (1 hour)
17 Football practice 1–3 p.m.	**18** Get feedback for term paper (1 hour)	**19** Football practice 1–3 p.m.	**20** Finish getting feedback for term paper (1 hour)	**21**	**22** Begin to rewrite and recheck final paper (1 hour)	**23** Lunch with Josh
24 Continue to rewrite and recheck final paper (1 hour)	**25** Continue to rewrite and recheck final paper (½ hour)	**26** Football practice 1–3 p.m.	**27** Continue to rewrite and recheck final paper (½ hour)	**28** Football practice 1–3 p.m.	**29**	**30** Finish final revisions of term paper (1 hour)
31 Term paper due tomorrow at 8 a.m.—have printout ready						

Exercise 3-4   Strategic Planning

This calendar-based system can be used for any task that requires multiple steps to complete. For example, using Figure 3-3, strategically plan how you would prepare a thirty-minute presentation for class. Let's say it was assigned on the first of the month. The due date is already listed on the calendar along with some other obligations that you need to plan around. First, list the steps necessary and estimate how long each one will take. Then fill them in on the mock calendar.

List steps needed with approximate times to complete:

_____

_____

_____

_____

Fill these steps in on the mock calendar in Figure 3-3.

Figure 3-3   Insert the steps from Exercise 3-4 to plan and complete the oral presentation

April   Year 2015

Sun	Mon	Tue	Wed	Thu	Fri	Sat
			1	**2** Soccer practice 3–5 p.m.	**3** Soccer practice 3–5 p.m.	**4** Soccer game 3–5 p.m.
5	**6** Steph's 21st birthday!	**7**	**8** Soccer practice 3–5 p.m.	**9** Soccer practice 3–5 p.m.	**10**	**11** Soccer game
12 Soccer practice 3–5 p.m.	**13** Soccer practice 3–5 p.m.	**14**	**15**	**16**	**17** Soccer final	**18**
19	**20**	**21**	**22**	**23** Get card for Gram & Pap	**24**	**25**
26 Dentist appointment 2 p.m.	**27**	**28** Gram & Pap's surprise party	**29**	**30** Oral presentation due!		

Time Waster 3: Personal Habits Do you have personal habits that waste your time? Worry and procrastination are two of the most common. We have talked about how worry is wasted negative energy. If you find yourself worrying a lot, please review the difference between *worry* and *concern*—remember, we even discussed how to turn worry *into* concern.

Procrastination
When you put off doing something until the last possible minute

Procrastination is another personal habit that can waste a large amount of time. Procrastination means you put off doing something until the last possible minute. In addition to wasting time, procrastination leads to poor quality work compared to when you plan ahead. Procrastination and worry are related. Procrastination robs you of time and power by causing stress in the form of guilt, embarrassment, and anxiety. The anxiety and fear of failure can cause worry. Both procrastination and worry are powerful enemies of time management and the stress they cause can hurt your mind and body. Studies have shown that students who procrastinate regularly are more stressed and have more health problems than those who plan their time better.

One cause of procrastination is fear of failure. However, in other cases, fear of success can be the reason. For example, success can lead to increased responsibility, which can be scary. If fear is a factor, we encourage you to review how to reframe your thinking. Procrastination can also result from not understanding the task, or simply not making the task a priority. Save yourself the unnecessary stress and develop better time management skills to combat procrastination.

Think about other personal habits that could be classified as time wasters in your life. How much daily time do you use talking on the phone or texting? Do you spend hours playing video games, aimlessly scrolling through social media, or getting wrapped up in the latest app or other trend? The internet, computers, tablets, and smartphones are among the most useful pieces of technology ever invented. These things have completely changed how we communicate and access information. However, many people let these devices control their lives. Don't let technology waste your precious time. You may be guilty of sitting down to do some schoolwork and thinking, "I'll just check my phone *real quick.*" How often does that lead to half an hour wasted on social media?

Spending hours online each day, texting during class, spending your whole night playing video games when you have an important test the next day—these are not effective ways to use your time if you want to succeed (as common as these behaviors might be). These behaviors also create problems outside of school. Using technology for personal reasons during work hours is a major reason for low productivity in the workforce and could also get you fired. Identify your personal time-wasting habits and ask yourself how you can improve. Remember, time is precious. Becoming aware of exactly how you use your time is a good first step in personal success with time management. Rate your personal habits in Exercise 3-5.

Rate the following statements based on how often you experience them.

3 = Often   2 = Sometimes   1 = Rarely   0 = Never

_____ I worry about many things in my life.

_____ I put off tasks until the last minute.

_____ I talk and text on the phone for long periods of time even when I have other tasks that need doing.

_____ I spend time on the computer, on my phone, or playing games even when high priority tasks need to be completed.

_____ I get bored easily with a task.

Now add up your score.   My total score _____

A score of 0–5 is very good. Even the best time managers have a rare occasion where they engage in some of these habits. However, if you only occasionally engage in these behaviors (1 point each), you have very good time management habits. A score of 6–10 ranges from fair to poor, and you could improve your habits with better time management strategies. A score of 11–15 is cause for concern, and you really need to work on your personal habits because they are wasting your time.

Now that you have assessed your personal habits, you will develop the single most powerful tool to combat all the "often" responses in Exercise 3-5, avoid procrastination, and become an effective time manager. This almost magical tool is called the *to-do list*. Be careful: Before you dismiss this as too simplistic or not very powerful, consider the following success story, which occurred in 1910.

Success Story

A Simple Time Management Idea, Worth $25,000 in 1910!

When Charles M. Schwab was president of Bethlehem Steel, he confronted Ivy Lee, a management consultant, with an unusual challenge. Paraphrasing the original conversation: "Show me a way to get more things done," Schwab demanded. "If it works, I'll pay anything within reason." Lee handed Schwab a piece of paper. "Write down the things you have to do tomorrow," he said. Schwab did it. "Now number these items in the order of their real importance," Lee continued. Schwab did. "First thing tomorrow morning," Lee added, "start working on number one and stay with it until it is completed. Next, take number two, and don't go any further until it is completed. Then proceed to number three, and so on. If you can't complete everything on schedule, don't worry. At least you will have taken care of the most important things before getting distracted by items of lesser importance. The secret is to do this daily. Evaluate the relative importance of the things you have to get done, establish priorities, record your plan of action, and stick to it. Do this every working day. After you have convinced yourself of the value of this system, have your men try it. Test it as long as you like, and then send me a check for whatever you think the idea is worth."

In a few weeks, Charles Schwab sent Ivy Lee a check for $25,000. Schwab later said that this lesson was the most profitable one he had ever learned in his business career. (And remember, $25,000 in 1910 dollars would be worth over $650,000 by today's standards.)

The problem with to-do lists, like anything else, is that they must be fully understood for you to get the most out of them. Even though making a to-do list sounds simple enough, it can be done incorrectly. If you've been making to-do lists wrong, you might mistakenly believe they can't help you. One of the biggest mistakes people make is creating a list that is too complicated. Then the list itself becomes a source of stress—not very helpful! Let's look at the proper way to develop this powerful time management tool.

Technique 1: The Daily To-Do List. Do you start each day without a plan? If you have a plan, do you understand how to prioritize (figure out what needs to be accomplished first)? Without a plan, your time can be easily wasted. Maybe you think you're too busy to sit down and plan out each day. What you may not realize is that the small amount of time it takes to plan your day will pay off by freeing up all the time you would have wasted without a plan.

That said, as we've mentioned before, *you must find a balance.* A few minutes spent planning your day will help to save you time later. But if you find yourself worrying about how many items to put on your to-do list or filling in three different calendars, then you've defeated the purpose of planning as a time-saver.

Like Charles Schwab in the Success Story, many successful leaders feel that making effective lists is the secret to their success. It allows them to plan and prioritize tasks, and it also helps them discover new ways to use their time efficiently.

There are several types of lists you can make and several places you can make them. The process of keeping different types of lists can become so confusing that you may get lost in all your lists. Therefore, we recommend a simpler way to organize your life. The first step is to gather the proper tools.

A large desk or wall calendar works well with a daily to-do list. It's a good idea to create your to-do list with your calendar in front of you for reference because it will already have important events written down. To construct this list, do the following:

1. Write down every activity, assignment, meeting, or promise that comes your way each day, and keep this list with you.

2. Prioritize each task based on how urgent or important it is. Number the most important thing "1," the next most important thing "2," and so on. (Exercise 3-6 will help you practice prioritizing.)

3. Over the course of the day, complete these tasks starting with "1" (the most important) and moving down the prioritized list. Cross them off as you finish them. This will give you a sense of accomplishment and pride, which will keep you motivated and dedicated to your list. Your goal for the day should be to have all top-priority items crossed off—but if you don't manage to get to them all, that's all right. Just move any remaining high-priority items to the top of your new list for the following day. Remember, stress and worry will accomplish nothing.

4. At the end of your day, reprioritize any remaining items on your list. Place those tasks that need to be done the next day at the top of a new list. Then list other tasks that you hope to complete. Remember, it would be best to do all of this in your study area or wherever you keep your big calendar so you can use it as a reference. Get in the habit of spending a few minutes each day planning for the next day. This process will help you greatly and will eventually become automatic and take only minutes to complete. Now go to bed, secure in the knowledge that you don't have to worry about tomorrow.

5. Assess your list and priorities the next day and make changes if necessary. Remember, things may come up unexpectedly throughout the day, so be a little flexible. Try not to overwhelm yourself. For example, some larger high-priority tasks may require breaks where you move on to a simpler task down the list, or maybe even rest for ten or fifteen minutes to refresh yourself. As we mentioned, it is about finding balance, and it may take several attempts before you see exactly how this style of planning will work for you.

Helpful Hints:
- Do not make your lists very long. Focus on three to six high-priority items and think of the rest as extra credit. This number may seem small to very busy people. If you accomplish three to six items each day, though, you will be amazed at how much you can do over time. It's worthless to write down ten to fifteen things and completing none of them because you're overwhelmed by the number of items. In other words, *keep it simple*!
- Find ways to make tasks interesting.
- Have a positive attitude.
- Do your most demanding work early in the day, when you're fresh and alert.
- Reward yourself when you get a job done.
- Organize your desk so you are not wasting time trying to find pencils, dictionaries, and other supplies.
- Control interruptions.
- Commit to finishing what you start.

Chapter 3: Managing Your Resources

Exercise 3-6 Prioritizing Tasks

Imagine that you have reached your long-range career goal and are now a successful employee. You have the following tasks to do in addition to your daily work routine. You start work at 8 a.m. Prioritize this list by writing numbers 1 to 5 on the line to the left of the item to indicate which you would do first, second, and so on.

_____ Prepare for important meeting scheduled from 9 to 10 a.m.
_____ Begin research for a report due in two weeks.
_____ Reserve a conference room for a departmental meeting by 11 o'clock.
_____ Call two clients to schedule appointments for next week.
_____ Meet with your staff members to assign their daily duties.

In summary, the combination of a daily to-do list with a large desk calendar at your study area can do much to improve your time management skills. See Table 3-1 for a list of some of the major benefits of this system.

Table 3-1 To-Do Lists and Calendars: What They Do for You

To-Do Lists

- Help you to begin your day with a written plan of action and prevent other people and distractions from wasting your time
- Combat procrastination
- Help you develop a prioritized list that prepares you for the next day and prevents you from jumping from task to task
- Allow you time to think and plan to increase efficiency
- Help to organize your life

Calendar

- Helps you see the big picture of what is coming up
- Assists in the strategic planning of getting larger, long-term tasks accomplished
- Notes important appointments, events, and deadlines
- Is a key tool when creating and accomplishing goals; think *measurable* from SMART

Exercise 3-7 gives you the opportunity to make a daily to-do list.

Using your desk calendar, make a daily to-do list for tomorrow. Keep it with you throughout the day. Does it feel good to cross off the items? Try this for at least ten days in a row, and then write about your results. Did it make you more productive? Did it help with your personal organization?

Things to do today   **Date** _____

Priority   **Task**

_____   _____

_____   _____

_____   _____

_____   _____

_____   _____

3.3   Additional Time Management Techniques

A few additional time management techniques and concepts will add *synergy* to your time management skills. Synergy means the whole is greater than the sum of its parts. To put it in mathematical terms, it's like $1 + 1 = 3$—a seemingly impossible equation. It simply means that if you combine these new concepts with what you already know, the impact will be even greater than what you imagined.

3.3a   Make Time Your Friend

Waste Time Productively   This may seem contradictory since we just told you it's important not to waste your time. However, it's also important to remember that time is not your enemy. It can be like a companion that travels along with us on our journey through life. For example, do you know people who continually complain that "There aren't enough hours in the day" or they "just don't have any time to get anything done"? Remember our earlier discussion on the power of the subconscious mind: If you continually plant the thought that you never have enough time, guess what? You won't!

So how do you turn time into a friend? One of the best methods is to learn to *waste time productively.* The best way this concept can be demonstrated is by revisiting the concept of *reframing,* which we covered in the goals and attitudes chapter.

Scenario 1   You were supposed to have a doctor's appointment at 1:00 p.m. You also have some errands to run and a big test coming up in two days, so you want to do some studying this evening. The doctor's office is extremely busy; it is 1:30, and there are still several people ahead of you. You begin to feel angry, your blood pressure rises, your muscles tense, and you begin to worry about all the things you must do and how this is going to put you behind. By 2:00, you are ready to explode. Finally, at 2:45, you see the doctor. The appointment doesn't go well because you are so mad. You even forget to tell your doctor some important information about your health. Then you run your errands, feeling upset the whole time, and when you get home, you have a pounding headache. You are unable to study effectively and have a rough time sleeping that night. Your grade on the test reflects these problems.

Scenario 2   You have a doctor's appointment at 1:00 p.m. You also have some errands to run and a big test coming up in two days, so you want to do some studying this evening. The doctor's office is extremely busy; it is 1:30, and there are still several people ahead of you. You are prepared for this. You calmly pull out your note cards to study for the exam. You study until your name is called at 2:45. You then go in and have good appointment with your doctor. They are able to help you with a health problem you've been having because you remember to mention it. You run your errands and then go home. Because you were able to study in the waiting room, you decide to go out and see a movie. You come home refreshed and ready for a good night's sleep.

In Scenario 2, you managed to *reframe* a bad situation into a good one. Having to wait for an appointment can be a *time waster*, but being prepared helped you to *waste that time effectively* by studying. You probably know of other times when you can apply this technique. This does not mean you constantly take your schoolwork with you, the idea is to do something productive when a situation threatens to waste your time so that you can free up some time later for something else, maybe even an activity that is fun and relaxing.

Capitalize on Peak Periods.   We talked about Albert Einstein's question during our *power of the subconscious mind* discussion, pondering why he always got his best ideas in the morning when he got lost in shaving. It also serves a purpose here. In the study skills chapter, you will learn why you should understand your *internal biological clock*—in other words, knowing the times of day when you are most effective. Most people are more productive in the morning, but we all differ. If you know what times of day are most productive for you, you may be able to schedule your more difficult tasks for these times. Maybe you come up with good ideas on your morning commute or walk to school. If so, it may be a good idea to carry a small recorder or notebook with you so you don't forget your ideas. Today almost all cell phones have voice recording and note-taking capabilities. Don't hesitate to use them, but also remember to periodically back up any form of electronic storage.

Conversely, there are times during the day when your mind may not be at its optimum level. For example, most people feel less productive and creative after they eat lunch. These are good times to sit back, relax a little, and read over your work instead of trying to come up with new ideas.

All of us have an internal biological clock, and if we pay attention to it, we can optimize our performance. Have you ever noticed how you may feel sicker or more anxious at night? Even seasonal changes can alter your productivity or feeling of well-being. That is why a bright and cheery study room in the dark of winter can be a more productive studying environment.

Plan for the Unexpected   You've done a great job planning with your daily to-do list and desk calendar. However, life doesn't always go as planned. This is why you must be flexible and positive. If something unexpected comes up, don't panic or worry—it won't help to react that way. Calm down, reorganize, and do the best you can to make the situation positive.

Also, know when you are overcommitted and learn to say "no." Saying no is difficult for several reasons. You might be afraid of letting someone down, of not being liked by others, or of missing out. However, if we say yes to everybody and take on too many tasks, none of them will get done well.

If you don't want to say no but are unsure if you can honestly say yes, be honest. For example, if someone asks you to do something, respond by asking, "Can I have some time to think about it?" You can still say no later, but now you can assess whether you really have the time to do this task. If you still need to say no, you have time to prepare a thoughtful response.

Just as important as learning to say "no" is learning *how* to say "yes." Let's say someone asks you to help with a large project. If you simply say yes, you may get several tasks dumped on you—more than you have time for. Instead, say yes in a way that limits how much the other person will ask you to do. For example, you can respond by saying, "I'm not sure how much time I have. What's the most important thing I can help you with?" This tells the person asking you for help that you can't do everything they may want you to; it also encourages them to think of the one task they think is most suited to your abilities and talents.

Finally, many unexpected things can happen to disrupt your well-planned lists. Remember, don't be a slave to your schedule or make large lists. Try to leave a little extra time each day in case something comes up, and have realistic expectations for how much you can get done. Stay motivated by rewarding yourself for getting all your tasks done. If you have a large task (such as a research paper), reward yourself along the way for each little step accomplished. A small reward will help your motivation and move you on to the next step. But remember to save the biggest reward for when your large task is done.

Managing Technology and Avoiding Its Distractions   It has been proven that when you physically write something down, you are more likely to remember it. But let's face it, as technology continues to advance, we will have to rely more on touchscreen devices (and beyond) to manage our lives. Adapting to this way of life is natural for some and maybe not so much for others. Regardless, if you can avoid the distractions these devices offer, you will also find there are many resources that will help with your personal time management using electronic devices.

For example, having a calendar that syncs between your phone and your email account is a great way to keep efficiently organized on the go. This way, you can update your schedule when you are at your computer or on your tablet or out and about with a smartphone, knowing it will all sync up. Then you can transfer this information to a desk calendar at a convenient time. In addition, when collaborating with others as part of a group project where you have to coordinate multiple schedules, you will have the ability to set up and sync shared calendars between all of you. This makes scheduling (and changing the schedule) easy and efficient for everyone involved.

Speaking of being efficient, as much as technology can help, it can also be a huge time waster. We've already mentioned some of these distractions, including social media, apps and games on your phone or tablet, online videos, series, and sitcoms—even advertisements that waste your time when you scroll through your news feed or watch a video. Be aware of this and always try your best to stay on task. One way to do this is to use a personal reward system where technology time wasters are the reward. For example, allow yourself twenty minutes on social media only after you've accomplished your top three priorities on the to-do list. Save being able to play your favorite video game for after you've finished studying and limit yourself to thirty minutes of play time. You will be more motivated to finish what is necessary so that you can relax afterward. You might even enjoy the activities more if you don't have the guilt of procrastinating hanging over your head.

Technology is constantly evolving, so it is up to you to seek out current methods that will work in your day-to-day life. Don't be afraid to test out new time management apps and different ways to use your devices to become more efficient. As always, be careful and avoid the many distractions you will surely come across.

3.4   Learn to Maintain Balance

You may be tired of hearing the word *balance* by now, but it is a key concept in many of the topics in this text. The happiest, most productive people combine work, family relationships, and time off to create a satisfying life. These people are *balance experts*. They know that if they only take care of everyone else, they will have little time or energy for themselves, and their stress will grow both physically and emotionally. See another connection between stress management and time management?

Balance experts pay attention when work demands intrude on family time or when family responsibilities distract them at work. It's a lot like recognizing when you're entering your bad stress zone, as we discussed previously for stress management. They also realize that time away from work or school is essential to recharge their batteries. Balance experts approach their commitments with well-defined goals and a positive attitude.

Table 3-2 shows you some of the signals that should alert you that you are drifting out of balance.

Table 3-2   How to Recognize When You Are Drifting Out of Balance

- Losing sense of humor, one of the first signs
- Lack of restful sleep (most people need eight hours)
- Excessive yawning or fighting sleep in class or at a meeting
- Tasks piling up to an overwhelming level
- Becoming easily annoyed

Food for Thought

We think technology will save us time, but that doesn't always happen. A Harris Poll taken between 1973 and 1987 showed the average American's amount of free time had shrunk from 26.6 to 16.6 hours per week. Do you want to guess where that average would be today?

Food for Thought

Wherever you go on vacation, you must take *yourself*. Make sure you are good company. In other words, learn to enjoy your time no matter what you are doing or where you are.

3.4a   Enjoy Your Time

When you're planning out your time on your large desk calendar or your daily to-do list, don't forget to include some fun things. Write them in a bright color or do something to make them stand out. This way, instead of looking at your calendar with dread, you now have fun things interspersed between productive tasks. Remember to take some time for yourself.

Just like your cell phone, you need to recharge your batteries or you will run down and be useless. This can be done in several ways. Research has shown that it's best to alternate between productive bursts followed by time to rest and brainstorm before starting a new task. Learning to take it easy is also good, if not essential, for productivity.

Vacations are another way to recharge. However, some people cram many activities into a stress-filled getaway and end up feeling like they need *another* vacation when they return just to recover from the first one. *Vacation* means "to vacate, or get away." Vacations should be refreshing and relaxing, not stressful. Only you know what kind of vacation works for you. For some, it may be a couple of days at the beach; for others, it may be mountain climbing; and for still others, it may be simply staying at home. Again, choose what works for you to recharge your batteries.

Exercise 3-8 Evaluate Your Personal Progress with Time Management Strategies

Now that we've discussed how to better manage your time, let's put these techniques into action. Over the next four weeks, incorporate as many of the strategies discussed into your academic and personal life as you can. Mark on your calendar a specific date one month from now to come back to this very page and complete the following questions:

How much free time do you feel you have each day? Has this changed over the past month? If so, by how much?

_____

_____

_____

How has using a calendar to keep track of upcoming events and deadlines changed your productivity and free time? Did you use a calendar in the past? If so, what specifically has changed when using one this month?

_____

_____

_____

Have you used a daily to-do list? Has prioritizing it helped keep you on task? Describe your personal routine when developing the list, and also describe how you go about completing tasks.

_____

_____

_____

Have you found that there are certain times of the day when you are able to work best? If so, when?

_____

What ways have you cut down on daily distractions in your life? Have you implemented any personal reward systems?

_____

_____

_____

Do you feel you have a better grasp on managing your time? _____

Now that you've had some time to develop these methods, how can you further improve your time management techniques for the future?

_____

_____

_____

3.5 Financial Wellness: Money Matters

Too often in our society, people think of money and the accumulation of material possessions as being the same thing as success. Although financial security may be one of your long-term goals, try not to make it your only focus. Many successful people in history had little or no money. Mahatma Gandhi is a good example of somebody who changed his entire country of India, as well as the world, yet he had only four possessions (glasses, a watch, sandals, and a homespun cloth robe). Think about your definition of success and your views on money by doing Exercise 3-9.

Exercise 3-9 What Are Your Views on Success and Money?

What is your definition of success?

_____

_____

_____

List some people who you think have successful lives.

_____

_____

What personal qualities helped them succeed?

_____

_____

_____

What characteristics do you have that will contribute to your success in life?

_____

_____

_____

List two success goals you will accomplish within a year.

_____

_____

List a success goal you wish to accomplish within five years.

_____

_____

_____ Do you equate money with success?

_____ Do you use money as a tool to improve your personal and professional life as well as the lives of those around you?

Money can be an effective tool to help you reach your goals. The more you understand money, the better you can manage it. Much like time management, your attitude toward money is important. If you continually tell yourself you will *never* have enough money, you *never* will. You must change these negative attitudes, understand financial concepts, and learn to use money as a positive tool that can enrich your life and the lives of others.

For most of us, money is a limited resource that must be managed much like our time. Everyone's financial situation is unique, so each budget needs to be personalized. Keep in mind that most people will always need to budget carefully no matter how much their incomes increase. This is because as your income grows, so will your financial responsibilities and, often, your wants. Even people who have millions of dollars go broke or live very sad lives. Of course, the opposite can also be true: Some people who are considered poor still manage to find happiness.

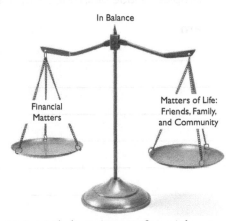

Maintain balance in your financial attitude.

3.5a   Understand the Basics of Money

The money you have "coming in" is called your *income*. Income can come from many sources, such as your salary or wages, an allowance, child support, government payments like welfare or social security, tax refunds, gifts, interest, money made on investments, and so on.

The total you have coming in from all these sources is your **gross income**. However, your employer probably withholds some of your pay for things like taxes, social security, insurance, union dues, parking, and other deductions. The money you actually take home is called your **net income**.

It's easy to know what your income is. Now for the hard question: "Where does your money go?" The things you spend your money on are called your *expenses*. There are two types: **fixed expenses** and **variable expenses**. Fixed expenses are the same each month. Examples include your rent or mortgage (home) payment, utility bills (phone, TV, internet service), and loan payments. Variable expenses, as the name suggests, *vary* or change from time to time. Examples of variable expenses include your food, clothing, entertainment, gas, car repairs, and educational expenses.

Ideally, your net income is greater than your total expenses! If you want to pay for your education or buy that dream house or car, you must understand your personal finances and come up with a successful plan for how to pay for these things. Planning and controlling the use of your money is called *budgeting*. Its many benefits include:

- Giving you an idea of where your money is going
- Decreasing and (hopefully eliminating) your anxiety and money worries
- Helping you focus on your goals and priorities in your life
- Helping control your spending
- Helping you figure out what you can spend on fun things and activities

Gross income

The total money you receive from all sources

Net income

Your gross income minus things like taxes, social security, and insurance, which are deducted; also known as take-home pay

Fixed expenses

Things that cost you the same amount every month, like rent or a mortgage

Variable expenses

Things that don't always cost the same amount, like food

Do you really *need* those $200 sneakers, or do you just *want* them? This is a question you must ask yourself if money is tight. Answer the following questions to help you distinguish between "wants" and "needs."

List all the things you spent money on this month, including all fixed and variable costs (see below). Examples include bills, rent, transportation, clothing, groceries, entertainment, and health and beauty items.

Item	Was It a Need or a Want?	Cost
_____	_____	_____
_____	_____	_____
_____	_____	_____
_____	_____	_____
_____	_____	_____
_____	_____	_____
_____	_____	_____

Did you spend more money on things you wanted or the things you needed? _____

Did you buy any of the items because someone made you feel you had to? _____

Did you shop for the best deal? _____

How much money do you think you could have saved this month if you'd shopped around or decided not to buy some of the things in the wants column? _____

Explain the following statement: "It is best to live within or even beneath your means." _____

_____

_____

HINT: If you are not sure if you want or need something, wait twenty-four hours and then decide.

3.5b   Steps to Budgeting

To keep things simple, here are two basic steps to budgeting. The first step is to gather all the facts by getting a good idea of your income and expenses. This takes time and good record keeping. Once you have all the facts, the second step is to analyze your situation and develop a budget. Of course, you will need to review your budget periodically and make adjustments as necessary. Let's work on Step 1 in Exercise 3-11.

Use this form (or create your own) to keep track of your income and expenses for three months.

Month _____   **Year** _____

Total Income for the Month

Wages/salary (net pay)   _____

Tips (if applicable)   _____

Financial aid   _____

Outside support
(parents or others)   _____

Other   _____

Total income for the month   _____

Total Expenses for the Month

Fixed expenses (rent, utilities, loans, insurance, etc.)

Expense	When It's Due	Amount
_____	_____	_____
_____	_____	_____
_____	_____	_____
_____	_____	_____
_____	_____	_____
_____	_____	_____

Total fixed expenses for the month   _____

(continues)

Variable expenses (This is the harder one. List everything, including food, transportation, entertainment, etc.)

Expense   **Amount Spent**

_____   _____

_____   _____

_____   _____

_____   _____

_____   _____

_____   _____

_____   _____

_____   _____

Total variable expenses   _____

Total expenses for month (add fixed and variable)   _____

If applicable, list any money you have in savings or investments _____

You now have a good picture of your monthly income, expenses, and savings. Now it is time for Step 2, analyzing your financial situation. There are several ways to do this. Some people like to break their expenses into larger categories and show how much of their money (what *percentage*) they spend on each category each month. Figure 3-4 shows a sample.

Another method is to ask yourself several important questions, as in Exercise 3-12.

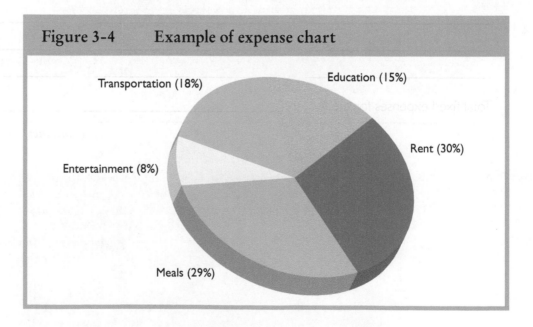

Figure 3-4   Example of expense chart

Transportation (18%)
Education (15%)
Rent (30%)
Entertainment (8%)
Meals (29%)

Exercise 3-12 Step 2: Analyzing Your Income and Expenses

Answer the following questions:

Do you have enough income to pay for your expenses? _____

Are you spending too much money? If so, where can you cut expenses? Is there one category in particular where you tend to spend too much? _____

Are you able to save money to put toward your goals (a vacation, tuition, a future large expense like a new computer)? Remember, you need to set aside a certain amount to pay those large but occasional expenses that will crop up during the year, such as car insurance or unforeseen maintenance or repairs.

_____

Don't worry. It's normal to feel like you will never have enough money to reach your goals. However, with a good plan, you can get there. The key is *consistency*. If you came up short when you compared your income to your expenses, there are many things you can do. First, consider where you can stop spending so much. We aren't talking about living off of instant noodles here or even giving up your phone. Most of us can easily trim $100 a month (often more) by making simple changes. Here are some suggestions that can add up to save you a lot of money. After you've read the list, do Exercise 3-13.

- Is there anything you can do to reduce your utility bills? Turn off lights when you don't need them, turn the thermostat down one or two degrees, set the temperature lower while you are sleeping, take shorter showers, look for a cheaper phone plan— even a few changes could mean major savings.

- If you currently live alone, consider sharing living expenses (like rent and utilities) with a roommate.

- Pack your lunch instead of eating out. Packing a lunch just three times a week can save you at least $12 to $15 a week—that's $60 a month!

- Walk, ride a bike, or carpool to save transportation costs. Cut down on driving and perform regular car maintenance to prevent costly repairs. Checking fluid levels and changing your car's oil on schedule is the single most important way to increase your engine's longevity.

- Save on food and clothing expenses. Buy nonperishable food in bulk, shop for clothes at discount and secondhand stores, compare prices, and look for items on sale. Find and use coupons. Eat out less frequently, so that when you do, it is a special treat.

- Find free or cheap ways to have fun. Examples include hiking, reading a book, or joining a club. Rent or borrow movies. Look for student discounts on entertainment.

- Consider not purchasing name brand things. Many generic or store-brand products are just as good.

Food for Thought

Reviewing the list, look at the examples that also relate to your physical health such as walking, exercise, and eating healthy. Your physical and financial health are connected. Little things add up. For example, packing healthy lunches instead of eating out, walking more, and cutting unhealthy habits like smoking, excessive drinking, gambling, and eating too much candy can benefit your health *and* wealth. If you saved just $10 a week, that would be $520 a year toward an emergency fund, a goal, or a fun reward.

- Don't try to impress anybody, especially friends who have more money. Someone will always have more money than you.
- Write down your financial goals. If you want a vacation, plan a year in advance by budgeting a little each month, and it will happen. Also, you can save money if you vacation with friends or family and share expenses. If your goal is very important (such as getting your education), a few years of frugal living will pay off.

Exercise 3-13   Pick *One* Idea

Select one idea from the list we gave you—or create your own—to save money, and track it for a month or two. Calculate how much money you saved. When this behavior becomes automatic, pick another idea.

Write your idea here:

_____

_____

See if you can now use the budgeting ideas from this text to develop your personal budget in Exercise 3-14.

Exercise 3-14   Chapter Summation

Construct Your Budget

Use information from this chapter and the exercises you've completed, in particular your answers from Exercise 3-11, to construct a budget for next month. Set a limit for your variable expenses—the amount you are able and willing to spend on each category for things like entertainment and clothes.

Clothing	_____
Entertainment	_____
Medical/dental/eye care	_____
Education (tuition, books, loans)	_____

Month _____   **Year** _____

Total Monthly Income _____

Expense	Budgeted Amount
Rent/mortgage	_____
Utilities	_____
Telephone	_____
TV/internet	_____
Loans	_____
Insurance	_____
Transportation/repairs	_____
Food	_____

Emergency fund (future expenses)	_____
Savings toward long-term goals (house, vacation)	_____
Other	_____
Total expenses	_____

Your total expenses should be equal to—or, even better, less than—your income.

Remember that things can change, or you may forget an expense. Your income may increase, or your goals may change. Don't worry. Just review and adjust your budget. Even on a small scale, budgets are powerful. If family members are supporting you financially, in addition to being very thankful, you should still budget and help out as much as you can.

3.6   Choosing Your Financial Institution

Here are some basics on finding a suitable financial institution. You need to find a financial institution that offers the types of services you need. You can go to a commercial bank, savings and loan, or credit union. It is best to make sure that the institution is federally insured (FDIC), which means it is backed up by the government in case of institutional losses. The services you need might include a checking account, debit cards, credit cards, or loans. Free checking and overdraft protection are also nice to have. Shop around for interest rates. Ideally, you want the highest on your investments (like your savings account) and the lowest on your loans and credit cards. Convenience is also a factor. Consider things like location and what hours they're open as well as services like direct deposit of your paychecks or mobile deposit for personal checks.

3.6a   Credit Cards, Friend or Foe?

It may seem like you get hundreds of credit card offers in the mail. When used properly, credit cards can be great, but the temptation of *easy* money can be dangerous. "Buy now, pay later" sounds good, but often, you end up paying much more later than you would've if you'd just paid now.

You certainly need loans to pay for school, a home, a car, and emergencies, but be careful of falling into a debt trap. When you borrow money, you must pay it back over time *plus* an additional amount. This cost of borrowing is called **interest**, and the amount you pay is determined by the annual percentage rate (APR). Sometimes there are extra charges and fees on top of interest, and these amounts can quickly add up. Be careful of charging items you do not need but simply *want*. Don't sign any credit card agreements unless you fully understand all the terms. Find a trusted person to explain if you are unsure.

Interest

The amount you must pay back in addition to the amount you borrowed

Credit cards are a big part of building your *credit score*, which we will discuss next. Without going into great detail, here are some very important tips when using a credit card:

- Only make purchases you know you can afford.

- Check your credit card statements regularly. You will be surprised at how quickly small expenses add up. You can check your balance at any time online; most banks offer secure mobile apps for this, as well. Check your balance often.

- Ignore the "minimum payment due" amount. This is usually a very small number and credit companies want you to think you can get away with only paying the minimum. You'll get away with it, but you will be charged interest on the remaining balance. As that interest adds up, you may find yourself in a position where you can no longer afford to pay off the full amount you owe on your card. Pay as much as you are able to as soon as you are able to.

- Find out when your monthly credit cycle begins and make sure you pay the entire balance at least a day or two before your next cycle begins. If you pay your balance all the way down each month, you will not be charged interest and your credit score will soar!

- Make sure you have an easily accessible checking account set up through your financial institution (and make sure there is enough money in it to cover your credit charges!). It is actually quite easy to link your checking account when you log in to your credit card website. Linking your accounts makes paying your monthly balance as easy as securely logging in, typing in the amount you wish to pay from your checking account, and clicking submit.

- Start with a low credit limit to protect yourself from borrowing too much, and look into rewards programs like cash back or airline miles. A good rewards program can be very beneficial, but don't let it trick you into spending more than you should.

Always consider the following question, "Would I buy it if I had to pay in cash?" If you don't think you are financially secure enough (or responsible enough!) for a credit card, we suggest sticking with a debit card, which is more like using cash since you need to have the money in your account in order to use it.

3.6b   Maintaining a Good Credit Score

Having a good credit history is important for getting loans, especially when it comes to getting a lower interest rate. It is very likely you will need loans in the future. Your credit history is a permanent record of bills or loans you have paid or failed to pay on time. It is gathered from your financial history with credit card companies, banks, collection agencies, and the government. This personal data creates your *credit score*, a number ranging from 300 to 850 that has a lot of influence on applications for loans, future housing, employment, and other important finance-related issues. The higher your credit score, the more money you can borrow for a house or car.

To maintain a good credit score, consider the following:

- Pay your bills on time and do not default (fail to complete payments) on your loans.

- When using a credit card, pay off the entire balance each month on time. Try to find a card with a low or no annual fee and the lowest interest rate.

- Do not go over your credit limit. In fact, the closer you get to your limit, the more it brings down your score. Pay your balance regularly so that you don't get close to your limit.

- If you cannot pay a credit card balance in full on a given month, at least pay more than the minimum amount due. Paying anything less than the minimum will result in a lowered credit score.

- Do not apply for credit cards or loans that you do not absolutely need; this can also lower your score.

3.6c   A Word about Taxes

You must also think about taxes when it comes to budget planning. Individuals are often shocked when they see their first paycheck and it falls way short of what they expected. Often, people expect to receive their *gross income*—their hourly wage multiplied by the hours they worked—but in reality, what you receive will be less. What you actually take home—your *net income*—is your gross income minus several *deductions*. You may wonder, "Who is FICA and why is he taking some of my money?" Actually, FICA stands for the Federal Insurance Contribution Act, which is Social Security, and sets aside a portion of your income to ensure you will have an income later in life when you retire. In addition, it would pay you and your dependents if you become disabled and could not work. FICA also deducts for Medicare, which is a government program to insure you have health insurance when you reach old age.

Other deductions include federal, state, and local taxes that are withheld at different rates according to the amount of your income and where you live. You may also have optional deductions that pay for health insurance, vision and dental coverage, life insurance, disability insurance, retirement contributions, and even employee parking. You can see how these will add up and reduce your take-home pay. Therefore, it is important to plan your personal budget factoring in the tax deductions and contributions that come out of your paycheck for your weekly or monthly income.

In addition, if you are making significant income, you are responsible for filing yearly taxes in mid-April. You may owe the government an additional amount based on your financial situation, or you may be eligible for a tax refund. Everyone's financial situation is different, so we suggest that when the time comes, do all you can to learn about the current tax laws, specifically about how they can benefit you (refunds, deductions, exemptions, etc.). Overall, taxes are another important reason to make sure you allow for extra buffer room in your budget.

3.6d   Financing Your Education

There are many ways to help finance your education. One obvious way is to get a job to earn some income for education and life expenses. Another is to receive financial help from family. However, even if you do both of these things, it is likely that you will still need to borrow money by taking out a loan that you must pay back later. Loans aren't the only option. Unlike loans, **grants** are a form of financial aid that does *not* need to be repaid later. Obviously, you should go after every possible grant you can find. Most are based on your financial need. **Scholarships** are also free money that does not need to be paid back. Some are based on your need; others can be based on your achievements, community service, or your ability to write an essay.

If you do need to take out a loan, **subsidized student loans** are a good option. Their interest rate is low because they are subsidized (supported) by the federal government. Typically, these loans don't need to be paid back until after graduation. Requirements change from year to year, but here are some basic tips:
* Meet *early* with a financial aid officer to find out about all the loans, grants, and scholarships your school and government (state and federal) have to offer. This is your best source of updated information and requirements. Find out the deadlines and apply early.

Grants

Financial aid that does not need to be paid back later; most are based on need

Scholarships

Financial aid that does not need to be paid back later; can be based on need, achievement, community service, or other factors

Subsidized student loans

Low-interest loans supported by the federal government; may not need to be paid back until after graduation

- Search your community for grants and scholarships.

- Search the internet for grants and scholarships, but be skeptical of companies that offer scholarship and grant services for a fee. You can find the same information with good detective work.

- Loans and gifts of money can come from relatives and friends. Borrowing money from friends or relatives can be uncomfortable. You should have a contract to define the terms of the loan and prevent future hard feelings.

- Understand that loans must be repaid or your credit will be ruined.

Remember that eligibility for financial aid, including grants and loans, is often tied to academic performance. If you do not maintain the required grade point average, however your institution defines it, you may lose your financial aid.

3.6e   A Word about Identity Theft

You can be the victim of identity theft and not even be aware of it. All someone has to do is gain access to your Social Security number or other personal financial information. Your credit score can be destroyed by another person borrowing money, and failing to pay it back, in your name. To avoid being a victim, take the following measures:

- Never give out your Social Security number unless you are absolutely certain it is for a secure reason. For example, you need to give your Social Security number when opening a bank or credit card account, applying for a job, and filing taxes.

- Likewise, be cautious of giving out your credit card numbers. Avoid throwing away any credit card statements or mail items with credit or Social Security information. Shred them first.

- Do not carry your Social Security card in your wallet. If you have a safe deposit box, keep your Social Security card there. At the very least, keep it in a fire-safe box in a secure place in your home. With either option, you'll have access to your card if you need it for a legitimate reason.

- Check your credit rating at least once or twice a year. Make sure it is free of errors. Even the most cautious consumers can have errors on their credit report or be the targets of identity theft. A personal credit check does not affect your credit score, so you can do it often if necessary, but you only get one free credit report a year from the major credit bureaus.

- Regarding spam emails: There are many scams, some designed to entice you ("Register now to claim your cash prize") and others designed to scare you ("Regarding your past due account"). These types of junk emails are referred to as *phishing* and should not be responded to. If one looks legitimate (e.g., it appears to be from your bank or your place of employment), contact customer service or human resources to find out if the message is real or fake.

Healthy Decision-Making

Sharlene has a test on Monday and some research she wants to do on a paper due in several weeks. She has scheduled time this weekend on her calendar to go to the library to gather some articles for her paper and meet with her study group before the test. Her friend Melissa has asked her to help out with a volunteer community event this weekend on teaching children about personal safety. Sharlene wants to help but is fearful of having a lot of work passed on to her. She also does not want to lose her library time. Can you give her some suggestions on how to say yes to Melissa without losing time for her schoolwork?

_____

_____

_____

_____

Can you suggest some tasks she could do before the weekend to help Melissa so she would still be free to go to the library and have some weekend time for herself? One hint would be making posters to advertise the event. Can you list others?

_____

_____

_____

_____

_____

Know Your School

Your school will have support services to help with financial matters. Research school resources that can help you. Examples include personal counseling services and financial aid offices. List the information here, and for quick reference, place the information in a prominent place, such as on your refrigerator.

Resource Name: _____

Office Location: _____

Phone Number: _____

Email Address: _____

Resource Name: _____

Office Location: _____

Phone Number: _____

Email Address: _____

Resource Name: _____

Office Location: _____

Phone Number: _____

Email Address: _____

Resource Name: _____

Office Location: _____

Phone Number: _____

Email Address: _____

Resource Name: _____

Office Location: _____

Phone Number: _____

Email Address: _____

Active Study Strategies

Learning How to Learn

Objectives

By the end of this chapter, you will be able to:

- Organize yourself to maximize your study success
- Listen for learning in a classroom setting
- Record lecture notes in different formats
- Describe various note-taking strategies
- Reflect on note-taking styles that work best for you
- Identify active reading strategies
- Recognize unique aspects of taking an academic course online
- Use different strategies to achieve online success

Why Learn This Skill?

Good study skills are one of the top reasons for student success. Even if you already have study strategies, this chapter will help you by reinforcing your existing strategies or introducing you to new ones. In addition, strategies that have worked for you in the past may need to be changed to meet the demands of more challenging coursework. If you've changed majors or career paths, you may need to learn different strategies than the ones you used before.

Keep in mind that study strategies apply to your life even after you graduate. Maybe you've heard of the importance of being a "lifelong learner." You may not have to worry about your teacher's grading policies once you are established in your career, but colleagues and supervisors will evaluate your work and your work habits. What you will learn in this chapter—about creating an organized space to study in—will transfer into your work environment. Active reading strategies will certainly help you read your textbooks, but they can also help with the reading you have to do on the job. Note-taking skills will help you in the classroom and during meetings and presentations. We could go on, but you get the idea: These skills are transferable beyond your academic success and can impact your professional success as well.

4.1   Introduction

This chapter covers several important ways to develop stronger study skills. These include organizing your study area and revisiting study schedules and some time management techniques. In addition, you will learn new methods for reading text material and taking good lecture notes. Let's begin by covering some strategies that will help you manage your study load more effectively. Exercise 4-1 will help you assess your current study skills.

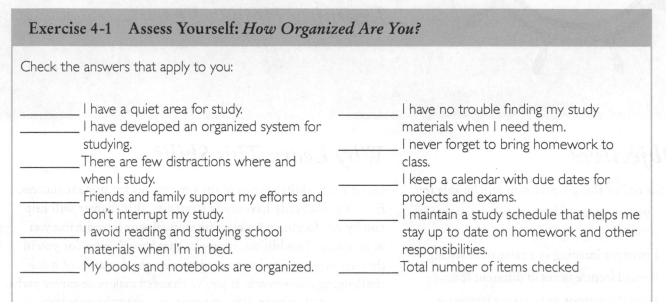

Exercise 4-1   Assess Yourself: *How Organized Are You?*

Check the answers that apply to you:

_____ I have a quiet area for study.
_____ I have developed an organized system for studying.
_____ There are few distractions where and when I study.
_____ Friends and family support my efforts and don't interrupt my study.
_____ I avoid reading and studying school materials when I'm in bed.
_____ My books and notebooks are organized.

_____ I have no trouble finding my study materials when I need them.
_____ I never forget to bring homework to class.
_____ I keep a calendar with due dates for projects and exams.
_____ I maintain a study schedule that helps me stay up to date on homework and other responsibilities.
_____ Total number of items checked

If you checked eight or more items, you're a pretty organized student and only need to work on one or two issues. Checking six to seven items indicates that this chapter could help you become more organized. Four to five checked items indicate that you would greatly benefit from becoming more organized, and three or fewer items indicates that you have some work to do and need to read the following ideas right away.

4.2   Organizing Study Materials

4.2a   How to Organize

Many textbooks will tell you the so-called *right* way to organize, and retail stores will offer to sell you the latest notebooks, calendars, tablets, and countless other organizers. If you're like a lot of students, you may have gone to your bookstore or the nearest discount store to buy these organizational tools—perhaps you even have a tablet to schedule your commitments. However, after a few weeks, despite your good intentions, you may find that these organizational strategies just don't *stick*.

Although we will give you many ideas on organization, there is no *one way* to organize. You simply have to create a system that works for *you*. The key is to keep it *simple, consistent*, and *systematic*.

Notebooks and Other Materials   Not submitting an assignment because "I left it in another notebook" doesn't cut it. Keep your materials organized so that you can access them with little stress and confusion. One recommendation is to keep a notebook for every class. For many classes, three-ring binders are simplest because you can easily keep everything in order and three-hole-punch handouts, exams, and such. If you're a full-time student, it is often easiest to have separate notebooks for each class so you don't have to cart all your materials to each class. Finally, many students find they need to have a different color notebook for each class to minimize the chances of taking the wrong one to class.

Laptops and tablets have become more acceptable for use in class. If you use one in class, keep your electronic notes organized in labeled and dated folders. Always remember to back up your information regularly. Once again, avoid all distractions that your device may tempt you with in the classroom or while studying!

Calendars In our discussion of time management, we discussed the importance of maintaining calendars for long- and short-term time frames. A calendar with room for writing to-do lists may be helpful. In addition, your calendar can help you keep track of deadlines and plan out large tasks over a period of weeks, as described earlier.

Study Area Where you study is also very important. Ideally, you should always study in the same place so you mentally connect that place to studying. It should have minimal distractions and good lighting. The table or desk should have all the necessary study tools, such as pens, paper, a calculator, a computer, and so on. Please see Figure 4-1. In particular, you should avoid studying in bed. Why? Because of something called *classical conditioning*. Russian scientist Ivan Pavlov did an experiment where a bell would ring right before a group of dogs were fed. Naturally, when the dogs ate the food, they *salivated* (or drooled). However, as the dogs began to connect the food with the sound of the bell, they reached a point where just the *sound* would cause them to drool—even if there wasn't any food. How is this relevant? When you're in bed, it's your body's natural response to get sleepy. If you study in bed, soon, you will connect *studying* with sleeping. When that happens, you may find

| Figure 4-1 | Which person is getting the most out of study time? |

that even when you are studying during the day (when you aren't tired), you still start to yawn and lose focus. That's because you have *conditioned* yourself to feel sleepy when you study. Plus, if the conditioning goes the other way and you associate your bed with studying, you might have a hard time getting a good night's sleep.

If You Live on Campus... Begin by thinking about how you study best. Do you concentrate best in total quiet, without interruption? Depending on your residence hall situation, you might need to find somewhere else to do your best studying. Perhaps there is a quiet space in the library or an empty classroom.

If You Commute... For commuters, it is equally important to maintain an organized study space. You may not have to deal with the typical residence hall distractions, but you still need to create a study area of your own. If you have to use your bedroom to study, avoid studying in bed. Use a desk or table in a well-lit area. Also, sit in a desk chair. This will force you to sit up straight (helping with concentration). If you study in a living room or dining area, try to avoid distractions such as the TV or loud music. If you live with others—family members or roommates—try to study at times when they are less likely to be a distraction. Also, see if your school has designated study areas reserved for commuters (or students in general).

       Now do Exercise 4-2.

Exercise 4-2   What's Wrong with This Picture?

Looking at Figure 4-1, identify three things the student in the poor study area can do to improve.

1. _____
   _____

2. _____
   _____

3. _____
   _____

4.3   Developing a Study Schedule

There are several ideas to consider when developing your personal study schedule. You should think about various time management techniques and personal aspects of your life to determine what methods will work best for you.

4.3a   The Importance of Time Management

As with any journey you are about to undertake, there is no substitute for good planning and preparation. The same can be said for your successful academic journey. Successful preparation includes developing a daily schedule with proper study time built in. Don't be discouraged if your first few schedules don't work well; flexibility is also important. And don't forget to schedule relaxation and recreational time because these are also important to academic success (and general well-being).

4.3b   Scheduling Study Sessions

In creating a study schedule, many students look for blocks of several hours during which they can study. Do not underestimate the value of finding small pockets of otherwise wasted time, like in the waiting room at the doctor's office. A few minutes here and there will add up. Another example applies to commuting students, who can record vocabulary terms and definitions and listen to them during their drive or bus ride to campus. If you have an appointment and the person you're meeting is running late, be prepared by having your math homework with you. If you complete one or two problems while you're waiting, it's time well spent.

4.3c   Alternating Subjects

Studying notes and other course materials over shorter periods of time in more frequent intervals is more effective than long cramming sessions. If you have several hours blocked off as study time, remember to take a short break every thirty minutes to an hour or so (whatever works best for you). Listen to a couple of songs, throw in a load of laundry, or check your email—anything that will take a couple of minutes and allow you to clear your head a bit. Then move on to another subject. A good way to see if you are studying efficiently is to ask yourself questions periodically about what you have just read. If you can't answer these questions, you are probably losing interest and need to take a short break to become more focused.

4.3d   Time of Day

The actual time of day that you choose to study can be very important. It may not be the same time for everyone. Some people are morning people; others are night owls. We all have different *biological clocks*, which simply means that our bodies prefer to be asleep and awake at different times. Becoming aware of your personal biological clock can help you to be a more effective and efficient learner. The message for now is to schedule as much of your study time as possible when you are most alert, awake, and focused. (Note: It is not always up to you when you get to study. Following our scheduling tips will help you to make the most of your study time, whatever the time of day.) In Exercise 4-3, you'll have the opportunity to revisit time management principles.

Exercise 4-3   Creating a Study Schedule

Use the weekly grid in Figure 4-2 to block out your class time along with dedicated study times that work best for your schedule. You can also include any other fixed obligations such as work or school activities. Don't forget to add personal and fun things, such as workout times, meals, and social time.

Write in your schedule of classes and include study time and free time as you see fit.

Note: Remember to switch subjects periodically (every thirty minutes to an hour or so). If you need to split segments into thirty-minute sections, draw a line to divide the segment in half.

Figure 4-2   Study grid

	Mon	Tue	Wed	Thu	Fri	Sat	Sun
6–7 a.m.							
7–8 a.m.							
8–9 a.m.							
9–10 a.m.							
10–11 a.m.							
11–12 a.m.							
12–1 p.m.							
1–2 p.m.							
2–3 p.m.							
3–4 p.m.							
4–5 p.m.							
5–6 p.m.							
6–7 p.m.							
7–8 p.m.							
8–9 p.m.							
9–10 p.m.							
10–11 p.m.							
11–12 p.m.							
12–1 a.m.							

Some additional words of wisdom:

- Don't forget to check your large desk calendar (or electronic version) for the quarter or semester, which should include due dates for assignments, test dates, meetings, and important events that must be added to your weekly schedule.

- Leave some open blocks of time. Your week probably won't go exactly as planned, and you will need flexibility. If you find that you often have to change your schedule, you may not be in control of your time; a review of the time management chapter can help.

- Remember the daily to-do list principles. Establish the habit of holding your own personal planning session each day. Take a few minutes in the morning to list what you need to accomplish (or at the end of the day to plan for the next day); then prioritize your tasks. Use Exercise 4-4 to assess your current study skills.

Exercise 4-4   Assess Your Current Study Skills

Answer the following questions. Be critical and honest in selecting the response that best answers the question.

3 = Always   2 = Sometimes   1 = Rarely

_____ Do you have an organized place to study?

_____ Is it quiet where you study?

_____ Are the conditions and lighting comfortable?

_____ Do you have all the tools (pencils, paper, electronic tools, etc.) you need to study at this place?

_____ Do you know when major exams, papers, and assignments are due?

_____ Do you make a specific study schedule for each academic term?

_____ Do you make the most of short time periods throughout the day?

What were your results? For now, it doesn't matter as long as you were honest. Remember, this is an assessment of where you are now. Your eventual goal should be to have all your responses be "Always." If they are already, great! If not, you need to develop an action plan to change all the responses to "Always" in the near future.

Considering your answers above, create an action plan that focuses on two specific goals for improving your study habits. In creating your goals, remember to follow the SMART model.

4.4   Reading Text Materials

You can also develop effective strategies to get the most from assigned readings. These strategies are powerful and will make studying for exams much easier and less stressful.

First, let's assess your current reading skills and strategies in Exercise 4-5.

Exercise 4-5   Assess Yourself: How Effective Are Your Text-Reading Strategies?

Check the statements that apply to you:

____ I preview my texts before classes begin to get a sense of the material.

____ I schedule time each day to complete reading assignments.

____ I stay up-to-date on reading assignments, rarely falling behind the schedule outlined on the syllabus.

____ I preview the assigned reading, taking note of subject headings and subheadings and carefully reviewing the introduction and conclusion.

____ I ask questions about, or debate the content of, the text.

____ I check my comprehension of text material, noting areas where I do not understand.

____ I review the chapter after completing the reading assignment, making note of concepts I may still not understand.

____ I underline and/or write notes in the margins of my text.

____ I write supplemental notes on assigned readings in outline or some other organized form.

____ I take advantage of supplemental material in the text, including end-of-chapter questions and summary material (when available).

____ Total number of items checked

If you checked nine or ten items, you use very good reading strategies for assignments. A total of seven or eight checked items indicates that your strategies could be better, and you will benefit from this chapter. A total of five or six checked areas means you need to improve your reading strategies; four or fewer checked items indicate that you *really* need to improve the way you read.

Regardless of age, academic background, major, or confidence level, students are all surprised by the challenges of reading assignments—both in terms of how difficult the reading can be and in terms of how much there is. Students generally improve by (1) managing time for reading assignments and (2) using *active* rather than *passive* reading strategies. By *engaging* with your reading, you will understand and remember more. We'll show you how.

4.4a   Managing Time for Reading Assignments

Let's take an example. You have to read a difficult chapter of fifty pages this week, and you feel overwhelmed by the amount of material. Fifty pages can seem like a lot for only one course, especially if you have the same amount—or more—for some or all of your other courses. However, if you commit to reading ten pages a day for a week, it seems more manageable. Further, if you break a ten-page assignment into two daily sessions of five pages each, it's even more manageable. The key is to use time management strategies to handle your reading load.

4.4b   Reading Strategies

We've given you several strategies that will help you keep up with your reading. However, you want to do more than simply read the material. You want to (1) understand it and (2) remember it. Students who read *passively* don't pause to check for comprehension, mark unfamiliar terms, or ask questions about the text. Have you ever read a page and stopped to realize you have no idea what you just read? This is an all too common example of passive reading. Students who read *actively* use a variety of strategies to check their understanding. Although active reading feels like it takes more time than passive reading, it actually saves you time because you understand the material better and need less review time for the exam. Active reading typically includes writing, both in marking the text and in taking notes. Most active reading strategies have the following features:

Previewing   Preview the assignment by skimming the chapter headings and subheadings and carefully reading introductions and conclusions. Notice key points written in italics or bold print. Some text chapters have summaries and discussion questions at the end. Many students like to read those materials first rather than last. Why? Because then they will know what they should look for while reading.

Highlighting or Underlining   Read a section and then highlight or underline the key points. Marking your text keeps you involved in the reading and forces you to pay attention to the key points. Generally, it is best to read a section and then go back over the material and mark it. If you mark as you read, you will very likely mark too much material, which will defeat the purpose of marking only the most significant information. Many people (including the authors) think that *outlining* (more on this soon) the chapter is more effective than highlighting because it forces you to write out the concepts instead of just "coloring them in." Not only does it help you to learn the material better but when you take the test, you often have to write out the answers. That said, always use the strategy that works best for you.

Margin Notes   In addition to highlighting, underlining, or outlining key information, it is a good idea to write notes in the margins. Such notes can include questions you have about the text, important terminology, or very brief *paraphrasing* (rewriting it in your own words) of important points. These notes can help you prepare for exams, and the very act of writing these notes can help you understand and remember the material better. See Figure 4-3.

Food for Thought

Many students want to sell back their books, so they hesitate to write in them. However, remember that your purchase is part of your investment in your education. Students who mark in their textbooks tend to learn the material better, and isn't that why you bought the book in the first place? If you buy the book, keep it unmarked and in near-perfect condition, and then earn a poor grade in the class, have you gotten as much from your investment? Besides, keeping your books in pristine condition doesn't help the cost all that much if you sell them back to buyers on campus.

Figure 4-3　　Sample textbook page with text marking and margin notes

10.3a　The Cabinet

Not like a parliament, president makes own decisions

Despite its prestige, the president's cabinet (see Table 10.2) is not a collective high level decision-making body. Because ours is not a parliamentary government, the president is not obligated to share responsibility with the cabinet. Its officers serve at the president's discretion, and the president is under no obligation to consult with them individually or collectively.

Individual officers can have great significance for the president. As will be discussed in Chapter 11, they serve as the president's arm in controlling the massive federal bureaucracy and in imposing his political priorities upon it. The cabinet also provides a mechanism for bringing into the administration people who represent different social, economic, and political constituencies. Often presidents will make appointments from constituent groups who did not support them but whose support they need.

Loyalty important, but also have to serve their constituent groups

After several years in office, presidents become more concerned with controlling the bureaucracy than with decorating their cabinet with people whose value is more symbolic than substantive. Thus, they look for cabinet officers who may be less well known but will be more loyal.

The selection of the right cabinet is a difficult problem. Few cabinet officers, whatever their temperament or background, can serve simply as the president's loyal agent. They must also represent to the president the perspective of their department and the *constituent groups* it serves. For example, the secretary of labor should have a good working relationship with organized labor; the secretary of the interior should have a solid relationship with the developers or the environmentalists, preferably both; and the secretary of agriculture must have a good rapport with farmers and the

Source: *Introduction to American Government,* ninth edition, by Charles C. Turner, D. Grier Stephenson Jr., Robert J. Bresler, Robert J. Friedrich, and Joseph J. Karlesky. Copyright 2017 by BVT Publishing. Used by permission of BVT Publishing.

Using Support Materials　Does your text have review questions at the end of the chapter? Try to answer them. Does your instructor post study guides and other materials online? Use them. Does your text come with a study guide or supplemental website? Use these to aid in your comprehension of the material.

Text Notes　Take good, accurate, and readable notes. Remember that the purpose of taking notes is to write down key points from the reading or lecture, not to write down everything. In addition to highlighting, outline your chapters so you can make the connection from your brain to the pencil. This is what you'll need to do on the test.

Outlining can be done in several ways. You can use bullet points, numbers, Roman numerals, or letters, or a combination. Outlines can also take the shapes of lists, diagrams, pictures, and flash cards. Making your notes visual can help you better understand relationships or how it all fits together. See Figure 4-4 for some examples. Test your knowledge in Exercise 4-6.

Food for Thought

In our previous discussion of time management, we spoke about wasting time productively. Carrying your flash cards with you, say to a doctor's appointment (or any appointment where you may have to wait), can save you valuable study time.

Figure 4-4   Sample of text notes

Chapter 10: The Presidency

Overview of the Executive Branch

1. Made up of people who help the president formulate and implement policy
2. Called the administration, these people include cabinet secretaries, under-secretaries, administrators and deputies of independent agencies, and senior White House aides.

Executive Branch Components:

Cabinet—Comprised of the heads of fifteen executive departments and other officials. Often divided into an inner cabinet (handles issues of broad national importance) and an outer cabinet (deals with sharply defined programs and subject to pressure from client groups). Vice president also participates in cabinet meetings.

White House Staff—Played no role in policy before FDR; now president's closest confidants, with loyalty only to president. George H.W. Bush used *multiple advocacy* (a system of advising the president in which all sides of an issue are presented) with his staff.

Executive Office of the President (EOP)—Created in 1939 as managerial arm of presidency. Structure reflects dominant issues of the time. Important agencies/councils include Office of Management and Budget (OMB), National Security Council (NSC), and Council of Economic Advisers (CEA).

Vice President—Mainly a ceremonial role until 1947. Walter Mondale was Carter's intimate adviser, Dick Cheney was George W. Bush's, and Joe Biden was Obama's.

Questions and Concepts to Know:
Who are the people that make up the executive branch and what do they do?

Study Tools:
Learn sidebar key terms
Use Table 10.2

Exercise 4-6   Test Your Knowledge on Text Reading

Do you schedule time each day to read text material?

Sometimes   Always   Rarely

Do you mark important points in your text?

Sometimes   Always   Rarely

Do you outline the important points in your text?

Sometimes   Always   Rarely

In your text notes, do you write in your own words?

Sometimes   Always   Rarely

If you answered *always* to these questions, that's great! For each one you answered sometimes or rarely, develop an action plan or goal for improvement. Remember to make SMART goals.

Reading Goal(s):

_____

_____

_____

_____

4.5 Taking Effective Lecture Notes

You may be tired of hearing the word *strategy* by now. However, it is an important part of success and, yes, there are note-taking strategies that will help you take effective lecture notes. First, assess yourself in Exercise 4-7.

Exercise 4-7   Assess Yourself: How Good Are Your Note-Taking and Classroom Strategies?

Check each item that applies to you:

_____ I can concentrate during lectures.

_____ I have strategies for coping with or minimizing distractions.

_____ I prepare for lectures by keeping up with my reading and other assignments.

_____ When given the choice, I sit where I am least likely to become distracted (near the teacher, away from the window or exit, etc.).

_____ My lecture notes are readable and easy to follow.

_____ I review my notes before the next class to make sure things are clear and to check for missing information or inconsistencies.

_____ My notes are organized so I can find information right away.

_____ I mark my notes by underlining or highlighting important information.

_____ I am willing to ask questions during the lecture or go to my teacher's office for assistance if I do not understand some of the lecture material.

_____ I volunteer to answer questions in class.

_____ Total number of items checked

If you checked nine or ten items, you're a pretty good notetaker and only need to work on items you didn't check. A total of seven to eight checked items means you're an all right notetaker, but there's room for improvement. If you checked five to six items, you should work on improving your strategies. Finally, four or fewer checked items means you need a drastic overhaul of your note-taking strategies.

Select an item you did not check and develop a specific action plan that will have you checking it in the near future.

Action plan:

_____

_____

_____

_____

_____

_____

4.5a   Note-Taking Tips

Listening   To become a good notetaker, you may need to sharpen your listening skills. You want your notes to be accurate, readable, and understandable; to capture main points, ideas, and relationships; and to identify questions. You need to be able to stay focused and manage distractions, daydreaming, and tiredness. Here are some methods for increasing your concentration during lectures:

- Sit in the front of the classroom. If you can choose where you sit during a lecture, try to sit at or near the front of the class. Students who sit in front are less likely to become distracted during lectures or to engage in side conversations with other students.

- Electronics like your phone or tablet should only be accessible if they are necessary for note-taking or for a good reason (like if you have young children or a sick family member who may need to reach you).

- Prepare for the lecture. Read the material, review your notes, and identify questions before class.

- Ask questions—of yourself and of the instructor. How can I use this? How does this relate? Listen for answers or raise questions with the instructor either during or after class.

- Handle distracting thoughts. If you think of something important but unrelated to class, you may need to write a quick note to yourself and set it aside until after class.

- Answer questions. Volunteer when the instructor poses a question to the class.

Organization   There are many good ways to organize your notes. As we told you at the beginning of the chapter, the key is to find a system that works for you without making it too complicated. Here are some suggestions:

- **Use the Cornell method.** The *Cornell method*, developed by Walter Pauk, provides a unique way to organize your notes and to check how well you remember and understand the material. Draw a vertical line down each page in your notebook about two inches in from the left side of the page. Write your notes on the right side of the line. Use the left side for brief comments, key words, questions you may want to ask, and for other notations that add emphasis or clarity. See Figure 4-5 for an example.

- **Organize your notebooks.** Keep your notes in a three-ring binder with dividers to separate the various subjects. Better yet, keep a separate notebook for each course. If you do this, make sure you label the notebooks, or perhaps have different colored notebooks for each class, so you are less likely to take the wrong notebook when you leave for class.

- **Analyze your notes.** Review your notes right after class whenever possible or at least within a day of the class. If you review your notes shortly after class, then you will be able to fix most errors and gaps yourself. You might also want to compare your notes with those of another student. If you're still missing essential points, you might want to ask your instructor to review your notes with you and make suggestions.

- **Mark your notes.** As you should with a textbook, underline or highlight key information or questions.

Figure 4-5   **Example of Cornell method compared with disorganized notes**

Disorganized Text Notes

Sentences

A complete sentence has two parts, a subject and predicate. Both can be more than one word. Subject includes noun or pronoun. Noun–person, place, or thing. Pronoun–substitute word for noun. Pronouns: personal, demonstrative, indefinite, possessive.

Verbs are action words. Forms change–person, number, tense. Person is first, second, third. Number is singular or plural. Tense is present, past, future, present perfect, past perfect, future perfect. Verbs are regular and irregular. Regular–add the correct ending to the base form. Irregular–change the entire spelling of the word. Some verbs need auxiliary (helping) words

Cornell Method of Text Notes

Simple Sentences: Subjects and Predicates

What are the two parts of a sentence?	A complete sentence has two parts: a subject and a predicate
What is a subject?	*Subject*: a noun or pronoun
What is a noun?	*Noun*: person, place, or thing
What is a pronoun?	*Pronoun*: substitute word for noun
What are the types of pronouns?	*personal* pronouns (he, she, it, they, we, etc.)
	demonstrative pronouns (this, these, that, those)
	indefinite pronouns (each, either, neither, anyone, somebody, etc.)
	possessive pronouns (mine, its, his, hers, theirs, ours)
What is a predicate?	*Predicate* includes a verb, the action of a sentence.
What are verbs?	*Verbs*: action words. The form depends on person, number, and tense.
Identify the components of verb forms.	*Person*: first (I, me, we, etc.), second (you), third (he, she, it, they, etc.)
	Number: singular or plural
	Tense: present, past, future, present perfect, past perfect, future perfect
Define regular and irregular forms.	Verb forms are regular and irregular. *Regular*—add the correct ending to the base form. *Irregular*—change the entire spelling of the word. Some verbs need *auxiliary* (helping) words, such as "have" in "have helped" (present perfect), "will" as in "will walk" (future), and "had" as in "had gone" (past perfect).

Summary: Simple sentences are composed of subjects (nouns/pronouns, which indicate person, place, or thing) and predicates (verbs). There are four types of pronouns. Irregular and regular verb forms depend on person, number, and tense.

Take the notes from one of your current lecture classes and convert them to Cornell method notes (leaving room in the left margin for questions and other comments).

Compare these new notes with your original ones and see which system you prefer. Answer the questions below:

Which version of your notes do you prefer?

_____

What are the strengths of your original set of notes?

_____

_____

What are the weaknesses in your original notes?

_____

_____

Keep it SMART—write a brief action plan for how you will change your note-taking strategies for the rest of the semester:

_____

_____

_____

_____

4.6 A Word about Attending Class

The importance of attending your classes cannot be overstated. Beyond the fact that skipping class is a waste of your tuition money, there are several other reasons. When you skip class, you miss class discussions, where instructors tend to highlight what they consider most important and what is likely to show up on the exam. Skipping class is not a very smart time management technique. It will take you twice as long to find out what you missed and copy someone else's notes than if you just had attended the class. Being on time and attending class tells the instructor you value what they have to say, and it shows respect.

4.6a Classroom Etiquette

In later chapters, we discuss the importance of making a good impression at job interviews. It is equally important to consider the image you communicate in class. Being on time and attending class is not the only way to communicate maturity and a positive attitude. You must also communicate respect for your peers and instructors (and yourself!) by remembering the following:

- **Avoid side conversations.** If you like to sit with your friends, sit up front so you're less tempted to talk to each other instead of attending to class material. (Your notes will be better, too.)
- **Refrain from text messaging.** As well as person-to-person side conversations, avoid electronic side conversations in the form of text messaging.
- **Silence cell phones.** Get in the habit of turning your cell phone off or on silent (*do not disturb* mode) before entering a classroom. If you must have it handy for an important reason, at least put it on vibrate. This habit will help you in the future (like during meetings or presentations at work) as well.

4.6b   Success Strategies for Online Courses

Online education can mean any learning that occurs over the internet. Other terms for online education include distance learning or education, virtual learning, e-learning, and web-based training. As online learning continues to grow and evolve, it becomes important to have both an understanding of online education and specific strategies for success. Distance learning has grown because of students who live far away from campuses, work full time, or have families or other obligations and need flexibility in their educational schedule. One of the biggest misperceptions about distance learning is that online courses are easier. In fact, these courses are usually more difficult for the average student because they require a lot of self-discipline and self-motivation. However, if you have these traits, you should do well in these types of courses.

Another misconception is that all online courses are similar. In fact, there are several types of online course formats and experiences. Currently, online courses are broken down into two main types: **synchronous** and **asynchronous distance education.** *Synchronous* courses could include video chat software where students have face-to-face contact with faculty on a regular basis. Basically, everyone in the class logs in *at the same time* alongside the instructor. *Asynchronous* courses use online bulletin board postings, chat rooms, and text dialogues to conduct the course. In these courses, you may never really see the professor (other than maybe a video introduction), but interact through messaging and postings. Some courses are hybrids and have some face-to-face interaction integrated with text dialogue and postings. In most courses, students sign in at least once a week for a live chat conversation. In addition, weekly assignments and session questions are posted in a "course room" or assignment outline. Tests are usually given in a secure online location where students can access the test or an assigned project or paper.

Online courses naturally have some technology requirements, such as a relatively new computer with internet access and the required software programs to successfully interact with the course.

Synchronous distance education

Where students and faculty log in at the same time, sometimes with face-to-face interaction over video chat

Asynchronous distance education

Where online bulletin boards, chat rooms, and text dialogues are the main form of interaction

Here are some specific strategies that will help ensure your success with distance learning:

- Stay self-motivated and read postings daily from your classmates and professor.
- Stay connected and respond to posts on a regular basis to contribute to the discussion.
- Practice good time management by balancing your personal obligations and meeting all your deadlines.
- Maintain an ideal study environment with all your needed technology and no distractions (remember to avoid the distractions your devices may tempt you with!).
- Use proper citations when writing or posting about things you've read.
- Participate in any online training or orientation sessions.
- Keep a backup copy of all your work.

Exercise 4-9   Is Distance Learning for You?

The following traits are most likely to help you succeed in an online course.

Answer the following questions with either "yes" or "no."

_____ I'm self-motivated and rarely procrastinate.

_____ I have good typing and reading comprehension skills.

_____ I typically get all my assignments done on time.

_____ I have access to the internet and all the technology and software needed for an online course.

To be really successful online, you should be able to answer "yes" to all these questions. If you do have a "no" answer and still want or need to take an online course, come up with a specific action plan to change it to a "yes."

Action Plan:

_____

_____

_____

_____

Healthy Decision-Making

Read the following case about a student who has difficulty keeping up with her classes. What advice would you give to Alison?

Alison is taking twelve credits her first semester, and she is struggling academically. At midterm, most of her grades are either C or D. She made B's throughout high school without much effort. She attends her classes and generally completes assignments on time, although just barely. She's never had to take notes before, at least not as much as she does now. Also, she doesn't understand why she does poorly on quizzes and tests because she does all the reading. Outside of the classroom, she is having a good experience: She's making friends and trying to get involved. Sometimes there are distractions in the residence hall, but she still tries to get her work done.

Your advice:

_____

_____

_____

_____

_____

_____

_____

_____

_____

Know Your School

Your school will have support services to help you with your study skills. Research what school resources can help you, such as peer tutors, learning skill centers, math centers, and so on. List the information here, and for quick reference, place the information in a prominent place such as on your refrigerator or bulletin board.

Resource Name: _____

Office Location: _____

Phone Number: _____

Email Address: _____

Resource Name: _____

Office Location: _____

Phone Number: _____

Email Address: _____

Resource Name: _____

Office Location: _____

Phone Number: _____

Email Address: _____

Resource Name: _____

Office Location: _____

Phone Number: _____

Email Address: _____

Resource Name: _____

Office Location: _____

Phone Number: _____

Email Address: _____

5

Learning Styles, Memory, and Test Taking

Making the Grade

Objectives

By the end of this chapter, you will be able to:

- Explain Gardner's Multiple Intelligences theory

- Describe your preferred learning style(s)

- Improve on a less well-developed learning style

- Select effective study strategies based on your learning styles

- Identify types of memory

- Use effective memory techniques

- Select strategies to improve your test-taking skills

- Develop strategies to interact positively with faculty

Why Learn This Skill?

Students often start college without memory or test-taking skills and without knowing or understanding their own learning styles. Soon they realize they need to improve their skills in these areas, particularly test taking. Exams now are often more challenging: Instructors cover more material in less time, and they ask higher-level questions than many of us experienced in our lives before college. Also, in some classes, your entire grade may be based on only two or three exams.

Developing the skills and knowledge explored in this chapter will help you not only at school but in your career. Once you graduate, learning—and testing—does not end. You will have to learn (and sometimes memorize) new information and techniques for your work. To do so, it is important to gain a new level of self-awareness, particularly when it comes to how you learn and remember new information best.

5.1   Introduction

To begin the chapter, we will discuss learning styles. Once you better understand your preferred ways of learning, you can develop the memory and test-taking techniques that work best for you. After exploring learning styles and memory techniques, we'll conclude with effective test-taking strategies and ways to interact positively with faculty.

5.2   Learning Styles

Have you ever thought about how you learn? Each of us has preferred styles of learning. Understanding this preference can help make us even better learners. Let's begin by exploring your preferences in Exercise 5-1.

Exercise 5-1   What Is Your Learning Style?

Answer the following questions regarding your preferences. Remember, there are no right or wrong answers. These questions are designed to evaluate your preferred methods for learning and studying. (Note: If you're a new student and haven't spent much time in a classroom recently, you may have difficulty answering some of these questions. Just put the answer that you think would most closely apply to you.)

1. I prefer classes with
   a. Lectures
   b. Visual aids, such as slideshows and videos
   c. Labs and other hands-on activities

2. I like to learn from teachers who
   a. Lecture for most of the classes
   b. Provide handouts, write on the board, and use other visual cues
   c. Interact with the class and promote group work

3. When I read, I tend to
   a. Read out loud or start to move my lips as I read
   b. Highlight or underline main points, using different colors
   c. Get bored or become restless easily

4. When taking notes, I benefit from
   a. Recording the class so I can listen to any lecture material again
   b. Organizing the material in a visually clear and appealing way
   c. Sitting near the front of the class so I don't get distracted

5. To memorize material, it is best if I
   a. Recite it out loud a number of times
   b. See it written down and review it repeatedly
   c. Use mnemonics (memory aids) or write it out

6. I concentrate best in an environment that
   a. Is quiet
   b. Is organized and neat
   c. Has limited activity around me

7. When studying for a test, I benefit from
   a. Discussing the material
   b. Organizing the material in outline or chart form
   c. Practicing concepts in a hands-on way

8. To learn something, I need to
   a. Hear it
   b. See it
   c. Practice it

9. I understand instructions best
   a. When someone explains them to me out loud
   b. When they're written clearly, perhaps with diagrams or charts
   c. If I can do it myself

10. In class, I like to sit
    a. Anywhere—it really doesn't matter as long as I can listen to what's going on
    b. Near the front, where I can see the board or slides
    c. Near an exit, so I can get up if needed

(continues)

Assessment

There are three primary learning styles:

- **Auditory**: If most of your responses were "a," your dominant learning style is auditory. **Auditory learners** understand material best by listening. They tend to like lecture classes. If they need directions to get somewhere, they prefer spoken directions to maps or written directions. Sometimes they like to record classes. (Be careful: Sometimes recording can make students less attentive during class if they think they can just listen to the file later, and always get your instructor's permission to record.)

- **Visual**: If you answered mostly "b," you may be primarily a visual learner. **Visual learners** understand material best by seeing it. They tend to be organized readers and notetakers, and they like to highlight or write notes in different colors. These strategies can help them to remember material better. If you're a visual learner, you might get frustrated if a teacher doesn't write on the board much or provide written directions. You benefit from sitting near the front of the class so you don't miss any visual aids.

- **Kinesthetic**: If you answered "c" most of the time, you are a *tactile*, or **kinesthetic learner**. In other words, you like to learn by doing. You might find yourself getting restless during lectures, and you may tend to prefer classes with lab work, group activities, and fieldwork.

Which learning styles are represented?

5.2a   Working with Your Learning Style

Although it is likely that you have one dominant learning style, you probably had answers in all three (or at least two) of the areas. That's because most of us use a combination of learning styles, and rightly so. Just as there are many ways to learn, there are many ways to teach, and students have to be able to adapt to all of them. You will use similar adaptation strategies in the workplace (and probably have already) when you have supervisors or colleagues with different approaches to working and learning. So, what do you do with this knowledge of your learning style? You can use it to adapt to challenging classroom situations.

Auditory Learners   In addition to using visual materials, perhaps you can record material. Caution: Be selective about recording class lectures. Many students record lectures and, because they know they'll have a recording to go back to later, they zone out during class. You may think, "I'm tired, and I don't have to pay attention—I can just go back and listen to the recording later." Unfortunately, "later" may never arrive. Also, you should always ask permission of your instructor to record their class.

A better idea might be to record your own study materials. For example, if you have to learn some new vocabulary terms, record yourself saying each term and its definition and listen to them on your commute to school (or while going to class or while on the treadmill at the gym). Studying in groups and discussing material with fellow students can be helpful as well.

Visual Learners   You might have difficulty with a lecture class that provides few visual cues, such as board work, slideshow presentations, or diagrams. In addition, you might struggle a bit to organize your notes. Find creative ways to write and organize your notes, such as color-coding or using concept maps (demonstrated later). It can be helpful to rewrite your notes within a day of the lecture so you get additional visual reinforcement.

Kinesthetic Learners   With your preference for movement and hands-on learning, you should incorporate movement into your studying. Moving a bit while you study and taking regular breaks can be helpful. You might want to alternate active study tasks (writing a paper, doing math homework, completing a lab assignment) with your reading assignments.

Remember, you might have one dominant learning style (or possibly two), but you have the capacity to use all three. Most successful students do. Do Exercise 5-2 to improve one of your less well-developed learning styles.

Exercise 5-2   Improving a Learning Style

Just like an athlete must have a "balanced game" and work on his or her weaker skills, so must a student to thrive in different learning environments.

Write in your least developed learning style from Exercise 5-1.

_____

Now, develop a specific action plan to strengthen this learning style.

Action Plan:

_____
_____
_____
_____

5.2b   Gardner's Multiple Intelligences

Do you have a preference between following a map or following written directions to get to a new destination? Do you enjoy math and science classes more than English and literature, or vice versa? Are you praised as a good listener, or do you tend to shy away from groups?

Your responses to these questions provide insight into the various intelligences you possess. That's right—*intelligences*, plural. Howard Gardner, a university professor, developed a theory of **multiple intelligences**. Basically, he argued that we have different types of intelligences and, within each person, some intelligences are better developed than others. If you are a student who prefers math and science classes over English, you have a well-developed logic/math intelligence. If you communicate well with others, your interpersonal intelligence is better developed.

Please do *not* take any of this to mean that if you struggle in an area, you cannot improve because of your intelligence. We have heard countless students say things like, "I don't have a mind for math" or "I'll just never understand chemistry." Rather than give up, most students need to work on these areas and take steps to develop these skills, perhaps by using what they are already good at.

1. **Linguistic Intelligence**   Someone with strong *linguistic intelligence* is good at using and understanding *language*. Writers, public speakers, and lawyers typically have great linguistic intelligence.

2. **Logical/Mathematical Intelligence**   Someone with *logical/mathematical intelligence* works well with *numbers* and *systems*. Scientists, accountants, computer programmers, and mathematicians rely on this type of intelligence.

3. **Musical/Rhythmic Intelligence**   Someone with *musical/rhythmic intelligence* can recognize *patterns* and *rhythms* with relative ease. Musical performers and composers are the most obvious examples of people who have this type of intelligence.

4. **Bodily/Kinesthetic Intelligence**   Someone with *bodily/kinesthetic intelligence* often does something *physical* to solve a problem or to learn. Examples include athletes, firefighters, and performance artists.

5. **Spatial Intelligence**   Someone with *spatial intelligence* is good at imagining and understanding the *three-dimensional world*. Airplane pilots and engineers rely on spatial intelligence in their work.

6. **Naturalist Intelligence**   Someone with *naturalist intelligence* understands the features of and differences among *living things* and the *natural world*. Farmers, foresters, and others who work outdoors and with animals demonstrate naturalist intelligence.

Multiple intelligences
A theory by Howard Gardner that we each have many different types of intelligence, some of which are more developed than others

Food for Thought

We Learn:

10% of what we read
20% of what we hear
30% of what we see
50% of what we both see and hear
70% of what is discussed with others
80% of what we experience
95% of what we TEACH to someone else

—Adapted from "A Word About Study Groups and Active Learning" by Edgar Dale from *Audio-Visual Methods in Teaching*, Second Edition, Austin, TX: Holt McDougal, 1963.

Although some may argue the percentages, the general concepts are still true today based on what research on learning has shown. The more senses you can involve in the process, the more you will learn. Therefore, text illustrations, website animations, and videos enhance the learning process. Lab experiences and interactive games and exercises will also increase learning.

Group or study discussions are highly beneficial. Effective study groups can help you in achieving academic success. An excellent method for learning material is to explain concepts to each other. If you have to teach the group a concept, you will really learn what it is all about. *You'll soon learn that there is no better way to learn something than having to teach it to someone else.*

7. **Intrapersonal Intelligence**   Someone with *intrapersonal intelligence* has strong *self-awareness*. Those with intrapersonal intelligence are very aware of their own strengths and weaknesses and often work at self-improvement. Researchers and philosophers demonstrate this intelligence.

8. **Interpersonal Intelligence**   Someone with *interpersonal intelligence* understands and relates well to other people. Educators, politicians, counselors, health-care professionals, and salespeople demonstrate interpersonal intelligence.

Applying Gardner's theory means using as many intelligences as possible when learning or teaching new information. For example, when learning about interest rates for borrowing money, you could read about it (linguistic), do mathematical problems (logical/mathematical), construct graphs (spatial), make up a song (musical), relate it to your personal finances (intrapersonal), discuss it with a group (interpersonal), and physically demonstrate with real money (kinesthetic). You don't have to use all eight to learn a concept, but the more intelligences you use, the better you will understand the material. Find out what intelligences are strongest for you in Exercise 5-3.

Exercise 5-3   Test Your Intelligences

Put a checkmark by those words or phrases that most closely describe you and then add up the total for each category.

Linguistic/Verbal Intelligence

_____ I am an effective communicator.
_____ I enjoy reading.
_____ I enjoy writing.
_____ I like word games.
_____ I like learning new words.

_____ Total

Logical/Mathematical Intelligence

_____ I like to discuss things logically.
_____ Math comes easily to me.
_____ I like science classes.
_____ I enjoy logic puzzles.
_____ I like to understand how things and systems work.

_____ Total

Musical/Rhythmic Intelligence

_____ I love music.
_____ I keep time with music.
_____ I create rhymes to remember things.
_____ I play music in my head.
_____ I notice when someone sings or plays off key.

_____ Total

Bodily/Kinesthetic Intelligence

_____ I like to exercise or play sports.
_____ I prefer a hands-on approach to learning.
_____ I enjoy lab classes.
_____ I learn by doing.
_____ I get restless easily.

_____ Total

(continues)

Spatial Intelligence

_____ I can draw things to scale.

_____ I understand how parts fit into a whole.

_____ I understand charts and diagrams.

_____ I understand cause and effect.

_____ I enjoy figuring out how things work.

_____ Total

Naturalist Intelligence

_____ I love spending time outside.

_____ I am realistic.

_____ I enjoy nature.

_____ I learn well in a "real-world" setting.

_____ I prefer not to be indoors.

_____ Total

Intrapersonal Intelligence

_____ I need privacy.

_____ I have strong self-awareness.

_____ I am reflective.

_____ I question things.

_____ I am selective about friendships.

_____ Total

Interpersonal Intelligence

_____ I am communicative or talkative.

_____ I am understanding.

_____ I love spending time with others.

_____ I am cooperative.

_____ I enjoy talking things over with friends.

_____ Total

What are three of your stronger intelligences?

1. _____

2. _____

3. _____

Now identify your most challenging course this semester: _____

Name three ways you can use your stronger intelligences to achieve success in this course:

1. _____

2. _____

3. _____

5.3   Aiding Your Memory

Although the purpose of education is to encourage thinking skills rather than memorization, memory is still important. The best way to measure what a student has learned is to test them on what they can remember. Therefore, a good memory makes it easier to succeed. Your memory can be broken down into *short-* and *long-term memory*. Things that are happening now or that have happened recently are stored in short-term memory. These memories aren't around for very long. For example, you can probably remember what you ate for lunch yesterday, but you might not remember what you ate for lunch this time last week. Long-term memory, as the name implies, stores experiences and knowledge for months, years, or even decades. Ideally, what you learn in school will be stored in long-term memory. To make sure you're using long-term memory storage, *focus* on the material and *engage as many senses* as you can while learning it. This is why effective discussion and study groups help long-term memory and test performance. Test your memory in Exercise 5-4.

Time yourself for one minute and try to memorize the following food items. Then, try to recite them from memory.

Meat loaf	Eggplant parmesan	Jam	Iced tea
Grapefruit	Kiwi	Lemonade	Hummus
Burrito	Frankfurters	Diet soda	Cherries

Were you able to memorize and recite them all? _____

If not, don't worry. This seemingly random list of foods would be hard for anyone to memorize. For one, the list is a little long. Also, some of these items might be more familiar to you than others. Finally, these foods don't necessarily "go together"—they aren't connected by anything in particular other than being edible. All these factors would make these items harder to remember.

At times, we all have to memorize information. The key is to have a system for memorizing things and it is even more important, to make sure you *understand* what you were meant to learn rather than simply being able to repeat it. Returning to Exercise 5-4, take the same items and place them in alphabetical order and in groups of three:

burrito, cherries, diet soda

eggplant parmesan, frankfurters, grapefruit

hummus, iced tea, jam

kiwi, lemonade, meat loaf

This memorization technique is called clustering, or grouping.

5.3a Grouping

There's a reason our phone numbers are written 555-1234. The dash in the middle helps make it easier for us to remember the numbers! Rather than remembering them all in one chunk, we can more easily remember two smaller groups of numbers (555 and 1234).

In the case of our food list from Exercise 5-4, we first grouped the items in alphabetical order and in clusters of three. We can also group the items by category:

Main course: burrito, eggplant parmesan, frankfurters, meat loaf

Fruits: cherries, grapefruit, kiwi

Drinks: diet soda, iced tea, lemonade

Spreads: hummus, jam

5.3b Mnemonics

Mnemonics

Words, rhymes, or other devices that help you remember

Another effective memorization technique is the use of **mnemonics**, which are words, rhymes, or other devices that aid your memory. For example, did you ever have to memorize the names of the eight planets in order (Mercury, Venus, Earth, Mars, Jupiter, Saturn, Uranus, and Neptune)? If so, perhaps you heard this mnemonic (or a similar one):

My Very Educated Mother Just Served Us Nachos.

This type of mnemonic is known as an **acrostic**: You take the first letter of every item to be memorized and form a sentence that will help you to remember vocabulary, terms, or concepts, especially when those items should be remembered in a special order.

Another mnemonic device is an **acronym**, which is like an acrostic. Acronyms are words or abbreviations formed from the first letters of the terms you need to memorize. For example, the ABCs of CPR remind you to A establish **A**irway, B rescue **B**reathing, and C establish **C**irculation. This mnemonic helps you to remember the steps and their proper order in a life or death situation. Another classic mnemonic is the word HOMES to memorize the names of the Great Lakes (Huron, Ontario, Michigan, Erie, and Superior). See Figure 5-1 for an illustration of the ABCs of CPR acronym. Can you think of any others?

Acrostic

Traditionally, when the first letter of each line of a poem or other written work together spell out a word; also when you take the first letter of each word you want to memorize, often in a specific order, and use them to create a sentence where all the words start with those initial letters

Acronym

When you take the first letter of each word you want to memorize and put them together to form an abbreviation or new word

Figure 5-1 An acronym and illustration of the ABCs of CPR

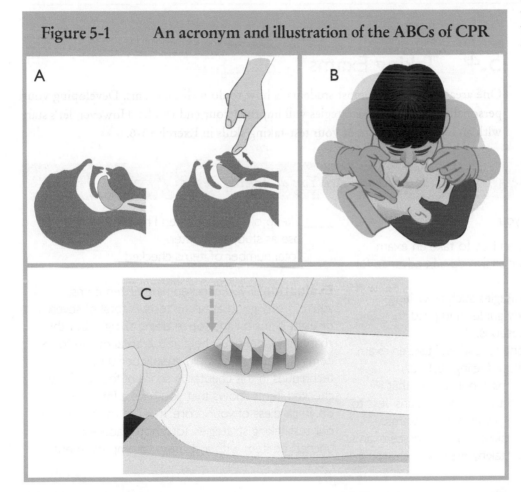

Rhymes are also helpful mnemonic devices. "In 1492, Columbus sailed the ocean blue." Many students in the United States are familiar with this age-old mnemonic. Formulas that appeal to your sense of logic can also help memory. For example, "Spring forward, fall back" helps us adjust our clocks accordingly for daylight saving time. You can also make up silly stories to help remember facts. In fact, the sillier the story, the easier it can be to remember. Try your hand at mnemonics in Exercise 5-5.

Exercise 5-5   Working with Mnemonics

Take the following list of animals: tiger, eagle, aardvark, snake. Create mnemonics to remember the items on the list. Use at least two of the strategies described under the mnemonic section.

Action Plan:

_____

_____

_____

_____

5.4   Taking Exams

One area that concerns most students is how to do well on exams. Developing your personalized test-taking strategies will improve your end results. However, let's start with an initial assessment of your test-taking skills in Exercise 5-6.

Exercise 5-6   Assess Yourself: *How Good Are You at Taking Tests?*

Check all that apply to you:

_____ I feel prepared when I go to take an exam.

_____ I study at least four or five days in advance for an exam.

_____ I use hands-on strategies such as writing answers from study guides and predicting and answering test questions.

_____ I feel calm, if not confident, when I take an exam.

_____ I finish exams without feeling rushed.

_____ I rarely get an exam back only to see that I missed questions I actually knew the answers to.

_____ I use my own strategies for taking exams.

_____ I have strategies for taking multiple-choice exams.

_____ I have strategies for taking essay and short-answer exams.

_____ I keep old exams (when I have the option) to use as study tools later.

_____ Total number of items checked

Evaluation: If you checked nine or ten items, you're pretty good at taking tests. A total of seven or eight items means you're doing all right, but this chapter will definitely help you. A total of five to six items indicates you would greatly benefit from the techniques in this chapter. A score of four or fewer checked items shows that you have a lot of work to do. Regardless of your score, most of us can improve our test-taking strategies. You should address any unchecked item with a strategy for improvement.

5.4a Active Test-Taking Strategies

Just as there are active reading, listening, and studying strategies, there are also active test-taking strategies. Do Exercise 5-7 to assess your current strategies.

Exercise 5-7 What Test-Taking Strategies Do You Use?

In which class have you most recently had an exam?

_____

Identify the strategies you used to prepare for the exam:

_____

_____

_____

_____

For Exercise 5-7, most students might provide the following answers: "I looked over my notes" or "I read the textbook." These strategies will only get you so far, even if you feel they worked for you in the past. It's better to use active strategies, which require you to do more than just "look at" or "read over" materials.

Active study strategies require you to *write* and *rehearse* materials—for example, by constructing flash cards and reviewing them—rather than merely "looking at" notes and other materials. The following are some examples of active strategies:

- Creating flash cards, problem/solution cards, or vocabulary cards (see Figure 5-2)
- Developing your own study guide
- Studying in small groups
- Outlining your chapters
- Drawing concept maps (see Figure 5-2)
- Creating charts or tables using the material
- Developing your own practice questions or mock exam

Developing these study materials and reviewing them at least a week before the exam will help you do well and can also help your stress levels because you will have a greater feeling of control. Use three or more different active strategies, preferably a week or so in advance, to prepare for your next exam.

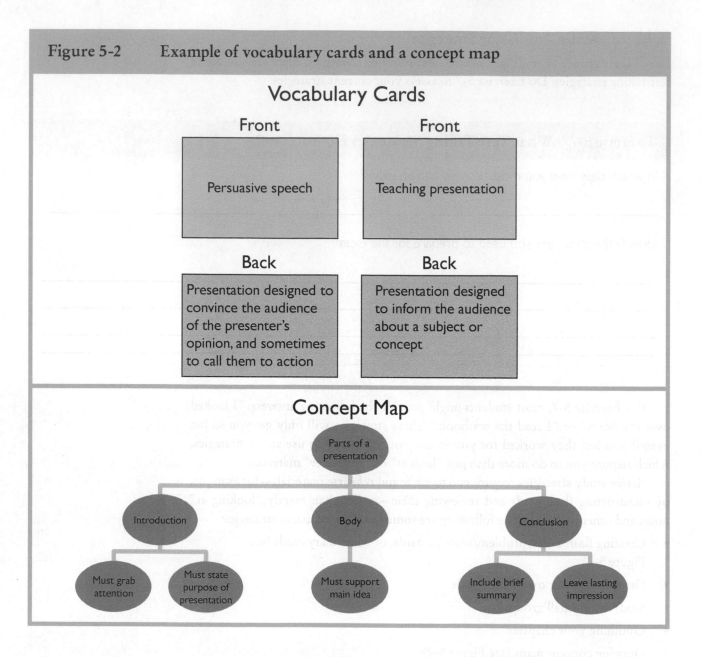

Figure 5-2   Example of vocabulary cards and a concept map

Vocabulary Cards

Front
Persuasive speech

Front
Teaching presentation

Back
Presentation designed to convince the audience of the presenter's opinion, and sometimes to call them to action

Back
Presentation designed to inform the audience about a subject or concept

Concept Map

Parts of a presentation

- Introduction
  - Must grab attention
  - Must state purpose of presentation
- Body
  - Must support main idea
- Conclusion
  - Include brief summary
  - Leave lasting impression

5.4b   Before an Exam

To reduce test anxiety, there is no substitute for simply being prepared. Preparing properly and using good study habits should help with how nervous you feel on test day. However, it is normal to have some anxiety about taking an exam, no matter how much you have prepared.

Begin to study at least a week before an exam, and schedule study time each day. Make sure you study all the material. Sometimes it is tempting to do what's comfortable and focus on the material you already know well instead of what is challenging. It is certainly important to study material you already "know" because *overlearning* (continuing to review material even once you know it) will help you do well on the test even if you're nervous. However, students sometimes avoid studying material they don't know as well, which is a mistake. Don't avoid difficult topics or ignore feelings of frustration and confusion. Seek assistance from your teacher, tutors, and classmates.

Exercise 5-8　Exam Action Plan

In the previous exercise, we asked you to reflect on a recent exam. Now we ask you to look to the future. Name a course in which you will have an exam soon.

Course: _____

If you know the date of the exam, write it here: _____

Which strategies do you think will be most helpful in preparing for this exam? The answer depends on you. For example, some students like to use flash cards, while others prefer outlines. The key is to use *active* rather than passive strategies and to use more than one strategy. For this next exam, commit to using three active strategies. Write them here:

Exam Preparation Strategies

1. _____

2. _____

3. _____

Use time management strategies to prepare for your exam. Set aside time each day on your weekly and daily schedules to study. If you're a full-time student, you may notice that exams seem to happen all at once. It is common to have no exams one week and several exams the next. Time management is key to making sure you can prepare for all of them. Exercise 5-9 can help.

Exercise 5-9　Prepare a Schedule to Study for an Exam

Write down a subject for which you have an upcoming exam: _____

How many days do you have to prepare for the exam? _____

In the space provided, write down tasks you will complete each day leading up to the exam. These tasks can include studying particular materials, re-marking information in your text, completing practice tests, and so on.

Name and date of exam _____

Date:	Tasks:
_____	_____
_____	_____
_____	_____
_____	_____
_____	_____
_____	_____
_____	_____

Now review the tasks in the right column. Have you covered all the exam material? Have you missed anything that may be on the exam? Have you given yourself enough time to learn more difficult material without forgetting about the easier concepts?

5.4c   During an Exam

Your strategies do not end once you begin taking your exam. Several strategies can be used during an exam to maximize your chance of success. These strategies begin with time management and include determining what kind of exam you will be taking.

Time Management Revisited   Arrive at the exam a few minutes early so you don't feel rushed. Pace yourself during the exam: Allow enough time to complete each section, but don't take so long that you run out of time and don't complete the entire test. If you finish early, use the extra time to review your answers. However, be cautious about making changes if you're not sure. It is usually a bad idea to change answers unless you know with 100 percent certainty that your original response was a mistake. More often than not, when students change answers, it turns out they had the right answer to begin with. Trust your gut.

Where to Start   Some people develop their own test-taking strategies. For example, they may do all the easy questions first and then return to the more difficult ones. Make sure you mark the questions you skipped or you may forget to return to them. Finally, do not destroy your old exams: Keep them and learn from them!

Hints for Objective Exams   An **objective exam** involves questions with definite right or wrong answers. Types of objective exams include multiple choice, true or false, matching, and other tests where the questions have answers that are either correct or incorrect. When taking objective exams, be sure you understand all the directions. Usually, your first idea about the answer is your best. Here's one good technique for multiple-choice questions: Read the question, but cover the options with your hand or a piece of paper. Answer the question in your head before looking at the options; then select the option that most closely matches the answer you came up with. Be aware of *qualifiers* in the question. These are words like *all, most, none, never,* and *mainly.* If the question asks if something is *always* true, the answer might be *no* even if that thing is *sometimes* true. For example, does March 1st *always* follow February 28th? The answer is *no* because during a *leap year*, February 29th would follow the 28th. These words are very important when it comes to figuring out the right answer.

Hints for Subjective Exams   A **subjective exam** can involve short-answer and essay questions, and is a test where *how* you answer can be as important as *what* your answer is. When taking subjective exams, plan your time. Questions asking for longer answers won't just take longer, they'll probably be worth more points as well, so plan accordingly. For short answers, stick to the main points that directly answers the question. Essays require more writing and usually more work. It almost always helps to take a few minutes and do some *prewriting*: Sketch out information you need to include, perhaps in an informal outline. You can then concentrate on writing without worrying that you'll forget important information. Organization is important in writing for exams. Look to the question for clues as to format. For example, essays often involve comparing and contrasting (see Exercise 5-10). For this type of essay question, first compare (write about similarities between the concepts) and then contrast (write about their differences). Here are some other key words that you will find in exam questions:

- **Explain**   This means you need to *demonstrate your understanding.*

- **Define**   This means you need to *provide a definition and precise description of a term or concept.*
- **Discuss**   This means you need to *consider possible points of view on a topic, usually more than one.*
- **Summarize**   This means you need to *present the main points of a topic.*
- **Argue**   This means you need to *present an opinion in an informed way* (you need to back your opinion up with facts or information from other sources).
- **Compare**   This means you need to *identify similarities.*
- **Contrast**   This means you need to *identify differences.*
- **Apply**   This means you need to *use a concept* or *show how it can be used.*

Some additional hints on essay exam questions:

1. Choose a title for your essay even if you don't use it. This helps to focus your thoughts and narrow your response.

2. Outline or map your response before you write it.

3. Make sure you have a good introduction, a body that supports your answers, and a strong conclusion.

4. Proofread your answers for spelling, grammar, sentence structure, etc.

5. Make sure you write clearly! If you make the instructor work harder to read and grade your paper, it usually means point deductions.

Exercise 5-10   Planning an Essay during an Exam

In this exercise, you'll practice writing informal outlines for essay questions. Compare your outlines with ones written by a classmate. Would this material satisfy the requirements of the essay?

Example from an Introduction to Literature course: Compare and contrast the modern and postmodern periods of American literature.

Introduction ⟶ Similarities between modern and postmodern periods. (Comparison) ⟶
Differences between modern and postmodern periods. (Contrast) ⟶ Concluding thoughts.

Now provide your own essay exam outlines for these possible exam questions from the content in this chapter:

1. Define and describe the three primary types of learning styles discussed in this chapter.

_____

2. Define the various types of memories and provide three or more examples to illustrate how you can use memory aids within your study strategies.

_____

3. Compare and contrast objective and subjective test-taking strategies.

_____

Which question(s) asks you to consider differences and similarities? Which question(s) asks you to describe a concept? Which question(s) asks for specific examples to illustrate your point? The same structure will not work for each essay. You have to consider the kind of question being asked.

5.4d   After an Exam

After an exam, some students eagerly look up the answers to questions they think they might have missed. Others avoid doing this, not wanting to face the facts. Regardless, many students do not take advantage of post-exam strategies that can enhance their learning over the long term.

Whether or not you did well on an exam, you should note the items you answered easily as well as those you struggled with or missed. This information will help if you have a comprehensive final or if the material comes up in other courses.

Right after an exam, evaluate the strategies you used. Did you spend enough time studying? Did you study everything you needed? Are there particular content areas where you were stronger (or weaker) than others?

5.4e   If You Did Poorly on an Exam

When one of your instructors returns an exam, take note of the types of questions you got right and those you answered incorrectly. Look at the areas where you did poorly. Were there particular ideas or sections that you got wrong? Were there specific areas where you could have studied harder? In addition, look at the types of questions you missed. If you struggled with particular types of questions, your instructor may be able to give you some suggestions for studying next time.

Psychologist Benjamin Bloom identified six types of test questions. **Bloom's taxonomy** provides a helpful framework for many students as tests become more advanced and complex. After you read about the method, do Exercise 5-11 to practice it.

Finally, if you do poorly on an exam, take the time to meet with your teacher. Reviewing the exam with your instructor may help you to improve in the future. Most instructors have office hours when they are available to meet with students. Many students do not take advantage of this opportunity. Showing positive concern about your performance on the exam will show that you care about your academics, as long as you make a good impression and avoid making excuses or coming off as defensive.

Bloom's Taxonomy

Six Types of Test Questions

Knowledge: These questions typically only require you to *recognize* information, like on a multiple-choice test.

Example: SMART stands for:
a. Specific, Measurable, Achievable, Realistic, Time-bound
b. Standard, Measurable, Action-oriented, Repeatable, Time-bound
c. Specific, Measurable, Approachable, Reasonable, Targeted

Comprehension: Similar to knowledge, comprehension questions require you to remember information.

Example: People with emotional intelligence
a. Manage their emotions well
b. Are geniuses
c. Are overwhelmed by their feelings

Application: This type of question requires that you apply what you have learned to a new situation.

Example: It's your first day at a new job and your boss hands you a list of tasks to complete. What organization and time management techniques can you use to ensure they all get done?

Analysis: Analysis questions require you to break a complex system or process into its parts.

Example: What are the parts of the Cornell method and how do they work together for effective note-taking?

Synthesis: Synthesis questions, like analysis, are often found in essay questions. Here you bring information and ideas together from different sources.

Example: This text has walked you through how to improve your stress management, attitude, and handling of resources (like time and money). How do these areas affect *one another* positively or negatively?

Evaluation: An evaluation is an informed opinion, "informed" being the key word. You have to explain your opinion by backing it up with information from the course.

Example: Are mnemonics a helpful tool for studying?

You might see all six of these types of questions on one exam or over the course of one course, but often, courses and professors will use one or two types more than the rest. As you take an exam, try to note the types of questions being asked.

Exercise 5-11   Applying Bloom's Taxonomy

Take another look at a course in which you will soon have an exam. Write a question for each area of Bloom's taxonomy based on material from that course. You'll gain a better understanding of the types of test questions, and you'll have the beginnings of a study guide.

Knowledge Question: _____

Comprehension Question: _____

Application Question: _____

Analysis Question: _____

Synthesis Question: _____

Evaluation Question: _____

5.4f   Faculty and Student Interaction

Positive communication with your instructor is important for your success. You can *interact positively* in several ways. For example, sitting near the front of the room, showing a genuine interest in the class, and actively participating in classroom discussions will go a long way toward establishing a good relationship with your teacher. Instructors are willing to help, but most expect you to be the one to ask for assistance. Don't be afraid to make an appointment or meet with faculty during office hours to discuss your concerns. Be sure to prepare by coming up with specific questions. Here are ten things instructors are looking for in a student:

Top 10 Qualities of Successful Students

Successful students…

1. Have a positive attitude
2. Actively participate in class
3. Are willing to learn and work hard
4. Take responsibility for their behavior and their learning
5. Have creative problem-solving abilities
6. Are dependable (they have good attendance and are on time)
7. Are respectful
8. Have the ability to work well with others
9. Have effective communication skills
10. Make education a priority

    How many would your instructor check off about you?

A positive faculty and student interaction will enhance the learning process and your academic performance.

Healthy Decision-Making

Mary knows she has a strong preference for visual learning and scored high on musical intelligence. However, one of her classes is all lecture with no slides and very little written on the blackboard. Mary feels there is a lot of information to know in this course but is finding it difficult to retain it. What suggestions would you have to help Mary succeed in this course?

_____

_____

_____

_____

_____

_____

_____

_____

Creative Thinking and Decision-Making Skills

Making Good Choices

Objectives

By the end of this chapter, you will be able to:

- Assess how emotional intelligence affects the thinking process

- Describe the relationship between critical and creative thinking

- Understand the integrated thinking process

- Improve your critical and creative thinking skills

- Analyze assumption and bias in information

- Learn how to turn problems into opportunities

- Develop action plans to become a better problem-solver and decision-maker

Why Learn This Skill?

Thinking is something we all do every day. We make decisions each day, which requires *critical thinking skills*. Often, we need to come up with new ideas or new ways to look at a situation, which requires *creative thinking skills*. Obviously, thinking is a vital tool we must use daily in life—not just in school.

However, most people pay little attention to *how* they think. Ask yourself the weird-sounding yet deep question: "Have I ever really *thought* about *how I think*?" Some people are *reactive thinkers*, waiting for a crisis to occur, whereas others are *proactive* and think ahead to avoid the crisis. Some people are *positive thinkers*, full of creative ideas; some people have a difficult time generating ideas or being creative. Some people make decisions confidently; others "can't make a decision to save their lives."

Thinking, like any other skill, can be assessed and improved to increase your academic and professional success. This chapter shows you how to improve your thinking skills in many areas, including critical and creative thinking, decision-making, and problem-solving.

"I think, therefore I am."

Descartes

6.1　Introduction

Psychologists specialize in studying *how* humans think. They have come up with several terms to describe the many complex mental activities that make up the process of *thinking*. These mental activities can include speaking and understanding language, reasoning, remembering, imagining, learning—and many more.

You can also break things down into the different types of thinking, including logical, deductive, critical, creative, directed, undirected, proactive, and reactive thinking, to name a few. While it's good to know these terms, the focus of this chapter is how to use this information to become a better thinker. As an effective thinker, you will be able to think creatively, problem solve, and make decisions to maximize your success in any situation. The development of these skills will make you an excellent student and a valued professional.

6.2　The Process of *Thinking*

Imagine this: Your stomach starts to rumble and it's feeling pretty empty. You think to yourself, "I'm hungry." Then maybe you start thinking about what you'd like to eat. You go to the pantry, the fridge, or look up takeout near you. Finally, you decide what you want and either cook or order it. Afterwards, you think to yourself, "I'm still a little hungry—what should I have for dessert?"

Integrated thinking

A model of the thinking process that breaks it down into five steps: (1) opportunity for positive change, (2) idea generation (creative thinking), (3) decision-making (critical thinking), (4) implementation and evaluation, and 5) feedback, all of which are affected by the environment

It's probably safe to say we've all been there. However, beneath this seemingly simple thought process lies what is known as **integrated thinking**, illustrated in Figure 6-1. Going back to our example, that initial stomach rumbling is an *opportunity for positive change*—you're hungry and you'd like to make a positive change by eating until you're full. This is the first step in the integrated thinking process. Next, you use your *creative thinking* skills to *generate ideas* (Step 2) about what you'd like to eat. After considering your options, you use your *critical thinking* skills to *make a decision* (Step 3) about what to cook or order and *implement* it (Step 4) by either preparing the food or calling the restaurant. After *evaluating* your meal, you get *feedback* (Step 5) from your body saying you're still a little hungry, so you consider what you might eat for dessert. Don't let the technical terminology fool you—you've been using the integrated thinking process in your daily life without even realizing it!

Notice we haven't yet mentioned the *environment* (shown in big, bold letters in Figure 6-1). The environment has a big effect on *what* and *how* we think. We will go into that more soon.

Chapter 6: Creative Thinking and Decision-Making Skills

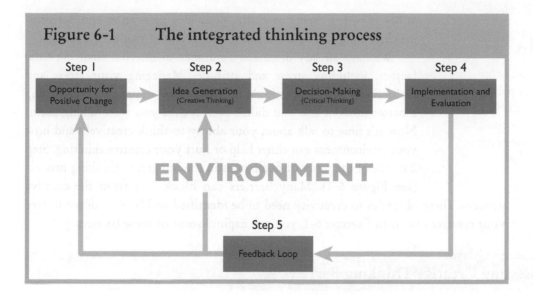

Figure 6-1 The integrated thinking process

Step 1	Step 2	Step 3	Step 4
Opportunity for Positive Change	Idea Generation (Creative Thinking)	Decision-Making (Critical Thinking)	Implementation and Evaluation

ENVIRONMENT

Step 5

Feedback Loop

6.2a   Emotional Intelligence and the Thinking Process

In 1990, Peter Salovey and John D. Mayer led the research in **emotional intelligence** or **EQ** as it has come to be known. They defined emotional intelligence as "the subset of social intelligence that involves the ability to monitor one's own and others' feelings and emotions, to discriminate among them, and to use this information to guide one's thinking and actions." To put it in simpler terms, emotional intelligence is about your ability to recognize, control, and evaluate emotions.

Emotional intelligence can affect your thinking, decision-making, and problem-solving processes. Let's demonstrate with an example. Think back to a time when you made a decision while you were really angry. Maybe it felt good to act on your anger at the time, but how did you feel later? Were there any consequences to your actions? If you had to do it over again, would you wait until you calmed down before making a decision or taking action? It takes EQ to recognize your anger in the moment and control it so it doesn't affect what you do.

There are many emotions, and they all affect how we think. For example, research shows that when someone becomes too stressed at work, it can take him or her up to four hours to recover and return to being productive. Think about how this applies to your studying and academic performance. This is why it is so important to assess your feelings and consider how they might affect your thinking.

6.2b   Your Environment and the Thinking Process

Your environment—both *external* (the world around you) and *internal* (your feelings and mental state)—can drastically change your thinking. Going back to our earlier example of feeling hungry, your options for that meal would be very different in downtown New York versus on a ranch in rural Montana. What if your fridge and pantry are empty? What if you reach for something to eat only to find out it's gone bad? What if you want to order food from the restaurant across the street, but then you find out they're closed? Other environmental factors are also important. If you're in a stressful environment, like

Emotional intelligence (EQ)

A kind of social intelligence that involves being aware of your own emotions and those of others and using that information to guide your thinking and actions

Food for Thought

You may be familiar with intelligence quotient (IQ) tests, but have you heard of emotional intelligence quotient (EQ) testing? It is designed to evaluate our ability to recognize and manage our emotions. Many successful people have a normal, or in some cases below normal, IQ but show a high level of EQ, possibly suggesting it is at least as important as IQ when it comes to success in life. In fact, some people with a high IQ may tend to "overthink" things, making it more difficult to make a decision.

at home with a crying newborn, your idea generation and decision-making might not be at their best—especially if you're also hungry.

We have already discussed a number of internal environmental factors, including stress and attitude. Managing your stress and maintaining a positive attitude were your first steps toward becoming a better thinker, and you didn't even realize you were taking them! Now it's time to talk about your ability to think creatively and how your environment can either help or hurt your creative thinking. Step 2 is one of the more difficult steps in the integrated thinking process (see Figure 6-1). Many barriers can block you from the creative process. These obstacles to creativity need to be identified and broken down to free your creative juices. In Exercise 6-1, you will explore some of these barriers.

Exercise 6-1   Assessing Creative Thinking Barriers

The following list represents the top four barriers to creativity. After the discussion of each barrier, answer the question to see if this obstacle is blocking your creativity. If the answer is yes, come up with a plan for how to break down that barrier.

Fear of Voicing Ideas

For the creative process to work, everyone must be free to share his or her ideas and perspectives because we all have different ways of viewing any given situation.

Are you afraid to speak up when you have an idea? _____ If you answered yes, you need to determine the root cause.

Why are you afraid to voice your ideas and what actions can you take to overcome this fear?

_____

_____

_____

Action Plan: _____

_____

_____

Fear of Losing Control

Sometimes people send signals to others, intentionally or without knowing it, that they really don't want to hear other ideas and will do it *their* way. This desire to control everything can act as a barrier to the creative process and it can stop everyone, the controlling person included, from coming up with new ways to do things. This stifling of creativity can cause companies to become outdated because they haven't found new and better ways to operate.

Are you afraid of losing control? _____ Do you feel uncomfortable in an environment where ideas are being tossed around freely? Are you threatened when others try to give you ideas? Do you feel a need to be in charge?

If you are afraid of giving up control or have been in a controlling environment that stifled your creativity, write your thoughts about it and come up with an action plan to overcome this obstacle.

_____

_____

_____

Action Plan: _____

_____

_____

(continues)

Premature Criticism

Premature criticism stifles creativity not only in the person who was criticized but also in anyone who witnessed it because they do not want to be criticized. You'll soon learn that it is important not to make quick judgments, good or bad, about someone else's idea in the creative process. Premature criticism can be a statement ("That's a stupid idea"), but it isn't always that obvious. It can be something as thoughtless and little as a heavy sigh or eye rolling after someone presents an idea.

Have you witnessed premature criticism? _____
Have you prematurely criticized others? _____

Describe how you can avoid giving premature criticism to others and come up with an action plan for what you can do if you witness or experience premature criticism.

_____

_____

_____

Action Plan: _____

_____

_____

Resistance to Change

New ideas bring change. This can be difficult when the change is to a technique, process, or situation that you have become comfortable with. However, change is both unavoidable and necessary in our lives. Instead of fighting change, learn to embrace it with a positive attitude.

When a change is suggested, do you resist it? _____ Do you think, "This is the way it has always been done; why should we look for a better way?"

Write about a time you were resistant to change and come up with a plan for how you can approach change with a positive attitude in the future.

_____

_____

_____

Action Plan: _____

_____

_____

Emotions Getting in the Way

When emotions are running high, it may be difficult to make clear or positive decisions. Feelings like fear, anger, or even excitement can cause us to act in ways that are not good for us or those around us. Understanding this about yourself is an example of Emotional Intelligence (EQ).

Do you act in the heat of the moment, letting emotions influence you to make bad decisions? _____

Think about a time when you made an emotional decision. Describe how you felt in the moment and the consequences of your decision. Come up with a plan for the next time you feel your emotions getting the better of you. (Hint: Think back to the section on stress management.)

_____

_____

_____

Action Plan: _____

_____

_____

6.2c   External Barriers to the Creative Process

Having assessed some of your *internal* barriers to the creative process in Exercise 6-1, you must also recognize that *external* barriers can interfere with your thinking. For example, if you are in a room that's full of distractions, like loud music, you might find you "can't hear yourself think."

Even how the room is arranged can affect the creative thinking process. If you're familiar with the tale of King Arthur, then you know about the Knights of the Round Table. The table was round so that all the knights would feel equal. This meant they didn't *fear voicing their ideas,* no one was *afraid of losing control,* and it helped prevent *premature criticism.* This kind of open discussion also helps people overcome their *resistance to change.* When we discuss teams later, we'll dig deeper into group creativity and brainstorming. Then we will revisit things like the arrangement of the room, distractions, and other *environmental factors* and how they can influence a discussion. Now that we've laid the groundwork, it's time to dig a little deeper into each of the five steps of integrated thinking.

6.3   Step 1: Opportunity for Positive Change

6.3a   Proactive and Reactive Thinking

Do you ever feel like you're struggling to stay on top of everything going on in your life? Maybe it seems like you are always "putting out fires," jumping from one problem to the next, never getting ahead. If that's the case, you might be relying on **reactive thinking**. You're using *reactive thinking* when you wait for a problem to come up and then try to fix it. By always waiting for the problem to find you, you can find yourself dealing with a crisis in which your emotions make it difficult to find the best solution. If you're always in crisis, you may find you get hit by problem after problem with no chance to get ahead.

Proactive thinking involves looking ahead and trying to predict what problems might occur. It's the difference between driving along, spacing out, and having to slam on the breaks when the car in front of you stops suddenly (reactive thinking) and driving along, alert and prepared, ready to slow down as soon as you see those tail lights (proactive thinking). Proactive thinking can help you prevent problems (and fender benders) from occurring. By thinking ahead, you can deal with potential problems calmly. Knowing that it's best to deal with problems when you're calm is an example of high EQ. Now that you understand the importance of looking ahead for potential problems, let's discuss what you can do when you see one coming.

6.3b   Reframing Your Problems

Have you ever heard the saying, "If all you have is a hammer, everything looks like a nail"? When the only tool you have is problem-solving, you can find yourself looking at every decision as a problem to be solved. Pretty quickly, it can start to seem like your life is full of problems, making it difficult to maintain a positive attitude. Instead, try reframing the situation. Maybe they aren't problems at all but rather *opportunities for positive change.* By looking at each major decision, or perhaps problem, as an opportunity for positive change, you are already on your way to a great outcome (see Figure 6-2).

Reactive thinking

When you wait for a problem to arise and then try to fix it

Proactive thinking

When you try to predict what problems might occur in the future and prevent them from happening

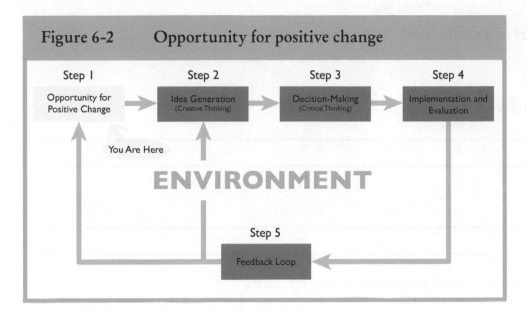

Figure 6-2   Opportunity for positive change

Let's practice reframing our problems with an example. It's important to get rid of any negativity and have a clear outcome in mind. For example, here is a problem statement that many students have either thought or said.

Problem: *"This subject is too difficult, I'm never going to pass this course."*

Stated like this, the problem might seem *insurmountable* or *impossible to overcome*. Words like *never* can lead to a *self-fulfilling prophecy* of failure. By deciding the goal of passing is hopeless, you've given yourself permission not to try and, therefore, resigned yourself to failure. You've guaranteed a negative outcome just in the way you've framed the situation! However, this challenge can be reframed.

Reframed as an opportunity for positive change: *"If I work hard, I can get better at this difficult subject, and in doing so, I will not only pass the course but also grow as a student and a person."*

Notice how the statement now presents an opportunity—in this case, more than one: You can get better at a subject you find difficult, you can grow as a student, and you can grow as a person! This statement then becomes a question: "What can I do to get better at this difficult subject?" This question will guide you as you come up with ideas concerning possible actions (Step 2: Idea Generation). This question may also lead you to look at the way things were done in the past to find a better way.

But before we move on to Step 2, let's come up with a few more examples together.

Problem: *"I'm too busy; there just aren't enough hours in the day!"*

Reframed as an opportunity for positive change: *"If I find a better way to deal with my busy schedule, I will be less stressed and I might be able to find time to relax!"*

Notice how the phrasing now presents the opportunity to handle a busy schedule while reducing stress and finding time to relax. When you go to the next step and ask yourself, "What can I do to manage my time better?" you are more likely to generate positive ideas that will result in a good outcome. Now do Exercise 6-2.

Exercise 6-2   Reframe the Problem as an Opportunity

Reframe the following:

Problem 1: *(fill in name) never listens to me.*

Restatement: _____

_____

Problem 2: *I'm always tired.*

Restatement: _____

_____

Problem 3: *I'm so afraid of math, and it's required by many of my courses.*

Restatement: _____

_____

Problem 4: *I can never commit to a study schedule.*

Restatement: _____

_____

Problem 5: *I can't figure out what program or career is right for me.*

Restatement: _____

_____

After clearly stating an opportunity for positive change, you are ready to move on to the next step and *generate ideas*. First, let's take a moment to make this process more personal by identifying an opportunity for positive change *in your life* in Exercise 6-3.

Exercise 6-3   Your Opportunity

State an "opportunity for positive change" (formerly known as a "problem") that you would like to work on as we continue our journey to success through integrated thinking. If you haven't chosen a career path, that might be a good place to start.

_____

_____

_____

Keep your chosen opportunity in mind as we work through the next steps.

6.4　Step 2: Generate Ideas (Creative Thinking)

Step 2 requires you to use creative thinking and come up with many ideas about how to embrace the opportunity you identified in Step 1 (see Figure 6-3). It can be tempting to come up with only one idea and move on to the next step immediately, but that would be a mistake. This step is not about deciding on the best idea—that's Step 3: Decision-Making. Rather, this step is all about coming up with as many ideas as you can, even if some of them seem a little "out there." This can be difficult for some people. Remember the barriers to creative thinking? Many of us are afraid of coming up with bad ideas, criticize our own ideas prematurely, and are resistant to trying something different. Try not to judge any of your ideas as good or bad at this stage. When it comes to generating ideas, try to be as free and creative as possible. You never know when a seemingly crazy idea might become a powerful solution.

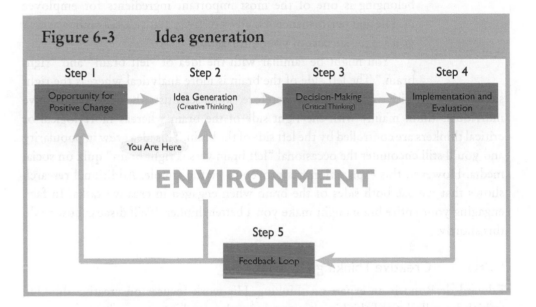

Figure 6-3　　Idea generation

| Step 1 | Step 2 | Step 3 | Step 4 |
| Opportunity for Positive Change | Idea Generation (Creative Thinking) | Decision-Making (Critical Thinking) | Implementation and Evaluation |

You Are Here

ENVIRONMENT

Step 5

Feedback Loop

Let's go back to our initial example of satisfying your hunger. What if you picked the first thing your hand touched when you reached into the fridge or the first item your eyes landed on when you opened the menu? You would have missed the opportunity to choose between many more delicious and satisfying options. Therefore, the purpose of this stage is to consider every possibility. Later, you might even consider combining some of your ideas—but now is the time to simply lay all your options out on the table.

6.4a　Background Information on Creative Thinking

If you struggle with **creative thinking**, you are not alone. For some reason, we do not focus as much attention on the creative side of thinking. Instead, most of your education and experience before now probably focused on critical thinking—which we'll get to in the next step. Right now, let's talk about creativity.

Many people feel they are not creative, but the truth is we are all creative and beyond that, we can *enhance* our creativity. You were being creative when you were hungry and came up with unique ideas for what to cook or order. Too many people

Creative thinking

Thinking that's designed to *generate* (come up with) *ideas* rather than judge them

believe *creativity* is limited to artists and eccentric geniuses. This attitude is unfortunate because it distances many people from their creative side. If we define creative thinking simply as "coming up with ideas," we can see that creativity relates to all of us. A worker who comes up with a better way to do their job, a parent who helps a child to learn a new skill or overcome a problem, or even someone who finds a better route to avoid rush-hour traffic are all being creative. We use creative thinking every day of our lives, sometimes without even knowing it.

Learning to enhance your creativity also benefits you in other areas. For example, increasing creativity also increases your self-confidence and motivation. Creative thinking can improve the quality of both your academic and professional work. If you feel free to contribute ideas, you will have a sense of belonging. This sense of belonging is one of the most important ingredients for employee morale and performance. Finally, creativity rejuvenates enthusiasm as you see the success of your efforts.

You might be familiar with the idea of "left brain" and "right brain." The left side of the brain is more analytical whereas the right side is more intuitive and creative. Therefore, some scientists thought that creative individuals think mainly with the right side of the brain whereas more logical or critical thinkers are controlled by the left side of the brain. This idea grew in popularity and you'll still encounter the occasional "left brain versus right brain" quiz on social media. However, this explanation has proven to be too simple. Additional research shows that we use both sides of the brain when engaged in creative tasks. In fact, engaging your entire brain might make you a better thinker. We'll discuss how to do this shortly.

6.4b   Creative Thinking Theories

Edward de Bono is an expert on thinking. His work focuses on creative thinking (which he calls *lateral thinking* because it involves making new, sideways connections) and critical thinking (which he calls *vertical thinking* because each idea relates logically to the next, step-by-step, in a line).

Critical thinking allows us to use our past experiences to inform us about the present and even the future. We discuss this type of thinking in the next step, decision-making. De Bono, in his book *Lateral Thinking*, discusses how creative thinking creates new ideas by making connections between things we had not connected before. As an example, take a look at Figure 6-4. You may be scratching your head, wondering how that cartoon relates to creative thinking. Picture your brain as a file cabinet. Somewhere you probably have a file that contains information on "the reason dinosaurs are extinct." Is this, by itself, funny? Of course not. Many species were lost forever. In another section of your brain, you have a file that contains information on how "drinking too much and smoking can kill you." This also isn't very funny by itself. However, when we connect these two previously unrelated pieces of information, we get humor—which is creative.

| Figure 6-4 | An alternate theory of dinosaur extinction |

The process of connecting previously unrelated bits of information is the power behind creative thinking. When two or more people are sitting around discussing ideas (brainstorming), *lateral* or *sideways* connections are being made from one idea to another. When you are sitting alone thinking of ideas, your brain is literally *storming* back and forth between the right side and the left side, making connections.

6.4c   Creative Thinking Techniques

Associative Thinking and Visualization   One method to encourage your brain to make connections is *visualization*. For example, you can write down your opportunity for positive change in the center of a piece of paper. Now, write key words and ideas all around the opportunity, and connect them all together. Use different colors and symbols to illustrate and emphasize certain points. Study this picture and see if you can find new relationships, patterns, or ideas. It may take time, but the more ideas you develop, the better your chance for a successful solution. See Figure 6-5 for a sample visual creative map. Draw your chosen opportunity for change from Exercise 6-3 in Exercise 6-4.

Figure 6-5

Figure 6-5   Example of a visual association related to finding a career

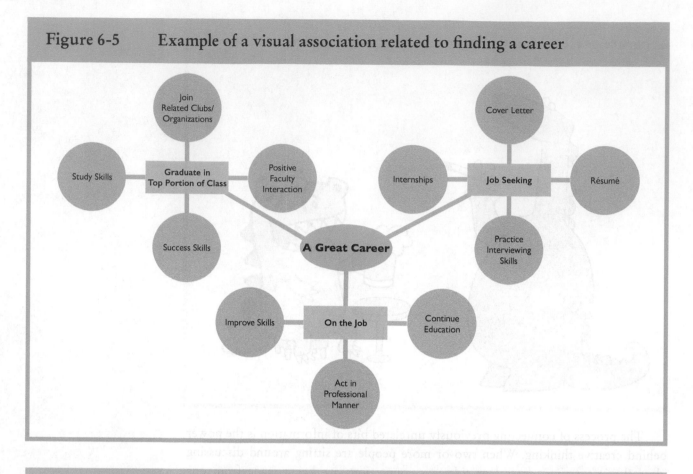

Exercise 6-4   Drawing Your Opportunity

Now take your "opportunity for positive change" from Exercise 6-3 and draw your own visual map. Include at least five connections between different ideas. More is better!

Personal Brainstorming Brainstorming is a powerful way to enhance creativity. Traditionally, this is a process in which a small group of people get together and come up with ideas concerning an opportunity or issue. We discuss this powerful technique more when we get to the chapter on group interactions. For now, the focus is still on you. It is helpful to meditate or slow your mind and then focus on the opportunity for change you selected.

Then, as ideas come into your head (the sideways connections discussed earlier), simply write them without judgment and follow the rules described below.

You can also discuss your opportunity with a trusted person. If done properly, this kind of collaboration allows you to benefit from that person's experiences, knowledge, and insights. Because each of you thinks differently, by working together, the total amount of creativity will increase. It is even better to choose someone who is successful in the area you selected as your opportunity for positive change.

The following are important rules to make sure this process is effective. Although mentioned previously, these rules are critical to the process and therefore deserve another mention.

- *Rule 1: Withhold premature criticism.* Don't tell yourself, "That's a stupid idea; I'm not going to write it down." Premature criticism will kill the creative process and should be avoided at all costs. Consider any idea, no matter how farfetched. Remember, the goal is not to come up with the best solution at this time. The goal here is to list all kinds of ideas to analyze and evaluate in the next step. You might combine some ideas later, or a crazy idea might lead you to come up with a more realistic one that you wouldn't have arrived at otherwise, so you never know which ideas will be helpful in the end.

- *Rule 2: The quantity, not the quality, of ideas is important at this stage.* The more ideas generated, the better the odds are that a truly great idea will emerge. There are no "right" or "wrong" ideas in creative thinking.

- *Rule 3: Get rid of distractions.* An environment free of distractions is best for creative thinking. Distractions can include noise, poor lighting, squeaky chairs, cell phones, and so on.

6.4d   Other Hints for Enhancing Personal Creativity

Allow your *subconscious* to work for you. If you remember from earlier, your subconscious is the part of the mind you aren't actively aware of. Calming your mind by meditating and gaining focus allows creativity to flourish. Sometimes it is important to get away from the issue for a while and let your subconscious mind work. Remember the times when the answer to an issue came to you suddenly, seemingly out of nowhere? Albert Einstein, one of the greatest thinkers of all time, said, "Why do I get my best ideas when shaving?" While his conscious mind was lost in the repetitive process of shaving, his subconscious mind was working on new ideas. Some people are more creative in the evening or in certain rooms or environments. Figure out where and when you are at your most creative.

6.4e   Analogies

An analogy is another way to create a connection between two seemingly unalike things. This can be helpful in generating new and unique ideas. Many inventions came about as a result of analogies. One day a man was walking through the woods when he got a bunch of burs (spiky seeds) stuck on his pants. Analyzing the burs, he envisioned an invention in his mind. Like the burs, it would involve little spikes designed to stick to things—but unlike the burs, it would be useful! That man developed Velcro®. Using analogies can be both fun and creative in developing unique solutions. Analogies are also a powerful learning tool. For example, when learning how the body regulates temperature, an analogy of the thermostat and heating/cooling system in your house can make the technical process of "homeostatic thermal regulation" much easier to learn.

Exercise 6-5   Generate Ideas

It's time to continue your personal journey through integrated thinking. Take your opportunity for positive change from Exercise 6-3 and, using concepts from our discussion, come up with a list of ideas related to your stated opportunity. This may take some time and several sessions. Use ideas from the visual exercise (6-4) to come up with at least ten ideas. (Remember to withhold judgment!)

_____

_____

_____

_____

_____

_____

_____

_____

_____

_____

_____

6.5   Step 3: Decision-Making (Critical Thinking)

In this step, we shift from creative to critical thinking to evaluate each idea or combination of ideas so we can decide how to move forward. Basically, you weigh the pros and cons of each idea to choose the best. See Figure 6-6.

6.5a   Critical Thinking

There are many definitions of critical thinking. In his book *Critical Thinking*, Robert Ennis explains, "Critical thinking is a process, the goal of which is to make reasonable decisions about what to believe and what to do." Diane Romain, in her book *Thinking*

Things Through: Critical Thinking for Decisions You Can Live With, argues, "Critical thinking consists of those activities of the mind that are indispensable to making decisions we can live with. The processes involved in critical thinking include becoming aware of our emotions and reflecting on them, identifying our values, assessing information and the authorities who provide it, analyzing and clarifying language, imagining solutions to problems, evaluating alternative solutions, and assessing and producing arguments."

What these definitions have in common is reasoning (assessing, analyzing, evaluating) and decision-making. **Critical thinking** is about looking at facts or ideas *objectively,* which means without emotion or opinion, and using logic to arrive at a decision. Note that critical thinking skills (like all thinking skills) can be developed and improved through practice.

Food for Thought

The word *critical* came from the Greek word *krinein,* which means "to separate in order to select." This step requires you to separate and evaluate your ideas and facts to select the best choice.

Critical thinking

Looking at facts or ideas without emotion or opinion, using logic to make a decision

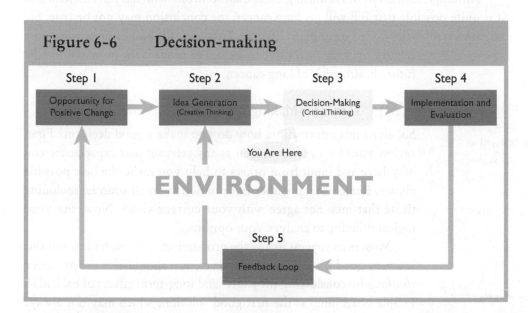

Figure 6-6   Decision-making

Critical thinking relies on *logical* thinking. Any time you evaluate, make judgments, or make decisions, you are using logical thinking. Just what is logic? One part of logic relies on your past experiences and knowledge. Another part of logical thinking relies on your ability to reason *deductively* and *inductively.*

Deductive reasoning is a form of logical thinking in which you reach a conclusion based on true facts called *premises.* For example, you may have the following premises:

Premise: Students who develop good study skills improve their grades.

Premise: Mary has developed her study skills by going to the learning resource center.

Conclusion: Mary's grades will improve.

In this example, you used deductive reasoning to reach a true conclusion. The conclusion in deductive reasoning is always true if the premises are true. Thanks to deductive reasoning, Mary should feel confident that with her improved study skills will come improved grades.

Deductive reasoning

A form of logical thinking where you reach a *definite* conclusion (or answer) based on facts, called *premises* (If the premises are true, the conclusion *must be* true.)

It's also worth pointing out that, by going to the learning resource center, Mary took action that could prevent a potential crisis, such as failing her first semester. As previously discussed, this represents *proactive thinking*, or thinking ahead, to prevent a problem. In contrast, many people wait for the problem to occur and then react to the crisis. This is called *reactive thinking*. Which do you think is better?

Another type of logical thinking is **inductive reasoning**. Here you make your *best guess* based on the premises or facts. Your conclusion is very likely to be true, but it isn't guaranteed. Here's an example of inductive reasoning:

Inductive reasoning

A form of logical thinking where you reach a *likely* conclusion (or answer) based on facts, called premises (If the premises are true, the conclusion is *probably* true.)

Premise: People who smoke have an increased risk of getting lung cancer.

Premise: Bill smoked two packs of cigarettes a day for twenty years.

Conclusion: Bill will get lung cancer.

Although the risk to Bill is much greater than someone who has not smoked, and it is quite possible that Bill will get lung cancer, the conclusion may not be true. He might never develop lung cancer in his lifetime. However, his best decision would be to stop smoking (proactive thinking) to prevent the potential for the future health crisis of lung cancer.

Food for Thought

Be careful of any *bias* you may have when gathering information or making a decision. Bias is defined as "prejudice in favor of or against one thing, person, or group compared with another, usually in a way considered to be unfair." How does this relate to decision-making? Consider someone gathering all their information selectively only from sources that share their views on certain subjects. Where people favor information that confirms their belief or hypothesis, this situation is called **confirmation bias**. Not truly looking at and considering all sides of an issue or gathering all points of view is not the best way to make an informed, unbiased decision.

6.5b   Decision-Making

So, given this information, how do you make a good decision? First, review your list of ideas as well as any relevant past experiences you may have and input from others to help you make the best possible choice. Remember to gather information from all sources, including those that may not agree with your current views. Now, use your logical thinking to analyze your options.

Most texts suggest listing the pros and cons for each idea, and this is a very good place to start. However, you should also use *proactive thinking* by considering the short- and long-term effects of each idea. People often jump at the first good solution, which may not always be the best in the long run. For example, in the business world, the short-term solution for making employees happier may be to give them all big raises, which certainly will result in a short-term positive effect. However, because of the raise, the company could go bankrupt or have to lay off some or all employees. This certainly would be a long-term negative effect. In Exercise 6-6, you will analyze the positive and negative effects of your ideas.

Exercise 6-6   Choosing the Best Idea or Set of Ideas

Continuing through your personal journey of integrated thinking, you need to choose from the ideas you generated in Exercise 6-5. Of course, you want to choose the one idea or group of ideas that will provide the greatest chance for success. You can test this by imagining each option individually. What would happen if you picked that idea? Consider the short- and long-term positive and negative effects of each of your ideas. Then pick the idea with the most positive effects and the least negative ones. Write the idea down and list its effects.

Your Chosen Idea or Group of Ideas:

_____

_____

_____

Short-Term Positive Effects:

_____

_____

_____

Short-Term Negative Effects:

_____

_____

_____

Long-Term Positive Effects:

_____

_____

_____

Long-Term Negative Effects:

_____

_____

_____

Note: You may have "none" for some of the above.

6.6　Step 4: Implementation and Evaluation

Wow, it seems like we took a long time to get to the point where we will actually put our ideas into action! However, consider that, with practice, these steps will become so automatic that you will go through the process rather quickly (depending on the size, complexity, and importance of the opportunity). If the opportunity for positive change is choosing the right meal, this process only takes a few minutes. If it is making a major change in your life, such as choosing a major and school to attend, it will take some more time. However, the end result will be worth the effort.

When putting your idea into action, you should take a moment to consider your approach. Beyond what you need to do to carry out your idea, is there anyone you should talk to? More important, how will you evaluate the outcome? The first part of this step is *implementation,* but equally important is the second part, *evaluation.* This is important not only to chart your progress (remember, SMART goals are measurable) but also to give you some feedback to kickstart the next cycle of integrated thinking (see Figure 6-7). Exercise 6-7 guides you through some questions that will help you make your idea a reality.

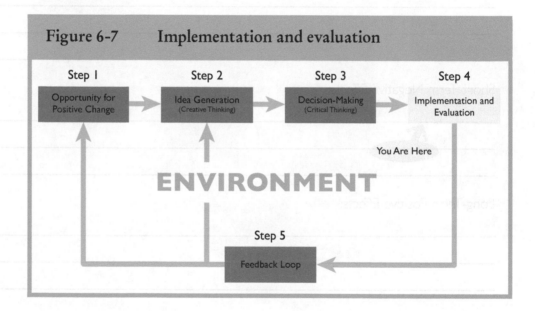

Figure 6-7　　　Implementation and evaluation

　　　Chapter 6:　Creative Thinking and Decision-Making Skills

You are nearing the end of your journey through integrated thinking, and it's time to put your idea from Exercise 6-6 into action. Answer the following questions to begin the process of implementing and evaluating your idea.

Does your chosen idea result in the positive outcome you imagined when you stated your opportunity for positive change? _____

Whom do you need to communicate with, and how, when implementing this idea?

_____

_____

What resources can assist you with implementing and evaluating this idea?

_____

_____

How and when will you evaluate (measure) your progress toward this opportunity for positive change?

_____

_____

When will you implement this idea?

_____

6.7   Almost the Final Step: Feedback

Notice that the feedback loop in Figure 6-8 can lead back to either a new opportunity for positive change or more idea generation. Once you implement your ideas, you may find they have opened related doors or opportunities that can lead you back to Step 1. This is a good thing. This expanding cycle of positive change is what carries you forward in life. Another possibility is that once you implement your idea(s) and gain some feedback, you realize you need to modify your plan. This might lead you back to Step 2, where you generate more ideas, potentially creating a cycle where you continue to assess and improve your plan. Of course, another outcome is when you reach a point where you have done all there is to do with an opportunity—there is no more room for change in that area or the problem is completely solved. Remember to get feedback from as many sources as possible. The more feedback you receive, the better your ability to evaluate the success of your idea and make adjustments if necessary. Although these five steps may seem like a lot, it is well worth the effort. More to the point, *you* are worth the effort. And with practice, these steps will become second nature.

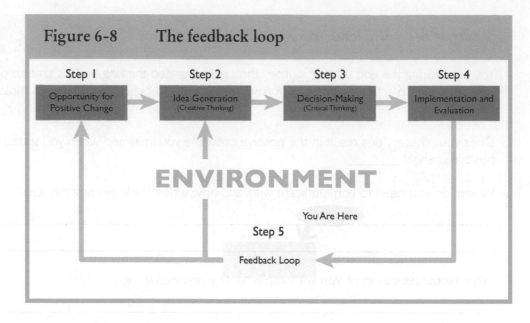

Figure 6-8   The feedback loop

6.8   Final Thoughts

Just the process of going through these steps will help you to understand and therefore improve your thinking processes. For most small issues, this formal process is done more or less subconsciously—you aren't even aware you're doing it. However, it can be very powerful to take one opportunity related to your professional life and one opportunity related to your personal life, and then work through the steps. The results will amaze you! However, it's best to choose only one issue in each area of your life to maintain a sharp focus and avoid becoming overwhelmed.

In Exercise 6-8, ponder one opportunity for positive change in your personal life and one in your professional life.

Exercise 6-8   Chapter Summation

List a major opportunity for positive change you would like to address in your personal life.

_____

_____

_____

List a major opportunity for positive change you would like to address in your professional or academic life.

_____

_____

_____

Healthy Decision-Making

Jerome is a senior in high school and unsure about what degree program he wants to enter. Because of this, he is having a difficult time choosing a school. He has taken tests to try to find the types of programs that might be a good match for his skills and interests. However, he still has many options and is getting anxious about making a choice. What would you do to help Jerome if he asked for your advice?

_____

_____

_____

_____

_____

_____

_____

_____

_____

Part Two

A Road Map for Professional Success

Communication in Action

Presenting Yourself to Others

Objectives

By the end of this chapter, you will be able to:

- Use effective communication skills

- Become a better listener

- Enhance your speaking and presentation skills

- Explain what *information literacy* is and why it's important

- Assess the challenges that come with internet research

- Improve your writing skills

- Describe strategies for finding and citing appropriate sources

- Use effective written and verbal communication in the workplace

- Develop effective communication skills for meetings

- Communicate a professional workplace image

- Follow workplace etiquette

Why Learn This Skill?

So far, we have focused our attention on *intrapersonal* skills—meaning skills that you use within yourself to understand yourself better and to manage your own thoughts and emotions. Now it is time to expand our journey into the *interpersonal* realm, where you interact and communicate with others. We will begin by defining *communication*; then we will work together to create action plans for how to improve your communication skills.

Communicating is not just something we do every day; it is a skill that we can hone and develop just like all the other skills discussed in this book. Have you ever sensed when you are losing someone in a conversation, or have stopped paying attention yourself while someone else was communicating with you? Have you ever received a written communication that you just didn't understand or gotten feedback that revealed you had been completely misunderstood? Lack of communication can cause big and small problems in both our personal and professional lives.

If you want to be successful, a key ingredient is effective communication. These skills should never be taken for granted; they are the means by which you present yourself to the world.

7.1 Introduction

Before we can begin improving your communication skills, we must first lay the groundwork. What is communication, exactly? You probably have a *working definition* in mind—meaning you know how to use the word, and you understand what others mean when they use it—but have you ever considered what the *formal* or *official definition* of communication might be?

7.2 A Model of Communication

Let's start with an example. When you are in class, your teacher communicates with you using things like lectures, videos, demonstrations, and slideshows. You listen (hopefully) and try to learn and remember what your teacher has communicated. Then maybe you ask questions, the class discusses the topic, or you take an exam. This should be a familiar situation by now. But let's look at what's really going on over the course of this day-to-day communication.

Take a look at Figure 7-1. The *person communicating* (in our example, the teacher) is the *transmitter*. The *thing being communicated* (in our example, the lesson) is called the *message*. The *audience* (in our example, the students) are the *receivers*. Notice that these *receivers* have a **filter** through which the message passes. This means that, in addition to having to talk over any noise or distractions in the room (more *filters*), the *transmitter* must also "get through" to the receivers. Some students might have short attention spans, some may find the topic challenging, some may be distracted, and all these filters affect how well they receive the message. Finally, the receivers can provide **feedback** to the transmitter about the message, in this case, by discussing the topic or asking questions.

Filter

In communication, any barriers the message must pass through (like noise, distractions, or a lack of attention on the part of the receiver)

Feedback

In communication, information sent from the receiver back to the transmitter about the message

---

Figure 7-1 The communication model

In an ideal situation, the teacher transmits a clear message that passes to the students with little filtration, and the students then give *feedback* in the form of a great grade on the exam. Do Exercise 7-1 to help you understand this model of communication.

Exercise 7-1   Understanding the Model

Give examples for the following:

Describe a situation in which you were the *transmitter* of a message. _____

_____

_____

Who was the intended *receiver* (or who were the *receivers*)? _____

What *filters* were involved? _____

_____

What type of *feedback* did you get? _____

_____

How could you have improved this communication? _____

_____

7.2a   Modes of Communication

This model of communication might seem a little complicated at first. However, it gives us the framework to discuss communication more deeply than we otherwise could. As you read through this chapter and complete the exercises, you will see common concepts and principles in all forms of communication.

Communication can be broken down into three broad categories: *verbal, nonverbal,* and *written communication.* Verbal communication includes all communication that uses sound. This can include conversations, lectures, songs, stories, animal sounds, grunts, and the list goes on. Nonverbal communication is communication *without* the use of sound. This can include a handshake, smile, wink, or people rolling their eyes in disgust. Nonverbal communication is very powerful even though people often forget about it. The third broad category is written communication. This includes text messages, tweets, letters, memos, reports, emails, charts, and pictures, among many others. We begin by assessing and developing each of these communication categories separately. Then we will take a look at specific examples. In Exercise 7-2, you will identify which of the three broad categories of communication each item or activity fits into.

Exercise 7-2   What Type of Communication Is This?

For each of the following, identify what type of communication is being used. Write **V** for verbal, **N** for nonverbal, or **W** for written. For some, there is *more than one answer*, so write down every type that applies. As you will see as we move through the chapter, there is a lot of crossover.

_____ cheerleading

_____ a mean look

_____ a TV commercial

_____ laughter

_____ a deep sigh

_____ a dog snarling and barking

_____ an email

_____ a speech

_____ grunting

_____ a to-do list

_____ a text message

_____ teaching a class

_____ a job interview

_____ a musical audition

_____ taking a test

7.2b   The Relationship between Verbal and Nonverbal Communication

Studies show that although the spoken word is important in communication, we rely even more on nonverbal communication when interacting with others (see Figure 7-2). This means that *how* you say something is often *more important* than *what* you say. This might seem like a pretty dramatic statement, but this chapter will show you how this idea works. See how well you interpret nonverbal communication in Exercise 7-3.

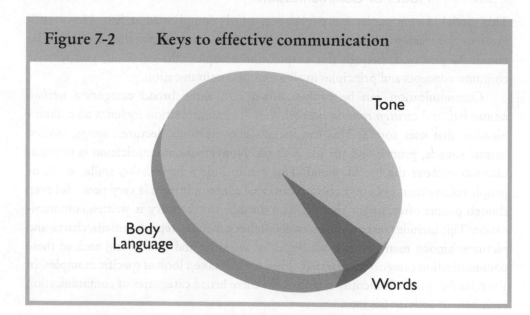

Figure 7-2   Keys to effective communication

Tone

Body Language

Words

Exercise 7-3   Body Language

Pair up with a partner and take turns trying to convey a feeling without using any verbal communication. See if you can guess accurately the nonverbal message.

Describe the nonverbal message you think your partner is sending in two separate instances.

Nonverbal communication 1 _____

Nonverbal communication 2 _____

Were you able to identify the nonverbal messages correctly?

Was it easy for you to communicate a nonverbal message in the exercise? It's time to put our new understanding of communication to work as we begin exploring how to improve our communication skills. Let's explore how verbal and nonverbal communication styles are interwoven.

7.2c   Informal Communication

Let's begin with a common experience: meeting someone for the first time. By now, you have probably figured out that your nonverbal gestures are an important part of your *first impression,* followed by your tone of voice and, finally, the words you speak. A positive approach would include a friendly smile, good eye contact, and (usually) a firm handshake (see Figure 7-3).

| Figure 7-3 | Who is making the better first impression? |

Your tone should be positive and friendly, your verbal communication should be clear, and you should introduce yourself by the name you wish to be called. This sounds pretty simple, but this first encounter often sets the tone for any future relationship, so it is important. There is no better way to learn than with practice. Please spend some time with Exercise 7-4.

Exercise 7-4   You Never Get a Second Chance to Make a Good Impression

Pair up with a partner and practice meeting each other for the first time. Keep practicing until your partner feels you have all the following items checked.

_____ friendly smile

_____ good eye contact

_____ good handshake

_____ positive, clear tone of voice

_____ well-spoken introduction

Just to reinforce this concept, repeat the introductions but change one element according to each scenario below. Describe how it makes you feel.

Scenario 1: No eye contact

Describe how this made you feel: _____

_____

_____

Scenario 2: No smile

Describe how this made you feel: _____

_____

_____

Scenario 3: Weak or poor handshake

Describe how this made you feel: _____

_____

_____

Of course, you usually have to continue the conversation after the initial meeting. Here is one helpful hint: *"People like to hear genuinely nice things about themselves."* If you pay attention, you'll notice their *appreciative* response. It could be a quick smile, a twinkling in their eyes, or the way their shoulders relax. When meeting people for the first time, it is also helpful to repeat their names back to them in greeting. This well-known memory aid will help you remember their names.

Chapter 7:   Communication in Action

7.3 Listening: The Often Forgotten Communication Skill

An often-neglected communication skill is listening. Many of us are too busy thinking of what we are going to say back or what we have to do that day to *truly* listen to somebody. There is a difference between *hearing* and *listening*. Hearing happens automatically, without you even trying. It's just sound reaching your ears. However, listening takes more work. For example, have you ever been in class or in a conversation where you could hear the words but got lost in other thoughts and didn't really know what the speaker was saying? You were hearing the speaker, but you were *not* listening.

Because *hearing* is a passive process (you don't have to try to do it, it just happens), most people assume that *listening* is too. This assumption couldn't be more wrong. Listening, when done right, is very active. **Active listening** means paying close attention to what the speaker is saying *verbally* and *nonverbally* and focusing on understanding the *message* (rather than on what *feedback* you'd like to give).

These are the key parts of active listening:

- Face the person who is speaking, maintain good eye contact, and even nod occasionally to show you are interested.

- Maintain an open posture (try not to hunch or cross your arms); you could even lean slightly toward the person to show that you are interested in what they are saying.

- Stay relaxed and confident.

- Think about what they are saying and ask for clarification if you don't understand. The best way to do this is to repeat what you *think* they are saying in your own words. This shows that you are listening and allows them to modify the message if a misunderstanding has occurred.

- Do not interrupt the speaker. Wait for them to finish and continue listening actively until it is your turn. If you need to, jot down a question or a response on a piece of paper so you won't be distracted by trying to remember it.

The benefits of active listening read like a recipe for world peace:

- Shows concern for others

- Leads to better communication

- Improves relationships

- Leads to better understanding and cooperation

- Can calm another person in a heated, tense situation

Listen well to other people's words and body language and show them that you understand their message, that they have gotten through to you. The payoff to listening well is that usually the other person will be more open to listening to *you* in return. Dale Carnegie, an author and motivational speaker, knew the power of listening in making connections with people. He once said, "You can make more friends in two months by becoming genuinely interested in other people than you can in two years by trying to get other people interested in you."

> *"Maybe if we did a better job of listening, history wouldn't have to repeat itself."*
>
> Author unknown but wise

Active listening

Paying close attention to both the verbal and nonverbal messages you are receiving and seeking to truly understand them

Consider this idea from the other perspective: What can you do to improve someone's willingness to listen to you? Try to maintain good posture while you are speaking, and speak clearly. If you slouch or your voice fades, you are telling the receiver that your message is not that important. Basically, you're telling them not to listen.

Put the principles of active listening to work in Exercise 7-5.

Active listening

Exercise 7-5   Active Listening

Working in pairs or small groups, make up a skit that shows all the wrong things to do in terms of active listening. It can be someone discussing a problem with a course or a funny incident that happened at work. Have fun with the skit, and see if the class can identify everything wrong with the interaction. Then follow up with the same skit, only now show all the *right* things to do in terms of active listening.

List of *wrong* things (Skit 1): _____

_____

_____

List of *right* things (Skit 2): _____

_____

_____

7.4   Speeches and Presentations

Now let's build on your knowledge of communication with a discussion of public speaking. Although public speaking takes training and experience, it all starts with our understanding of basic communication.

7.4a   Types of Speeches

There are several different types of speeches. You can give an *informative* speech, in which you explain something to a person or group of people. Examples include teaching a class, giving a workshop, or demonstrating a technique such as CPR. A *persuasive* speech is where you try to convince or influence an audience. The goal of a persuasive speech is to get others to share your opinion or do something that you've asked them to do. Examples could be a political speech or sales pitch. An *evocative* speech is meant to *evoke* (a word which here means create) a certain feeling in your audience. Evocative speeches can entertain or inspire; they can make people angry or sad. Examples can include a sermon, a rallying cry, or a comedy sketch. In fact, most comedy acts are actually well-rehearsed speeches that only look like they are *impromptu*. Impromptu (which simply means *spontaneous* or *unplanned*) speeches are, by definition, unrehearsed. If you were asked to stand up in class and give a speech on world economics, that would be an example of an impromptu—and probably pretty scary—speech. Some speeches fall under more than one category. For example, a political speech may be mainly persuasive (vote for me), but it can also tell about issues (informative) and stir up certain feelings (evocative) in the crowd.

So how do you go about preparing a speech? Keep in mind that the steps and principles for public speaking and written communication are very similar. These are both examples of *formal* communication—as opposed to *informal* communication, like texting with a friend, talking to a family member on the phone, or introducing yourself to someone on campus.

7.4b   Preparation

Long before you give the speech, and even before you write it, you need to select and analyze your speech topic, purpose, and type. Think about the audience for your speech. What are their backgrounds, and what will most appeal to them? Are there any special considerations? For example, a presentation for preschool students might require special strategies for keeping their attention. Do Exercise 7-6 to practice speech preparation.

Answer the following:

What is the topic of your chosen speech? _____

What type of speech are you presenting? (Note: It can be more than one type.)

_____

Who is the audience? _____

Are there any special considerations? _____

Where will you find information for your speech? _____

_____

_____

_____

Next, you need to research your topic by looking in the library and at reliable and accurate sources online. You could even conduct personal interviews. Citing your sources during your speech gives you *credibility* (shows people you are telling the truth) as a speaker. We will cover how to gather good information in greater detail later, but for now, please consider the following when researching any topic:

- *Locate* information using accurate and trustworthy sources.

- *Analyze* the information using critical thinking skills and consider how it fits with your chosen topic.

- *Question* the information—maintain a healthy *skepticism*. Be careful not to quickly believe everything you find. Compare multiple sources.

7.4c   Composing a Speech

There are three parts to a good speech—or a good paper, for that matter: an *introduction*, a *body*, and a *conclusion*.

The Introduction   The main purpose of the introduction is to state your purpose and get the audience's attention. The goal is to have them *want* to hear what you have to say. This sets the tone for everything that follows. Keep it short but powerful. One example is a rhetorical question (one you really don't want the audience to answer, just think about).

For example, "Do you think smoking only kills people who smoke?" could be an opener for a talk about the hazards of secondhand smoke. You can also lead with a startling statistic. For example, if you were giving a talk to a group of women about breast cancer, you could say, "Without early detection, it is estimated that 1 out of 5 women will die of breast cancer. That means four people in this room of twenty. Who will it be? Hopefully, nobody, if you follow the recommendations I will be presenting in my talk."

The introduction can also contain a related personal story or even a joke, but be careful because the joke could bomb or even offend someone. A brief demonstration could also be used, depending on the topic. The introduction should be well rehearsed, and the speaker should have direct eye contact with the audience to make a good first impression. In Exercise 7-7, you'll brainstorm ideas about a compelling introduction.

Exercise 7-7   Coming up with a Great Introduction

Working in pairs or small groups, brainstorm ideas for an attention-getting introduction for the speech you chose in Exercise 7-6. Write or explain it here.

_____

_____

_____

Rehearse your introduction in front of your group and have *them* answer the following questions.

Does it grab the audience's attention? _____

Is the purpose and relevance of the speech clearly stated? _____

You have the audience sitting on the edges of their seats (or at least curious) thanks to your great introduction. Now what? You need to support what your introduction said you were going to do with well-organized facts and information. This is the *body* of your speech.

The Body   The body of a speech usually makes up about 75 percent of it and should cover three to five main points, depending on the time you've been given. Trying to cover too much will lose your audience's attention, so, in most cases, we suggest limiting yourself to three main points. Support these points with facts, theories, statistics, or expert testimony. Use analogies or visual imagery to make the material more familiar and personal. Cover each point fully before going on, and use a transition, or bridge, between the points for a smoother speech. During the body of your presentation, try to keep the audience on their toes with an unexpected viewpoint or vivid language. Whenever you can, help your audience *visualize* or *imagine* your content, perhaps by using metaphors or detailed descriptions. Short sentences, personal stories, unusual statistics, appropriate humor, rhetorical questions—all these things will make your presentation pop. Different speeches require different strategies. The key is to keep your speech interesting. Exercise 7-8 will give you some practice.

Exercise 7-8   The Body of Your Speech

Research and list three main points you want to cover in your chosen speech, along with one startling fact, statistic, interesting story, or something similar, for each. Finally, add transition sentences between the main points and to your conclusion.

Point 1: _____

Interesting fact, story, etc. _____

_____

Transition sentence to Point 2: _____

_____

_____

Point 2: _____

Interesting fact, story, etc. _____

_____

Transition to Point 3: _____

_____

_____

Point 3: _____

Interesting fact, story, etc. _____

_____

Transition sentence to your conclusion (which we'll write in Exercise 7-9): _____

_____

_____

Now that you have completed the body of your speech, you need to end with a conclusion. It is a good idea to review the main points briefly. If possible, present them in a different way instead of simply repeating yourself. Be creative. Provide closure with a strong final statement that will leave a lasting impression. Sometimes a powerful quote or story will work. If you are giving a persuasive speech, your ending statement should be a *call to action*—you need to tell your audience what you want them to do. Do Exercise 7-9 now.

Exercise 7-9　Your Conclusion

Write or describe your conclusion for your chosen speech: _____

_____

_____

Now practice your conclusion in front of your group and have *them* answer the following questions:

Did the conclusion summarize the main points? _____

Was the summary interesting/creative? _____

Was there a strong final statement that brought closure to the speech? _____

What will the audience take away from this speech? _____

7.4d　It's Show Time: Delivering Your Speech

Now that you have prepared your speech, you must decide on your *delivery style*. Although you can try to memorize a speech word for word, this is not recommended because it has the potential to end in disaster (forgetting parts) or to be painfully boring because it has no *spontaneity* (the parts of the delivery—including nonverbal elements like gestures or pauses—that you come up with in the moment because they "feel right").

At the other extreme, you should avoid reading your speech word for word off a piece of paper (some speeches must be read, but we'll talk about that in a moment). This makes it difficult if not impossible to make eye contact with the audience and will result in a boring presentation.

Instead, the best approach is right in the middle. Use a brief outline, note cards, or a slideshow presentation to keep you organized and to remind you what to say next, but have the speech pretty much memorized, at least in terms of the content. You should still rehearse, and just like you shouldn't read your speech from a script, avoid simply reading your slides aloud—the main points are there to jog your memory so you can then provide the audience with more information without sounding stiff. With this style, you can maintain good eye contact and have a more *dynamic* presentation.

As we hinted above, another style is the *manuscript* speech, where you read words from a script—usually using a *teleprompter*. This style is needed when *accuracy* is important, like a presidential speech where even a small change in wording can have global effects. It takes practice to make this style of speech look natural. Certain techniques, such as weaving personal stories or humorous comments throughout the speech, can give it a more "off-the-cuff" feel.

7.4e Vocal Delivery Skills

Practice your speech by paying close attention to the following vocal skills:

Volume: Is the volume of your voice loud enough so everyone can hear you (without being too loud)?

Rate: Is your *rate of speech* (how fast you talk) so fast you are hard to follow? This is a common mistake. Is your rate so slow that you put your audience to sleep? A good speaker watches the audience and varies the rate to maintain interest.

Pitch: *Pitch* is the highness or lowness of your voice. Sometimes nervousness will cause your pitch to get very high and squeaky. Too high or too low a pitch can be distracting.

Rhythm: This is a combination of your pace and the pauses you use to emphasize main points or new ideas. Use pauses that differ in length and try not to fall into a pattern of pausing at regular intervals. If your delivery is too rhythmic, it will put people to sleep. It takes practice to become skillful at maintaining a good rhythm throughout your speech.

Word emphasis: Just like you can highlight a written word in boldface type to emphasize it, you can highlight a spoken word or key point by changing your volume, varying your rate or pitch, or by pausing afterward.

Dynamic speakers develop their vocal skills through practice. They use variety in volume, rates, and pitch and always factor in the type and content of the speech when considering their delivery.

7.4f   Physical Delivery

There is more to giving a speech than your vocal skills. Remember the importance of nonverbal communication. Your appearance will say a lot about you and your topic. Decide the kind of message you want to send to your audience when it comes to your clothes, hairstyle, and accessories because these things directly affect your credibility. Imagine someone giving a talk on investment strategies with frayed jeans, tennis shoes with holes, greasy hair, and T-shirt stains. Would you be eager to take this person's advice? What about someone giving the same speech dressed in a nice suit and tie or business outfit?

You don't always have to dress like a high-powered CEO, of course. The way you dress should reflect your topic. For example, if you are giving a speech about the importance of fitness where you also plan on demonstrating a new exercise technique, it might make sense to wear workout clothes.

Movement during your speech is also important. Formal speeches usually take place behind a podium. However, if you are teaching a class or workshop, staying behind a podium can create a barrier between you and your audience. Instead, walk around a little to create a more conversational tone.

Facial expressions are critical. If you know your material well and you are connected to it emotionally, your facial expressions should occur naturally. This is similar to smiling while talking on the phone. Even though the other person can't see you, the *smile* comes through on the other end. Make sure your expressions agree with your speech because smiling while you are talking about the stages of death and dying may seem insensitive. Gestures and hand movements can also emphasize points and keep the speech interesting. Be careful not to overuse gestures, however, as they could become distracting to your audience.

Some Other Tips:

- When trying to explain a difficult concept, start off with the simple parts and use analogies the audience can understand.

- Avoid overloading the audience with too much information.

- Space out things like humor and stories throughout your speech to keep it interesting.

- Use presentation aids (like slideshows) to help keep you organized and provide engaging imagery.

- Visuals should be large and uncluttered. These can include charts, slideshows, and posters. Make sure you have good color contrast.

- Know how to use your technical equipment, and have backups of all your electronic presentations. I always load my presentation on a laptop and have two separate backups kept in two separate places when I speak. Imagine going to do a speech and your computer crashes with no backup!

7.4g Final Words of Wisdom

There are three important concepts in presenting a good speech:

1. Practice
2. Practice
3. Practice

Get the point? And do not practice just the day before (or the day of!) your presentation. Giving yourself plenty of time to digest and reflect on the material is essential to remembering what you need to say (and how you plan to say it) and your level of comfort when it comes to actually presenting. Practice in front of helpful and trusted reviewers, such as family and friends (or even dogs because they will usually wag their tails supportively). The importance of rehearsing in front of a mirror or camera cannot be stressed enough. If you can record or take a video of yourself, you will get more of a feel for being in your own audience, and you might surprise yourself: "Like, I had no idea I said 'like' so much!"

Keep in mind that being nervous about your speech is normal. To reduce your fears, know your topic well and practice daily. Use the relaxation techniques from the stress management chapter, and remember that a little stress to get you geared up for your speech is good. Replace any negative self-fulfilling thoughts, such as, "I'm going to mess up my speech and forget what to say," with "I know my material well and have practiced it out loud several times."

If, during your speech, you start to get worked up (and hopefully you won't), you can use a technique called *redirection*. This means turning your fear into power. For example, you could use all that nervous energy to project your voice and create a dynamic impression by moving around and gesturing (within reason) instead of panicking to the point where you run away. In Exercise 7-10, you'll have a chance to identify the tasks you find most intimidating and develop an action plan for how to tackle them.

Exercise 7-10   Assessing Your Comfort Level with the Following Tasks

Put the following steps in order from what scares you the most to what is a piece of cake by numbering them 1 (easiest) to 9 (most difficult).

_____ Deciding on the type of speech

_____ Researching the material for the speech

_____ Choosing the main points of the speech and putting them in order

_____ Writing engaging and memorable content for the speech

_____ Finding and using visual aids

_____ Wrapping up the speech

_____ Speaking in front of people

_____ Making eye contact with the audience

_____ Answering questions after the speech

For the most difficult steps, don't stop here. It's time to come up with a solution to make those steps easier for you. Make sure your solution is actually "doable" for you. What will your action plan(s) be?

_____

_____

7.5   Written Communications

The comedian Eddie Murphy has been quoted as saying, "Anything you have to acquire a taste for was not meant to be eaten." You're probably wondering why that statement is here. Well, if you think about it, whether you agree with Mr. Murphy's approach to food, his advice has value. When it comes to writing, unless you're dealing with advanced subject matter, *the reader shouldn't have to work hard to understand you.*

If you remember this simple fact any time you have to write something, you will find that your readers appreciate it. By writing in a way that's easy to understand, you are being considerate of your audience's time and energy. Good writing is a necessary skill throughout life because it is yet another way you present yourself to the world. In fact, in almost any career, some people in your life will know you *only* through your writing!

When you sit down to write, always know two things: the *purpose* and the *audience.* Sounds a lot like what you do when preparing a speech or presentation! Also like a speech, most written communications contain an introduction, body, and conclusion. See how communication principles are universal? Do Exercise 7-11 to assess your skills.

Exercise 7-11   Assess Your Writing Skills

Check each sentence that applies to you.

_____ I am confident in my ability to complete writing assignments.

_____ I write some type of outline, even an informal one, before I begin a writing assignment.

_____ I am aware of my strengths in writing.

_____ I am aware of the areas where I need to improve my writing.

_____ I am aware of the expectations and conventions about citing sources.

_____ I always check my writing for a clear introduction and powerful conclusion.

_____ I ask friends or family members to give me feedback on my writing.

_____ I am willing to approach a faculty member with questions about writing assignments.

_____ I am comfortable writing under time constraints.

_____ I organize my time, so I am not rushed to complete a writing assignment at the last minute.

Eight or more checked answers indicate that you're pretty confident and quite likely prepared for writing assignments. Six or seven checked answers indicate that you would benefit from some of the ideas in this chapter. If you have five or fewer checked answers, pay close attention to the advice that follows.

7.5a   Examples of Workplace Communication

Before discussing a formal research paper, it may be useful to start off with two smaller, common written communications you are likely to encounter in the workplace: memos and emails.

Memos   A memo is an excellent way to get across a brief idea, an "FYI" (for your information), or a request for information to one or more people. In printed (hard copy) form, it should always begin as shown in Figure 7-4.

The text should be brief and to the point. Pretend you have to pay by the word for the memo like you would if you took out a newspaper advertisement. Lists are okay if they are not wordy. Remember that a memo's information should be easy to grasp at first reading. Also, don't overlook the importance of a *concise* (short and meaningful) subject line. Recipients should know at a glance exactly what your memo is about *before* they read it.

Before you distribute your hardcopy memo, you must sign it. Some people like to sign at the bottom of the memo, directly below the body. Others simply put their initials next to their name at the top (next to FROM).

Email   Emails are one of the most common forms of written communications in the workplace. You can think of work email like an electronic memo where the top portion (the template from Figure 7-4) is more or less handled by your email program. That said, you should still remember the following: The person to whom your memo is directed goes in the "To" section; if it is directed to more than one person equally, put them all in there (do not put just the first addressee in the "To" section and the rest in the "CC" section if the email is equally important to all); anyone included as just an FYI should be listed in the CC section.

Figure 7-4   Heading section of a memo

Template

TO: *[the main addressee or, if two or more are equally important as addressees, list them here separated by commas]*

FROM: *[you]*

SUBJECT (or RE): *[should be a brief statement of memo's subject, like a heading]*

DATE: *[current date]*

CC: *[anyone else who should receive the memo as an "FYI"]*

Example

TO: Members of the Business Society

FROM: Maria Sanchez, Chairperson

SUBJECT (or RE): Organizational Meeting

DATE: March 10, 2018

CC: Faculty Advisor

Once again, pay attention to the value of your subject line. The subject line is perhaps even *more* important in an email because many people organize their emails or search for previous emails by subject line. If you are forwarding an email to a third party, be *absolutely sure* you are not forwarding any personal, confidential, or proprietary information from the original sender to that third party. The consequences can range from losing a friendship to losing your job. Some people hit "Reply All" carelessly. Always make sure only people who need to be included are included. On the flip side, be sure to "Reply All" if you do want everyone to read your response. Simply clicking "Reply" will direct your message to only the individual sender.

It is always appropriate and polite to open the content of your message with a greeting, even in an email that is just a memo or a note to a friend. Start the message with a brief but appropriate greeting: "Hi folks," for holiday pictures to scattered family, and "Good morning, club members," if you're sending out a calendar of events, for example. Even just a "Hi Cathy," (providing, of course, that the person's name is Cathy) is a good way to start. (Speaking of Cathy, is it supposed to be *Kathy*? Always be certain of spelling, especially with someone's name!) Also, it is wise to use an email address that reflects your name clearly. For instance, firstname.lastname@provider.com is preferable to something informal and possibly inappropriate like bballplayer99@whatever.com. This says a lot about your professionalism (or lack thereof). Luckily, educational institutions and most businesses will provide you with an email name template (and perhaps an account) to use that is straightforward and clear in identifying you.

Professional emails should always include contact information in the signature under your name. Most email programs can format several different signatures for different situations; for the more formal ones, repeat your email address below the other contact information as a courtesy. Finally, make sure your spelling, grammar, sentence structure, and other writing elements are correct. In large companies, people might form their first impressions of you based on your emails before they personally meet you. Think about what those impressions will be if you send emails where names are misspelled, sentences are incomplete, other spelling errors are common, nothing is organized, and where you've included unprofessional information.

Food for Thought

CC stands for *carbon copy*, and it refers to a time when, to make copies of a memo, you would put a special piece of carbon paper between two sheets of regular paper (or you could create a stack of alternating regular and carbon paper). Then, when you wrote on the top sheet of paper, the pressure of the pen or pencil would cause the black carbon to transfer to the piece of paper below, duplicating your writing. A *blind carbon copy*, or BCC, is where the recipients cannot see each other's names or contact information in the email or memo. It's a good idea to use the BCC field when emailing a group of people who may not be acquainted with one another. It's polite to always let all recipients know when others are being CC'd or BCC'd.

7.5b   Writing That Big Paper

Writing, for class or for work, is challenging for many reasons. Perhaps the main difficulty is the need to do several things at once. Writing a paper, in a sense, is like driving a car. When you drive, you have to steer, accelerate or brake, check for oncoming traffic and traffic behind you, and pay attention to traffic signs and signals all at the same time. If you tried to do these tasks separately, you wouldn't get very far (to put things mildly).

Writing is similar. You have to work on the "big picture" aspects of the paper like organization and development of ideas, but you also need to consider sentence-level issues like punctuation, grammar, syntax (sentence structure), and semantics (word choice). You need to do well in all these areas to earn a good grade. It's no wonder many students find writing to be stressful. However, following the advice in the following sections will help put your mind at ease.

Gathering Good Information Once you have your assignment and have chosen a topic or title, you must find information on that subject. Finding information about, or researching, a topic requires **information literacy**. This is the technical way of saying "being able to figure out *what* you need to know, *where* that information can be found, *whether* the information you find is accurate and credible, and finally, *how* to use it." When you think of it that way, you can see why *information literacy* is an important skill to have not just when it comes to writing a paper but also for life in general. Information literacy can be broken down into the ability to *locate, analyze,* and *question* information. You should always maintain a healthy skepticism (don't believe everything you see, hear, or read). The goal of *analyzing* and *questioning* the information you gather is to make sure it's *accurate* (represents the truth) and *credible* (trustworthy). This kind of critical thinking is vital to every part of your life because with these skills, you will always be able to find good information whenever you need to perform a task or make an informed decision.

Coming back to your research paper, ask yourself what you know about your topic, what information you need, and where you can find it. Sources of information can include books, journals, credible websites, and expert individuals. Make sure you know the difference between *fact* and *opinion,* and that you can recognize *bias.* As you may remember from Chapter 6, bias is when someone lets their opinion change the way they present the facts. Online resources like Google search and Wikipedia® may be good places to *begin* to gather information, but you must seek out sources beyond these that are credible, scholarly, and reliable. Your professors and advisors will have a wealth of resources for you to choose from; do not hesitate to ask for assistance in this area if you are unsure where to look for valid sources of information.

Prewriting Once you have gathered all your sources, you can put together a rough outline. One suggestion is to color-code the different headings in your outline and highlight your sources with the same color where it is relevant. This helps you save time when looking for that portion of an article to talk about in a particular section of your paper.

Remember there are three main parts to any written paper: the *introduction, body,* and *conclusion* (sound familiar?). The introduction catches the reader's attention and states the purpose or topic of the paper. It is followed by the body of the paper, which presents the supporting facts. Finally, the end of the paper contains a summary and conclusion about your chosen topic. Given this simple overview, let's get a little more specific.

Your paper should begin with a *thesis statement,* which is a sentence that introduces the topic and lets the reader know your *point of view.* For example, a paper about the challenges of taking essay exams might start with: "An essay exam is like the driving test you have to take to get a license." This statement tells the reader that this is a paper about essay exams (the topic) and that you are going to argue that the challenges are similar to those involved in taking a driving test (point of view).

Your thesis statement should also tell readers a little about how you're going to organize your paper. In our example, readers can figure out, based on the thesis statement, that your essay will *compare* the two things. They might expect to read several body paragraphs demonstrating the similarities, followed by a persuasive conclusion.

After the introduction, you should have several paragraphs that support your thesis statement. It's a good idea to outline, even briefly, the ideas you'll discuss. An informal outline will suffice:

- Introduction and thesis statement:

  "An essay exam is like the driving test you have to take to get a license."

- Point 1: The writer, like a driver, must demonstrate many skills simultaneously.

- Point 2: Like taking a driving test, a student writing an essay exam has to demonstrate his or her skills in an artificial situation, not the ideal environment.

- Point 3: Both situations involve working under time constraints and under the eye of a critical examiner.

- Point 4: In both testing situations, students can improve their odds of performing well with practice.

- Conclusion

Drafting the Paper   Many students have a hard time writing a specific part of the paper. For some, it's the introduction. For others, it's the conclusion. Some students struggle with titles. The good news is you do not have to start from the beginning. Feel free to start in the middle. If you were writing the example essay comparing writing and driving, you could begin by developing the last body paragraph about the benefits of practice.

Peer and Faculty Review   Ask another student or trusted friend to read your draft and to give you feedback and suggestions. The more feedback you receive, the better—as long as your reader is honest with you. Some peers may hesitate to criticize your work. One strategy might be to tell the person what *you* think the strengths and weaknesses of the draft are. Then they can respond by either agreeing or disagreeing with your assessment, and you can build from there. You might also share examples of feedback you've received from instructors so the peer reviewer will know what kinds of suggestions to make.

Whenever possible, ask questions of your instructor. Some instructors respond best when students ask specific questions about an assignment rather than just handing over a draft and asking if it's OK. Prepare for a meeting with your instructor by asking specific questions about the assignment.

Revision   *Revise* (edit and rewrite) your paper several times before submitting it. With each revision, seek feedback. If your school has a writing or tutorial center, take advantage of that service to have a trained professional consult with you on your writing assignments.

Be careful not to count on the spell-check feature on your computer. It isn't always correct, and it may not be able to help you identify certain typos. For instance, you may have typed "form" instead of "from," and your spell-check will view it as correct. Consider printing out a hard copy of your paper; sometimes it is easier to see your mistakes on paper versus the computer screen. You can also try reading it aloud. This has two main benefits: It forces you to slow down your reading, making it easier to spot mistakes, and hearing the words out loud can help you identify where the wording might be awkward, among other style issues (like an overused word or repetitive sentence structures).

Time Management and Writing Many of your writing assignments will take time to do, so it's important to revisit time management principles. One of the key principles of time management is good strategic planning; in this case, we mean creating a time line for completing all the parts of writing a paper. Practice doing so in Exercise 7-12.

Exercise 7-12   Planning Your Time for a Research Paper

Situation: Your instructor gives you a writing assignment that's due in three weeks. This means you have twenty-one days (counting weekends) to work on it. Figure out what you would need to do each week by completing the chart provided. For this example, pretend you have to write a ten-page research paper on a topic from one of your classes this semester. The steps involved would include the following:

- Select a topic
- Come up with a thesis statement
- Decide the point of view you will present on that topic
- Research and gather information
- Retrieve print and other sources
- Read your sources and decide which ones are most appropriate

- Develop a working outline
- Write a rough draft
- Get feedback from peers and others
- Revise the paper
- Turn in the final draft

Now place these items on the chart along with the approximate time you need to do each one. You know that you have to come up with a topic first (and you should do that right away) and that you have to turn it in on the day it's due. The other tasks should be spread out strategically in between to maximize your chance of success. Compare your answers with a classmate. Do you feel you might have underestimated the amount of time it will take to complete each step? Did you leave enough time for prewriting and drafting? Did you leave enough time for revising and editing?

Week 1	Amount of Time	Week 2	Amount of Time	Week 3	Amount of Time
Select a topic					
				Turn in final draft.	

Plagiarism   **Plagiarism** is using someone else's work (part of it or the whole thing) without giving credit, including trying to pretend it's your own. You should always *give credit where credit is due*. Complete Exercise 7-13 to learn more about plagiarism. You should also be careful to avoid *self-plagiarism*, which means reusing your own work in a different context without telling others where or how that work was used before. Many people assume you can't plagiarize yourself because it's your content, but misrepresenting an old essay from one course as a new essay in another course is still plagiarism.

Exercise 7-13   Plagiarism Quiz

Place a checkmark by each action that would count as *plagiarism*.

___ Submitting someone else's paper as your own
___ Purchasing a paper and submitting it as your own
___ Purchasing a paper on the internet and borrowing some of the ideas for your own paper
___ Submitting the same paper for two or more courses

___ Using sources without providing endnotes, footnotes, or parenthetical citations
___ Using a direct quote without citation
___ Using your own words to explain another person's ideas without citing the information
___ Using a direct quote and changing one or two words without citing the source

Answer Key: Believe it or not, *all the above* are examples of plagiarism!

7.5c   Citing Your Sources—Giving Credit Where Credit Is Due

Many of your assignments will require the use of *primary* and *secondary sources*. Primary sources provide firsthand information. A scientific article is an example of a primary source if it contains the author's original research with information on the experiments conducted and their results. However, something like a work of art can also be a primary source because it presents the artist's vision without any additional analysis. Secondary sources *interpret* or *draw conclusions* about primary sources. To give an example, if you were asked to write a paper about a movie, the film itself would be the primary source; a critic's review of the film would be a secondary source.

Different *academic disciplines* require different systems for *citation* (giving credit to and listing your sources). Most humanities disciplines, including English, use MLA (Modern Language Association) style, whereas psychologists, educators, and social scientists often use APA (American Psychological Association) style. Historians rely on Chicago style (Chicago Manual of Style), and chemists use the citation rules of the American Chemical Society. Here, we will focus on the common elements of research writing across disciplines.

In-Text Citation It is important to cite any material that isn't your own. If you use direct quotations, use quotation marks—or a block indent (where the quote is a separate paragraph that gets indented) if the quote is longer than four lines or so—and cite your source. In other words, tell the reader where you got the information. Depending on the format you use, you can use footnotes (numbered citations at the bottom of the page), endnotes (numbered citations placed at the end of the paper, before the reference page), or parenthetical citations (citing the source in parentheses at the end of the quoted or paraphrased passage).

References Depending on the style, your reference page may be called Works Cited, References, or Bibliography. Regardless of the title, this is a list of all the sources you cited in your paper. Always be sure you know how your teacher wants your paper formatted and your references cited and listed.

7.6   Running an Effective Meeting

Meetings represent another important workplace interaction that requires verbal, nonverbal, and written communication skills. Running a meeting involves skills used both in writing a paper and giving a speech; in fact, all the communication skills you've learned up to this point are relevant when it comes to running an effective meeting.

Just like you can have many types of speeches, there are many kinds of meetings held for many reasons. For example, meetings can be used to share information, deal with difficult issues, influence attitudes, solve problems, and plan events. Your education will continue in the workplace, so meetings can also focus on educational programs such as lectures or workshops.

Meetings require solid proactive thinking in the planning process. Proper planning will ensure you have a productive meeting where people feel their attendance was worth their time and effort. The planning process should include deciding who will be invited, the purpose and objectives of the meeting, the theme or title, and a proposed *agenda* (you can think of it like a loose schedule). The location and date of the meeting should be established as early as possible so you can reserve a location and let all the attendees know the time, place, and purpose.

What are some of the things you can do to run a good meeting? First, a warm, friendly atmosphere should be established. Refreshments and name tags may be appropriate along with a comfortable seating arrangement. At the beginning of the meeting, you should provide a sincere greeting, perform introductions if appropriate, and clearly describe the purpose of the meeting. Most meetings are run from an *agenda,* which lists what is to take place during the meeting. Agendas should include at least:

- The date and time of the meeting
- The location of the meeting
- New and old business
- Discussion topics
- Any assigned premeeting tasks

However, more formal business meetings often use a standardized agenda with a set way of running things. **Parliamentary procedure** is a set of rules, such as those in *Robert's Rules of Order*, that describe how to run larger group meetings. In parliamentary procedure, most actions require that a *motion* be made, seconded, discussed, and then voted on. This may sound confusing, but after attending a meeting run by these rules, it does begin to make more sense. We won't go into the details here, but if you find yourself attending a larger formal meeting, it would be wise to read up on Robert's Rules so you understand what's going on. You should also watch what happens during the meeting carefully because you might learn more from the experience than you would from reading alone.

Parliamentary procedure

A set of rules that describe how to run a large group meeting

Regardless of whether the meeting is formal or informal, the person running it must pay attention to the verbal and nonverbal communication cues of the people attending. In most meetings, just like any communication, far more is expressed nonverbally than verbally, and you can make the meeting more meaningful to the people attending if you respond to these cues. Are people struggling to hear or see? Is it too warm or too cold? Are there any distractions? Is a break needed? Are heads nodding in agreement? Does there seem to be a lot of buzzing about a controversial topic? Is the topic boring, or is it time for a change of format or a change of pace? Is the energy level running low?

After the meeting is over, you need to write up what happened. This written record of the meeting is referred to as the *meeting minutes*. Minutes help keep track of what was discussed, what decisions were made, and what actions need to be taken. They can also help people catch up if they were not able to attend. Minutes should include:

- Date and time of meeting
- Members present, absent, and excused
- Acceptance of previous minutes with any corrections
- Announcements
- Brief description of discussions, decisions, and actions that need to be taken
- Date, time, and location of next meeting
- Time of *adjournment* (when the meeting ended)
- Signature of the person preparing the minutes (and/or the chairperson)

7.7 Workplace Etiquette: Communicating a Professional Image

We end this chapter with a very important but often overlooked communication concept. No matter what you choose to study or what job you find yourself in, you need to communicate a positive, professional image. This is just as important for *keeping* your job as it is for *getting* one. A professional image tells your coworkers and your employer that you take your position seriously and it can help you move onward and upward in your chosen career. To communicate a professional image, it is important to show that you have these attributes:

- Strong technical expertise and a willingness to share it (in other words, you "know your stuff" and are willing to share that knowledge with others)
- Good *interpersonal* skills (you get along well with others)
- Pride in your job performance and your organization
- Willingness to put up with the dull and boring aspects of your job (we all have them) without complaint
- The capacity to work unsupervised and still meet your commitments
- The confidence to put forth new ideas
- The insight to give credit to all who help you
- A desire to constantly improve (in what you know, how you interact with others, etc.)
- A positive attitude toward change as an opportunity and *not* as a threat
- Common sense and common courtesy in your dealings with others
- The desire to get involved and make yourself useful to the organization

If this is the attitude you project, you will be a success in any career!

In addition, it is important to maintain a day-to-day positive attitude in the workplace. Follow company policies and demonstrate good manners. Here are some general etiquette rules you should always follow:

1. Follow your office dress code—or consider dressing just a step above the norm. As they say, you should "dress for the job you want, not the job you have."

2. Stand and sit up straight. It shows you're paying attention. Make eye contact and use active listening techniques during communication.

3. Be on time or even a little early for work and all appointments.

4. Learn people's names as soon as possible and use memory techniques if needed.

5. Keep your personal space (office, cubical, or desk) clean and organized and respect the personal space of others.

6. Return phone calls and emails within twenty-four hours, even if all you say is that you will get back to them later.

7. Write emails and all correspondence in complete sentences with no spelling or grammatical errors.

8. Ask permission before putting someone on speaker phone.

9. Practice good manners and etiquette at lunch meetings. A good hint is never order any food that is messy to eat, especially if the lunch meeting has you a little nervous.

10. Follow your company's policy on cell phone and technology use!

11. Be kind and courteous and do not participate in office gossip.

12. Pay attention to your social media use, it can affect whether you get hired and could cause problems at your job if your online presence is unprofessional. We will talk a little more about this issue in the next section.

7.7a   A Word about Social Media

Within the past decade or so, social media sites have had a big impact on our culture. Our daily lives and activities are easily documented publicly. There may be many benefits in your social life; however, social media can also have disadvantages in the professional and academic world and the consequences can be devastating. Companies routinely screen social media sites when hiring new employees and to check up on current employees. University admissions staff have been known to screen their applicants by using social media sites. It may seem unfair, but the bottom line is this: If you are making your personal life public through social media, then your professional image will be shaped by what you put online. Privacy settings on these sites are important and we suggest you make good use of them. However, the best way to maintain a solid professional image is to make sure any information shared about you is positive and appropriate.

Healthy Decision-Making

Maria does well on her written exams and papers. She is very personable in small groups and is well liked by the rest of the class. However, she is quite anxious about getting in front of a group to give a speech. The class she is taking requires her to do a presentation that counts for 20 percent of her grade. Her presentation is due in one month, and she is getting very nervous. If you were Maria's friend, how would you try to help her?

_____

_____

_____

_____

_____

_____

_____

_____

Group Interaction and Team Building

Working Together Works

Objectives

By the end of this chapter, you will be able to:

- Contrast the differences between a group and a team

- Distinguish types of teams

- Understand team-building

- Appreciate diversity and describe its benefits

- Enhance group creativity through brainstorming

- Assess team effectiveness and improve team performance

- Recommend strategies for team leadership

Why Learn This Skill?

At work and at play, we see countless examples of individuals interacting in groups large and small. This process, commonly referred to as *teamwork,* is very natural. So many examples come to mind: sports teams, the cast and crew of a television show, local volunteer firefighters, our families, our coworkers, and fellow students working together on a school project. Think about your own activities and actions and how each of us participates in groups or teams.

The familiar acronym Together Everyone Achieves More reinforces the importance of being part of a team. We benefit from teamwork in many ways. This chapter reveals the value of teamwork on all levels. Teamwork can provide a sense of belonging, responsibility, accomplishment, unity, support, motivation, satisfaction, and both individual and team pride. Teamwork is truly a *sensory* experience, and we hope this chapter will be eye-opening.

8.1   Introduction

As Monty Python would say, "And now for something completely different!" In other chapters, we discussed *individual* attributes that contribute to success, including stress management, time management, and study skills. However, in the real world, you won't always be able to ensure your success alone. Both on campus and on the job, you will be required to work with others. Knowing how to collaborate successfully is as important to your success as knowing how to do well on your own. When it comes to understanding teamwork, it's best to experience as well as read about these ideas. Therefore, your learning experience in this chapter will come from your group and team interactions.

> *"People never learn anything by being told, they have to find out for themselves."*
>
> Paulo Coelho

What is the difference between a group and a team? We want *you* to come up with that answer as we work together. Our hope is that your initial groups will develop into effective and energetic teams.

8.2   What Is the Difference between Groups and Teams?

We join groups for different reasons. In Exercise 8-1, you will look more closely at why you've joined groups in the past. It is our hope that this will provide insight into what group participation has meant to you. With a better understanding of why people join groups, we can move on to exploring the difference between *groups* and *teams*.

Figure 8-1	Teams build on each other's strengths and support each other's weaknesses

The best way to understand groups is to experience them in action (see Figure 8-1). With this in mind, let's complete some activities (Exercises 8-1, 8-2a, 8-2b, and 8-2c) to remind you of your experiences with groups up to this point. Please complete these exercises *on your own*.

Exercise 8-1   Self-Assessment: Why We Join Groups

Remember a time (maybe recently) when you agreed to join a group. The group may have been a social organization, a school club, several students working on a class project, a committee, or a group of friends who play a sport together at lunchtime. Here is a short list of possible reasons you decided to join this group. Label each one with the number that best describes your reasons for joining.

5 = The main reason why I joined
4 = Part of why I joined   2 = Not why I joined
3 = Possibly why I joined   1 = Not relevant

Group I joined: _____
I joined because I was…

_____ 1.   … looking for people who share my interests and goals.
_____ 2.   … feeling like others were counting on me.
_____ 3.   … hoping to share the "thrill of victory" or "agony of defeat" with others who tried their hardest and pulled together.
_____ 4.   …looking for people to encourage me and help me so I would feel good about myself.
_____ 5.   … hoping the work or activity would be easier and more successful with a group than if I worked alone.
_____ 6.   … eager to be recognized as a member and contributor.
_____ 7.   … hoping to share the feeling that "we did more than we thought we could."
_____ 8.   … hoping to feel inspired, energized, and powerful when working with others toward a goal.

Evaluate Your Choices

_____ 1.   Add your scores for statements 1 and 4. The higher this number, the more you are motivated by a sense of *belonging and support.* Security in social relationships is important to you.

_____ 2.   Add your scores for statements 2 and 8. The higher this number, the more you are motivated by a sense of *responsibility.* The need to serve and help others motivates you more than going it alone.

_____ 3.   Add your scores for statements 5 and 6. The higher this number, the more you are motivated by a sense of *accomplishment and satisfaction.* You understand that more can be accomplished by a group than by an individual, and accomplishment is important to you.

_____ 4.   Add your scores for statements 3 and 7. The higher this number, the more you are motivated by a sense of *pride and unity.* Esteem (feeling good about yourself) and cohesiveness (fitting in with a group) matter to you.

Further Questions for Discussion

1.   In which area did you have the highest score? _____
In which area did you have the lowest score?

2.   What is one more reason, in addition to the ones mentioned, for joining a group?

_____

Exercise 8-2a   Types of Groups

List examples of groups that you see every day at home, school, or in your community.

1. _____
2. _____
3. _____
4. _____
5. _____
6. _____
7. _____

Exercise 8-2b   Groups You've Joined

List groups in which you are a member.

1. _____
2. _____
3. _____
4. _____
5. _____

Exercise 8-2c   Group Memories

Describe your most memorable group experience.

_____
_____
_____
_____
_____
_____

The words *group* and *team* are often used to mean the same thing, but they have important differences. It's important to remember that while *all teams are groups, not all groups are teams.* Keep this thought in mind as we continue to explore the differences between the two. Now do Exercise 8-3.

Exercise 8-3 List the Top 10 Benefits of People Working Together

Team up with a partner and compare your lists from Exercises 8-2a, 8-2b, and 8-2c.

Together, using your responses, discuss the benefits of being in a group. Once you agree on the Top 10 benefits, write them below.

1. _____
2. _____
3. _____
4. _____
5. _____
6. _____
7. _____
8. _____
9. _____
10. _____

Got your Top 10 list? Excellent! Now that you know the benefits of working together, it's time to go from being a group to becoming a team in Exercise 8-4.

Exercise 8-4 Building Teams from Groups

Group together with two or three pairs of students who completed Exercise 8-3. Arrange your desks or chairs for easier interaction and communication with one another.

Situation: You have been charged with developing ideas to market your school and attract qualified applicants.

Instructions

1. Introduce yourselves to each other and decide on a name for your group. Inform your instructor of your name. This begins to brand your team.

2. All members must work together, with each of you contributing ideas.

3. Assign someone to record the ideas.

4. After the allotted time, select someone to present your ideas to the class.

After the presentations are over, answer the following questions about your efforts:

What did each member contribute?

_____

(continues)

Did people interrupt at any point?

_____

Did each person feel free to voice an opinion?

_____

Was there disagreement at any point? How was it handled?

_____

When did everyone agree?

_____

Identify *verbal behaviors* (think back to the section on verbal communication) that helped you work together.

_____

Identify nonverbal behaviors (think back to the section on nonverbal communication) that helped you work together.

_____

Did suggestions from other members help you come up with new ideas? _____

Did a leader emerge in the process? _____

What were the benefits of working together on the project?

_____

_____

What, if anything, could you do better next time?

_____

_____

Did your class as a whole generate ideas that could help your school?

A team is a good example of *synergy*—you can accomplish more together than the total of what each individual could do alone. In a team, each individual's performance is less emphasized and the focus becomes the team's performance. This suggests that a team is something more than a group of individuals interacting. Did you think you were in a *group* or a *team* during Exercise 8-4? Let's improve our understanding by considering the definitions of *group* and *team*.

8.2a   What Defines a Team?

Look at your earlier description of a memorable group experience (Exercise 8-2c). If the experience was a positive one, you probably enjoyed a sense of *camaraderie*—a feeling of togetherness and the inspiring enthusiasm, devotion, and respect for the group that is felt within a team. Team members might not be able to explain the feeling, but they definitely know when they experience it.

A **group** is simply two or more people who interact with each other to complete tasks, achieve goals, or fulfill needs. A **team** is a group whose members interact with *focused intensity* to complete a shared, specific, primary goal. The key word in this definition is *intensity*, which is the main difference between groups and teams. To demonstrate this difference, let's compare a team to a magnifying glass on a sunny day. If you look at Figure 8-2, the rays of sunshine represent the individual members. The specific goal is to start a fire to survive in the wilderness. Without the concentrated and intense focus of the magnifying glass, the goal of starting the fire would never be accomplished because the rays of the sun (team members) do not, at least individually, have enough intensity. A group is simply a collection of members who interact without that focus or intensity. Figure 8-2 illustrates the point that every team is a group, but not every group is a team. That said, any group can develop into a team under the right circumstances.

Group

Two or more people who interact to complete tasks, achieve goals, or fulfill needs

Team

A group whose members interact *with focused intensity* to complete a shared, specific goal

Figure 8-2	The focus and intensity of the group members toward a goal determine if it is a team.

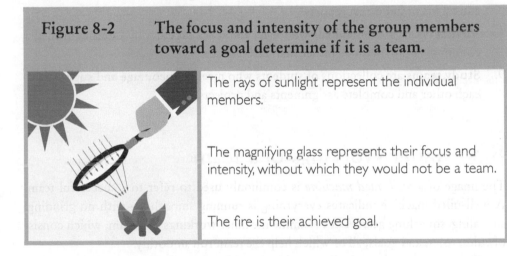

The rays of sunlight represent the individual members.

The magnifying glass represents their focus and intensity, without which they would not be a team.

The fire is their achieved goal.

8.2b   Different Types of Teams

Go back and look at the list of groups you created in Exercise 8-2a. You probably see a variety of types. Can you identify which were *teams* and which were *groups*? Looking at the teams, what do they all have in common? What differences do you see? Not all teams are the same. Let's look at some of the different types of teams in more detail.

The two main types of teams have to do with how the team started. *Formal teams* are set up by an authority figure who selects and assigns the members to work on a specific task. *Informal teams* are when the members get together on their own because they share a common interest. Again, keep in mind the *intensity level* is what differentiates a team from a group.

Most other team types focus on the team's activity or purpose. *Work teams* usually form around a specific process or function.

Examples:

1. **Advice teams** seek and provide information or research material, such as political advisers polling issues for popular opinion among voters.

2. **Project teams** produce, build, or create a new service or product, such as design teams who create new cars.

3. **Action teams** perform a specific operation or process for an organization, such as the organ transplant team within a hospital.

4. **Production teams** perform specific operations for producing a finished product, such as the shift crew at a fast-food restaurant.

5. **Maintenance teams** perform repair or preventative measures on equipment, such as the pit crew at a NASCAR race.

6. **Sports teams** are formed by members participating in their chosen sport, such as softball, football, soccer, bowling, or volleyball. A friendly pickup game would be a group, but a team has a schedule, a roster, and a competitive intensity to perform at their collective best.

7. Top **management teams** are executives who manage a company, such as a CEO and all his or her direct reports.

8. **Virtual teams** are individuals who meet and work together by internet or media communication methods rather than face-to-face.

9. **Study teams** are collections of students who meet to encourage and support each other and complete assignments and projects.

8.3 Inner Workings of a Team

The image of a *well-oiled machine* is commonly used to refer to a successful team. A well-oiled machine indicates everything is running smoothly—with no grinding, squealing, squeaking gears. Let's examine the inner workings of a team, which consist of rules, roles, and goals, all of which help the team run smoothly.

Team rules are the guidelines and instructions that all members agree to when they join the team. The rules lay out what actions and behaviors are acceptable as a member of the team.

> **Example:** *If you are on a sports team, you must learn and follow the rules of the game or your team will get repeated penalties and most likely lose.*

Refer back to the marketing team created for Exercise 8-4. Did your team establish any rules? What were they?

Team roles are those behaviors and tasks that a team member is expected to perform for the overall progress of the team. Have you ever been on a team and really didn't know what your job was? The technical term for that situation is *role ambiguity,* and it can greatly decrease your team's effectiveness.

Real-Life Application

What Is Synergy?

An effective team creates *synergy*. Remember, synergy is the sum of the individual parts creating a greater whole. Let's look to nature for an example of synergy that is often used in team-building seminars. Please see Figure 8-3, a flock of geese flying in V formation.

Figure 8-3	Geese in V formation exemplify a cooperative team

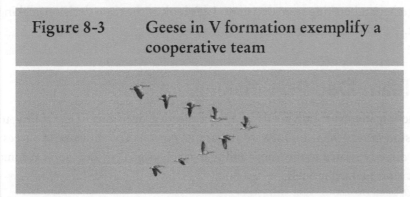

What we learn from the team of geese is that overall performance and productivity increase significantly when a team works together to generate synergy. When you see geese flying in a V formation, you might wonder what scientists have discovered about why they fly that way, and why these beautiful birds illustrate *teamwork* at its best:

FACT 1: As each goose flaps its wings, it creates an *uplift* for the birds that follow. This makes it easier for the birds in the back to fly, allowing the whole flock to fly farther, faster.

Lesson *People who share a common direction and sense of community can get where they are going more quickly and easily because they are traveling with the support of one another.*

FACT 2: When a goose falls out of formation, it suddenly feels the drag and resistance of flying alone. It quickly moves back into formation to take advantage of the lifting power of the bird immediately in front of it.

Lesson *If we have as much sense as geese, we will stay in formation with those headed where we want to go. We are willing to accept their help and give our help to others.*

FACT 3: When the lead goose gets tired, it moves toward the back of the formation and another goose flies to the point position.

Lesson *It pays to take turns doing the hard tasks and sharing leadership responsibilities. Like geese, people are interdependent on each other's skills, capabilities, and unique arrangements of gifts, talents, and resources.*

FACT 4: The geese flying in formation honk to encourage those up front to keep up their speed.

Lesson *When team members encourage each other, more gets done.*

FACT 5: When a goose gets sick or wounded, two geese drop out of formation and follow it down to help and protect it. They stay with it until it can fly again. Then, they fly off with another formation or catch up with their original flock.

Lesson *If we have as much sense as geese, we will stand by each other in tough times as well as when we are strong.*

Example: *The role of a point guard on a basketball team is to bring the ball up court and run the offense. The expected tasks and behavior include low or no turnovers, good passing, good shooting, and team spirit.*

In Exercise 8-4, which role did each person fill?

Team goals are specific and measurable (remember SMART) outcomes a team is trying to accomplish.

Example: *A sports team's goal is to win the championship.*

In Exercise 8-4, what goal did your team want to achieve?

This trio of inner workings (rules, roles, and goals) must be determined by a team working together and making team decisions. Let's look at the team decision-making process next.

8.4   Team Decision-Making

Team interaction involves individuals making collective decisions. This ability to make a decision moves the team forward toward its goal(s). The measure of success for a team is directly related to the team's ability to reach its goal(s). Let's look at some different decision-making models.

8.4a   The Three C's of Team Decision-Making

1. *Command decisions* happen when a leader (either an official leader chosen by the group or one who was *self-appointed*, meaning they took on the leadership role without being asked) decides something for the group. The group goes along with the decision because the leader pressures them to. A command decision can be helpful and necessary in a crisis where a decision must be made right away (e.g., in a fire or an accident). Because the leader made the decision more or less alone, the rest of the team members don't necessarily feel responsible for it.

2. *Consultative decisions* happen when team members *consult* one another about (or *discuss*) the issues at hand. Usually the individual who knows the most about the subject leads the consultation, and others may be left out of the discussion—especially if the team is large. Based on the discussion, a decision is made. Some team members may disagree with the final decision. These kinds of decisions take longer to make because information has to be collected and discussed.

3. *Consensus decisions* happen when the entire team participates. Every member expresses a view and has a say in the final decision. Everyone believes that the results of the decision are shared and they are equally responsible. This type of decision takes the most time to complete; however, because the entire team participates, individuals become more committed to the decision. In addition, because everyone is involved, implementation of these decisions is usually faster and more effective.

Each of the three C's can be used in different scenarios. No one decision-making type works well in every circumstance. The two greatest factors that impact these three types of decision-making are *time* and *responsibility*:

Time: How much time is available to reach a decision? Is there a deadline? Balancing time and teamwork can be challenging.

Responsibility: Does each team member feel a sense of commitment to the project and to other team members? Without that sense of shared responsibility, your team is just a group.

One other potential outcome is that the team can't make a decision at all. This can happen if team members do not want to speak up and progress stalls while everyone waits for someone else to take action and make a suggestion. When team members don't want to participate in the decision-making process, the whole team suffers. In other cases, the team can't make a decision because they don't have the information or resources they need. *Sometimes, doing nothing is the best thing you can do.* Sometimes the team decides to do nothing right away, but other times the discussion can drag on until finally the team decides to drop it without reaching a decision. In Exercise 8-5, you'll think about types of team decisions. Look at Figure 8-4, and then complete the exercise.

Figure 8-4	Team decision-making

Command decisions take the least amount of time, but the team's feeling of shared responsibility may be small because only one person is involved. The decisions the team makes through consensus take the longest to reach, but everyone shares responsibility and the time for implementation is shorter. Cooperation and collaboration are increased, and the results are likely to be more positive.

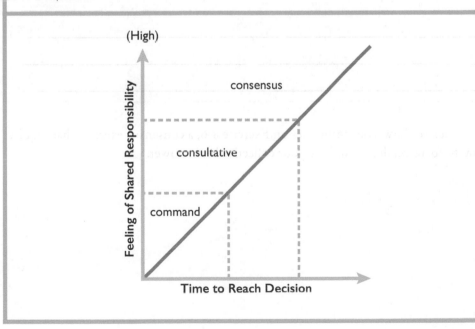

List some examples of the different types of team decision-making you have encountered in your own team experiences.

Command decision example: _____

_____

How did you feel about this decision? _____

_____

Consultative decision example: _____

_____

How did you feel about this decision? _____

_____

Consensus decision example: _____

_____

How did you feel about this decision? _____

_____

If you ever encountered a situation where a team could not make a decision, describe it and explain the reasons behind the situation.

_____

_____

_____

_____

Let's see how your team does on Exercise 8-6, a consensus exercise that requires you to focus on details and use your collective brain power.

Exercise 8-6 Consensus Exercise

Form teams of four to eight members. Here are eight questions that should get you thinking. First, answer each question on your own. Now that you have completed this task individually, you must consider each question as a member of your team. You must decide by *consensus*—meaning you all must agree—the best answer for each question. Do not change your individual answers even if you change your mind in the group discussion. Both individual and group solutions will later be compared with the "correct" answers provided. These answers can be found in the Appendix after you complete the entire exercise—DO NOT LOOK AHEAD AT THE ANSWERS AS THIS WILL RUIN THE RESULTS.

You have fifteen minutes to answer the questions individually and thirty minutes as a team. Appoint a team member to watch the time for your team.

1. You are trapped in a cold wilderness and are nearly frozen when you come across a primitive cabin. Inside you find a kerosene lamp, a candle, and a stove with some wood and paper. You find only one match. Which do you light first?

Your Answer _____

Group Answer _____

2. If a *leukocyte* is a white blood cell and an *erythrocyte* is a red blood cell, and if *dysphagia* is difficulty swallowing and *dyspnea* is difficulty breathing, what is a *phagocyte* and what does it do?

Your Answer _____

_____

Group Answer _____

_____

3. How many different combinations of coins, excluding pennies, add up to forty cents?

Your Answer _____

Group Answer _____

4. A lost camper saw smoke from a campfire on a cliff a distance away. Cupping his hands, he yelled as loud as he could in the direction of the cliff. Four seconds later, he heard an echo. If sound travels 1,100 feet per second, how far away was the cliff?

Your Answer _____

Group Answer _____

5. If a certain breed of chicken averages laying an egg and a half a day, how many eggs would you expect to get from that breed's roosters in one week?

Your Answer _____

Group Answer _____

6. A farmer had nine ears of corn stored in a barn. Every day, a squirrel went in and left with three ears. Yet it took the squirrel nine days to remove all the ears. Can you explain why?

Your Answer _____

Group Answer _____

7. Maria's mom has four daughters. Three of their names are Autumn, Winter, and Spring. What is the fourth daughter's name?

Your Answer _____

Group Answer _____

8. How many of each animal did Moses take on his ark?

Your Answer _____

Group Answer _____

(continues)

Question	Mark which questions you answered correctly (answers are in the Appendix).	Mark which questions your team answered correctly (answers are in the Appendix).
1		
2		
3		
4		
5		
6		
7		
8		
Total	( )	( )

Consensus decisions should be the best ones. None of us are as smart as *all* of us.

Now that you and your team have completed the consensus exercise, answer the following questions:

Which score was higher, the team's score or yours?

_____

How did your team do? Did one individual score higher than the collective team? Why? _____

_____

_____

Did your team members listen to each other's suggestions and comments?

_____

Did your team members adopt different roles? Examples: Leader, timekeeper, recorder, encourager.

_____

_____

_____

What have you learned about interactions between people attempting to solve a task? Did you reach consensus? If so, how long did it take?

_____

_____

What could you do differently to have a more effective outcome?

_____

8.5   Understanding Team Dynamics

Team dynamics refers to the basic nature of the team and how different personalities combine to create an evolving team personality. Just as every individual has a unique personality, each team forms a collective personality all its own. The growth of a team follows five steps, which are nicely demonstrated and explained by the stages of group development developed by Dr. Bruce Tuckman. (See Figure 8-5.)

Figure 8-5　A representation of Tuckman's stages of group development

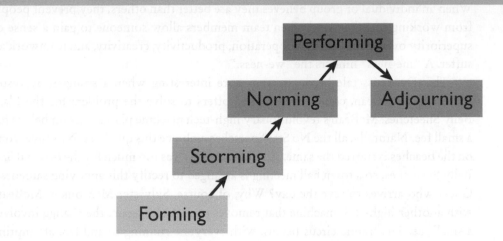

Stages	Forming	Storming	Norming	Performing	Adjourning
Individual Member Thoughts	Am I welcome? Can I trust these folks? Do they care about me? How do I fit in?	What is my role? Who leads? Why is that person in charge? Not ready to volunteer! Find someone to align with	What do you want me to do? Hey, these folks are OK! What's our goal and purpose? I can do that!	Enthusiasm Excitement Self-worth Belonging to part of something special Relying on teammates	Look at what we did! Next? Sorry it's over! Going to miss my teammates What a great memorable experience!
Group Thoughts	Why are we here? Who are these people? Better not be any more work!	Disagreement over who leads! We won't get anything done this way (politics) Who does what?	Respect for one person to lead develops A spirit of teamwork begins to emerge	All tasks will be assigned and completed. Synergy is felt. Teaming is fun! Wow, look at us!	We were part of this! Hope next group works this well Need to find another project
Outcomes	Introductions Meet and greet Form opinions from first impressions Forming team identity	Testing of members and roles Leader emerges Awkwardness leaves Cliques form	Group trust builds cohesiveness Me-ness becomes we-ness Roles solidified	Open communication Conflicts resolved Cooperation Collaboration Goal/purpose met	Example of the power of teamwork Potential new team leaders trained

8.5a　Diversity

Let's look at a story about teamwork and diversity authored by Dr. Seuss. An excerpt from *The Sneetches and Other Stories* describes a fictional community of strange-looking, long-beaked, spiky-haired, ruffled-necked, tall, bright yellow critters who live on a beach. A significant difference exists within this group of critters. Some have green stars on their stomachs and some do not. Surprisingly, the "star-bellied" Sneetches believe they are much better than the Sneetches with "plain bellies." This simple and clever children's story demonstrates a divided community with prejudice between the two groups of critters. The Stars are aloof and arrogant toward the meek and humble No Stars. Neither group socializes or interacts with the other.

This divided community is an example of what happens when one group or individual believes they have an edge and bring more to the group than anyone else. When an individual or group believes they are better than others, they prevent people from working together. And when team members allow someone to gain a sense of superiority over them, energy, cooperation, productivity, creativity, and teamwork all suffer. A "me-ness" hinders the "we-ness."

This Dr. Seuss tale becomes even more interesting when a stranger, Sylvester McMonkey McBean, comes to town and offers to solve the problem for the Plain Belly Sneetches. McBean's revolutionary high-tech machine places stars on bellies for a small fee. Naturally, all the No Star Sneetches embrace this quick fix. Now everyone on the beaches is starred the same. All this sameness was too much for the original Star Belly Sneetches, so a town hall meeting is arranged to rectify this annoying sameness. Guess who arrives to save the day? Why, of course, Sylvester McMonkey McBean, with another high-tech machine that removes stars. Once again, the change involves a small fee. The frantic circus begins, with everyone running to and fro, attempting to modify themselves differently from the other Sneetches. Into one machine and out the other machine the Sneetches scurry all day long. After the vicious cycle begins, the results become rather confusing: No one knows who is who. But, with all their money spent, they collectively watch Sylvester McMonkey McBean drive off into the sunset with a grin of satisfaction, proclaiming, "They never will learn. No. You can't teach a Sneetch!"

Sylvester McMonkey McBean actually served as a *catalyst* between the different Sneetches. When all the money was spent and McBean got up and left, the Sneetches discovered a simple truth: We are all equal, and no one should determine our self-worth. The me-ness became we-ness that day on the beach, and diversity was well within everyone's reach!

This children's story teaches us a lot about teamwork and diversity. Sameness is not needed for equality. We should celebrate our differences. Often our team members look, think, act, and communicate differently. An effective team embraces these differences. Reflect on celebrating diversity in Exercise 8-7.

Chapter 8: Group Interaction and Team Building

Exercise 8-7   Celebrating Diversity

Answer the following questions, and then share your results with your team.

What are you most proud of concerning your heritage? _____

Describe a favorite food that reflects your heritage. _____

What is your favorite family tradition? _____

Explain what diversity means to you. _____

_____

Share your answers with others on your team. Discuss these differences, and focus on the positives that grow from this diverse collection of team members.

REMEMBER: A team is a collection of people who have numerous differences, but the key is that they share a common goal. Let the richness of these differences add to the solutions and ideas you come up with to meet the team's goal(s).

8.5b   Embrace the Power of Diversity

Advances in technology and the global economy have brought the people of our world closer together than ever. Businesses have learned the importance and power of embracing diversity for the many new ideas, talents, and rich experiences it brings at the individual and team level. Organizations of all types have adopted practices that embrace workplace diversity. So, on an individual level, it is important to understand what it means to embrace diversity. One of the first places to start is understanding what a **value** is. Every individual, group, and society has *values*. These are the standards that people use to assess themselves and others, the principles by which they live their lives, the things they think are important. You must realize that values differ from person to person, group to group, culture to culture, and country to country. You shouldn't assume your culture's values, customs, and behaviors are admirable, sensible, and "right." Keeping an open mind to other cultures and beliefs is essential for cultural diversity to be a positive force. It is also important to understand that we are all unique and diverse even if we live within the same culture. Diversity includes race, ethnicity, gender, age, religion, disability, and sexual orientation.

Value

A standard used to assess oneself and others; a principle that you consider important and by which you live your life

So, what can you do to embrace diversity and benefit from its power? First and foremost, be open to the differences in your world and learn from them. Understand that other cultures have unique views on many parts of interaction, including appropriate eye contact, nonverbal communication, personal space, and expressing emotion, to name a few. Some cultures are quite comfortable with silence, while others consider it appropriate to speak before the other person has finished talking. Get to know the members of your team and consider how their different backgrounds contribute to the group dynamic. The key to embracing diversity is getting to know and understand your fellow students, coworkers, and team members and demonstrating genuine concern and interest in them.

8.6   Team Brainstorming

Now let's look at a strategy for generating breakthrough ideas and solutions. Of course, we know that for a team to successfully achieve its goals, it has to come up with ideas and solutions. *Brainstorming* is a great way to get the entire team involved in generating ideas.

8.6a   Team Creativity and Innovation: Brainstorming

A brainstorming session is an energetic, enthusiastic way to collect ideas and potential solutions for achieving a goal. Remember, the number of ideas is important—the more you come up with, the better—so try to build on the ideas of others and encourage ideas even if they seem crazy. After studying the following list, do Exercise 8-8.

How to Conduct a Team Brainstorm

1. Define your goal (your opportunity for positive change) so all team members understand the objective of the brainstorming session. (Keep the SMART acronym in mind when goal setting. If your goal is not specific, measurable, achievable, realistic, and time-bound, you won't be focused enough to come up with useful ideas.)

    a. Good goal: How can we increase the number of applicants to our school for next year?

    b. Too broad goal: How can we improve our school?

2. Establish a time limit for the session. Depending on the subject, twenty to thirty minutes should be long enough.

3. Choose a person to take notes (preferably where everyone can see them, like on a whiteboard). Ideas should be limited to only a few sentences to keep things moving quickly. This is not the time to discuss the ideas, so once an idea has been suggested, move on to the next one.

4. Someone should run the meeting. This means signaling the start of the process and rotating around the group in one direction to seek input. This person should also sit with the group and contribute.

5. Teams participating in an active brainstorm session are like bags of microwave popcorn, only they are "popping out ideas." Once the popping begins to slow— the ideas stop flowing—the process is complete. Also, if the predetermined amount of time is up, begin to bring the session to a close.

6. The person running the meeting should help the team participants categorize the collected ideas.

7. Then the person running the meeting should lead the team to make a consensus decision about which are the top five ideas.

8. Then the team should focus on finding a workable solution using the potential ideas from the top five list.

9. An action plan (including *who* will do *what* and *when*) should be developed to implement the idea or ideas.

An interesting class discussion would include listing the best of the best ideas from the entire collection of ideas from all the teams. Your entire class can then be considered a team. This process of small teams evolving into one large team is often used within an organization to gather ideas and maximize the participation of a greater number of people. Let's say one of the ideas your class came up with and agreed upon to "increase the number of applicants to your school next year" is to hold a large community festival at your school celebrating the diverse cultures represented in the student body. This festival would showcase your school and its program and it would provide a community service and an appreciation of cultural diversity. What a great idea! Your class could then be broken back up into multiple teams to further pursue and implement this great idea.

Do Exercise 8-8, and then use Exercise 8-9, to assess overall team performance.

Exercise 8-8   Brainstorming in Action

Have your team brainstorm the following: Your school would like to host a festival to celebrate diversity, involve the local community, and market the school and its academic programs. Organizers have asked your class to help them brainstorm ideas for this event. They have given you a list of areas to consider:

1. Location
2. Theme
3. Music, food and refreshments, activities
4. Marketing ideas
5. How the students can contribute
6. How the school can contribute

Conduct a brainstorming session for each element of the festival. In brainstorming, no idea is too unrealistic or far-fetched. Don't judge one another's ideas—just throw them out there. Go for it!

Complete the festival planning table below with your team's final answers.

Topic Areas	Top Ideas
1. Location	
2. Theme	
3. Music, food and refreshments, activities	
4. Marketing ideas	
5. How the students can contribute	
6. How the school can contribute	

Exercise 8-9 Assessing Team Effectiveness and Performance

Rate how your team did on each of the following.

3 = Fantastic   2 = Good   1 = Poor   0 = Missing

Clear goal or purpose	_____	Open and effective communication	_____
Team energy and enthusiasm	_____	Team spirit and pride	_____
Number and types of ideas	_____	Comfort level	_____
Level of participation	_____	Mutual respect	_____
Support and encouragement	_____	Ability to resolve conflict	_____

Total _____

Scoring

25–30:   You were a very synergistic and effective team.

20–24:   You were a good team that, with work, could become a great team.

15–19:   Your team was OK but needs some work in the low-rated areas.

10–14:   Your team needs a lot of work to improve.

Below 10:   Hope you used this as a learning experience!

8.6b   Strategies for Team Leadership

Applying what you've learned in this textbook will help you become an effective contributing member of a team and, perhaps, a team leader. In a leadership role, you must successfully set expectations for your team and communicate those expectations to them; you must also draw from members' individual strengths to accomplish your goal.

Set your expectations high and get to know your individual team members. Be sure to recognize and reward contributions and achievements. Create an environment where all team members can voice their ideas without fear of ridicule and premature criticism. While everyone won't agree all the time on team decisions, it is your responsibility to convince as many people as possible (or *build consensus*) about each team decision. You should also understand why members may oppose that decision or at least feel unsure about it.

One of the most important attributes of team success is that everyone feels they can contribute equally. It is your responsibility as team leader to create an environment that encourages this feeling. One final word of advice is to make sure that, even though you are the team leader, you share in the responsibilities instead of simply "dumping work" on all your team members. The single best piece of advice is the old adage, "The best way to lead is by example."

8.7 Teamwork at School, at Work, and in Your Community

A parable about masons (builders who work with stone and brick) best summarizes Chapter 8:

> One day while out for a carefree walk, I came across three bricklayers working on the same project.
>
> I asked the first bricklayer what he was doing. "Laying bricks," he told me.
>
> I asked the second what he was doing. "Making a brick wall," he told me.
>
> I asked the third.
>
> "Building a cathedral," he explained.

—From *Wisdom Distilled from the Daily: Living the Rule of St. Benedict.* Today by Joan Chittester, New York, NY: HarperCollins Publishers, 1999.

Everyone approaches work, tasks, and assignments from a unique perspective. Some people focus only on the task at hand (laying bricks), others focus on an immediate goal (building a brick wall), and still others have a long-term goal (building a cathedral) in mind. The question you must ask yourselves, as a team, is, "What are we going to do with the new skills that we've learned? Lay bricks or build cathedrals?" An effective team doesn't stop when a task is completed, or even when they reach their first goal—instead they look for and embrace the next challenge, building on each success until the cathedral is complete. Use your new knowledge about teamwork in every facet of your life. *Working together works*—at school, at work, and in your community.

Complete Exercise 8-10 Chapter Summation to assess a team at your school and one in your community.

Exercise 8-10   Chapter Summation

Describe a team at your school. _____

_____

What is its purpose? _____

What are its strengths? _____

How can it be improved? _____

Describe a team within your community. _____

_____

What is its purpose? _____

What are its strengths? _____

How can it be improved? _____

Healthy Decision-Making

Dave and Selma joined a study group for a particularly difficult class. Their time is very limited because they both work outside of school. However, when this particular study group meets, other members spend a lot of time complaining about the class and gossiping about other classmates. Dave and Selma feel the group should be more of a study *team* and approach their goal of doing well in the course with more *focus* and *intensity*. What can Dave and Selma do?

_____

_____

_____

_____

_____

_____

_____

Remember, *"All of us can do more than each one of us."*

9

Career Seeking and Leadership Development

Your Future Begins Now

Objectives

By the end of this chapter, you will be able to:

- Identify interests and how they relate to coursework and potential careers

- Analyze and develop transferable skills

- Identify and develop effective career search strategies

- Create and promote your personal brand

- Explain different résumé formats

- Build an effective résumé for a chosen career

- Identify components of portfolios and electronic résumés

- Create effective cover letters

- Demonstrate an understanding of how to complete an employment application

- Contrast different types of interviews

- Properly research and prepare for an interview

- Apply effective verbal and nonverbal skills during the interview process

- Understand the characteristics that develop career leadership potential

Why Learn This Skill?

In this chapter, you will learn strategies to enhance your career opportunities in four specific areas:

1. Self-discovery: Matching your personality, interests, and skills to a potential career.

2. Academic preparation: What to do beyond getting good grades that will transfer to career success. You will learn how to *brand* yourself, increasing your marketability. Involvement in your community, clubs, and organizations will, in turn, develop your leadership and organizational skills.

3. Finding your first career position: How to secure that great first career position by writing effective résumés, applications, and cover letters, and performing well during your interview.

4. Leadership: Some ideas about leadership and how to develop the leader within *you*! This skill will help you advance within your career of choice.

Preparing for your career is not something you do right before you graduate. Rather, preparation for your career begins early, while you are still in school. The first step is to select your career or major; for most students, this is not a one-time process. The overwhelming majority of students change their minds at least once, even if they feel certain about their initial decision.

The reality is that most people change not just jobs but also career tracks several times in their lives. Today's economy isn't your grandparents' economy where employees often worked for the same organization from the start of their working career until retirement. Workers need to be able to adapt to changes in the workplace. One way to prepare for working in the twenty-first century is to explore and develop a wide range of knowledge, skills, and abilities.

9.1   Introduction

This chapter is all about self-discovery and developing the skills to land that first great career position after graduation. There are two very important things you can do to ensure your success. First, understand that you must begin your search for your ideal career position on *day one* of college—*not* your last semester! Second, understand the four steps in a successful career search and how they are related. The four steps are illustrated in Figure 9-1 along with concepts and skill development that will be covered in this chapter to maximize your career success.

If you have chosen your career and feel this section doesn't apply to you, you're wrong. This information might confirm your choice, which is a great motivator to continue. However, some of you might find you aren't as committed to your choices as you thought you were, and this exploration will help you with your decision-making process. Of course, for those of you who haven't got a clue what you want to do, this is a great place to start.

Although you are just starting college, you can do a lot right now to start building a great résumé or portfolio, networking for future opportunities, branding yourself positively, and developing transferable skills that will help you succeed in your chosen career. Let's begin this chapter with some myth busting in Exercise 9-1.

Figure 9-1   The process of finding a successful career and position

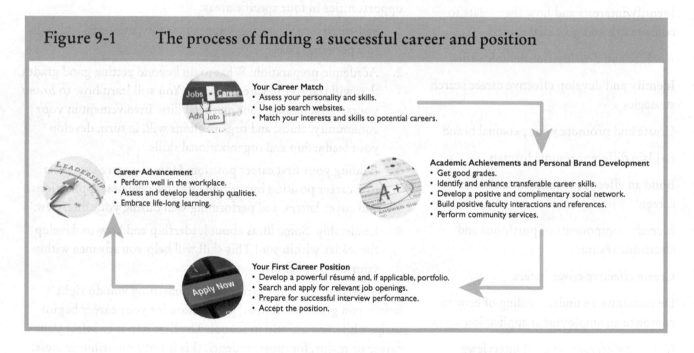

Your Career Match
- Assess your personality and skills.
- Use job search websites.
- Match your interests and skills to potential careers.

Academic Achievements and Personal Brand Development
- Get good grades.
- Identify and enhance transferable career skills.
- Develop a positive and complimentary social network.
- Build positive faculty interactions and references.
- Perform community services.

Career Advancement
- Perform well in the workplace.
- Assess and develop leadership qualities.
- Embrace life-long learning.

Your First Career Position
- Develop a powerful résumé and, if applicable, portfolio.
- Search and apply for relevant job openings.
- Prepare for successful interview performance.
- Accept the position.

Mark each statement with a "T" for true or "F" for false.

_____ 1. Good grades are the only factor behind getting a good job after graduation.

_____ 2. Students who enter school with a chosen major or career have an advantage over those who do not.

_____ 3. For most professions, there is only one major that can prepare a student for an entry-level job.

_____ 4. Liberal arts majors such as English, psychology, and philosophy do not prepare students for professional careers.

_____ 5. Changing career plans requires a change in major.

_____ 6. Most technology employers are not interested in skills like speaking and writing when they make hiring decisions.

_____ 7. Newspaper advertisements are the best way to find a job.

_____ 8. If you interview well, you do not have to be as concerned with the appearance and format of your résumé.

_____ 9. You should join as many clubs and organizations as you can, even if you do not attend any meetings or plan to be actively involved.

_____ 10. Volunteer experience is never as valuable as a paid job in terms of your professional and career development.

All of the above are… false! Each of these statements is a common myth about preparing for the work world after school.

9.2   The Academic Curriculum and Your Career Search

9.2a   Selecting a Program That Fits You

You may have already chosen a program of study. However, circumstances may change, or you may change your mind. You need to consider the following issues in selecting or changing your program:

• Why did you select your current program?

• Who, if anyone, influenced your choice?

• What do you know about the program and the opportunities in it?

No matter what your program, you will likely need to take courses in a number of areas. Requirements typically involve developing and demonstrating skills in writing and mathematics as well as knowledge in humanities, social sciences, and natural sciences.

Many students choose programs without knowing much about them. This chapter will give you the tools you need to make informed decisions about your academic and career options, starting with Exercise 9-2.

Food for Thought

The average student changes his or her career choice or major at least once.

Exercise 9-2   If I Had a Million Dollars...

If you were independently wealthy and could study anything, what would it be? For this activity, don't worry about limits like what programs your school offers, what others think, and the needs of other people like your parents, spouse, or children. This exercise is about imagining possibilities, so be as impractical as you would like to be.

_____

Now that you've answered the question, do some homework. Using a search engine, go to the U.S. Bureau of Labor Statistics *Occupational Outlook Handbook* website. There is a search box on every page. Search for your dream career. (Please note that you should be flexible with the wording. If you type "English literature" [with quotes], you will not find many results. You will, however, find several results for English literature [no quotes], English, and literature.)

Let's use art history as an example. If you search art history, you will find links on the following:

1. Archivists, curators, and museum technicians

2. Graphic designers

3. Advertising, marketing, promotions, public relations, and sales managers

4. Artists and related workers

If you chose health careers, you will be amazed at the number of professions in addition to nurses and doctors. There are more than eighty allied health professions alone. Some of the results of your search might not interest you, but others likely will. Write down the search items that are either interesting or pleasantly surprising to you:

_____

_____

Let's go back to our art history example and look at the third category of advertising, public relations, and related careers. You will see links to the following:

What They Do	How to Become One	Job Outlook	More Info
Work Environment	Pay	Similar Occupations	

Now it's your turn to explore. Go to the *Occupational Outlook Handbook* website. Complete this exercise by researching a career path that looks interesting to you. Summarize the key points under each heading:

Pay: _____

_____

_____

What They Do: _____

_____

_____

Job Outlook: _____

_____

_____

Work Environment: _____

_____

_____

Similar Occupations: _____

_____

_____

How to Become One: _____

_____

_____

More Info: _____

_____

_____

9.2b   Matching Your Skills

Achieving career success requires you to demonstrate certain skills. The term **transferable skills** refers to those skills you can carry from one job to another or use in various careers. These skills can come from courses within your program of study, but often courses and experiences outside your major also provide you with marketable skills. For example, students interested in business careers will do what seems to be obvious and take accounting and marketing classes. However, many of these students would benefit from liberal arts courses that might teach them a second language because in this global economy, such skills would help them write and communicate more effectively and can give them a more international view of the world.

To illustrate the importance of assessing and developing skills for the workplace, the U.S. Department of Labor identified the skills needed for career success in the *Secretary's Commission on Achieving Necessary Skills (SCANS)* report. This government document summarizes workplace *competencies* and *foundation skills* that any worker needs to be successful in the rapidly evolving modern workplace.

9.2c   SCANS Workplace Competencies

According to the *SCANS* report, effective workers can productively use:

Resources: They know how to allocate time, money, materials, space, and staff.

Interpersonal skills: They can work on teams, teach others, serve customers, and lead, negotiate, and work well with people from culturally diverse backgrounds.

Information: They can gather and evaluate data, organize and maintain files, interpret and communicate, and use computers to process information.

Systems: They understand social, organizational, and technological systems; they can monitor and correct performance; they also can design or improve systems.

Technology: They can select equipment and tools, apply technology to specific tasks, and maintain and troubleshoot equipment.

9.2d   SCANS Foundation Skills

Competent workers in the high-performance workplace need:

Basic skills: Reading, writing, mathematics, speaking, and listening.

Thinking skills: The ability to learn, to reason, to think creatively, to make decisions, and to solve problems.

Personal qualities: Individual responsibility, self-esteem and self-management, sociability, and integrity.

Beyond the *SCANS* report, several groups, including the Partnership for 21st Century Skills, have conducted a survey of four hundred U.S. employers to identify critical workplace skills for success for both the individual and business. This survey confirmed the *SCANS* report and emphasized that soft skills are important to teach in any academic program along with the technical knowledge of the profession. **Soft skills** are personal attributes that enhance career prospects and performance on the job and include things like communication and teamwork. Unlike **hard skills,** which are about a person's knowledge and ability to perform a certain type of task or activity,

Transferable skills

Those skills you can carry from one job to another or use in a variety of careers

Soft skills

Personal attributes that enhance career prospects and performance on the job

Hard skills

Skills related to one's knowledge and ability to perform a specific task or activity

soft skills are more widely applicable, are often *inter-* or *intrapersonal*, and can be harder to define.

Some key soft skills include:

- Effective written and oral communication
- High degree of professionalism and work ethic
- Teamwork
- Critical and creative thinking
- Problem-solving and decision-making

It's often said that hard skills will get you an interview, but soft skills will get you the job. These are the skills that many employers want to see, and many programs can help you to develop these skills. General education courses, taken in addition to technical and professional training, are a common way to develop soft skills. Experience in a wide range of areas helps you develop into a well-rounded and educated person and can also make you more employable. Begin thinking about how to develop your skills by doing Exercise 9-3 now.

Real-Life Application

Top 10 Attributes Employers Are Looking For

The National Association of Colleges and Employers (NACE®) released a perspective employer survey in 2016. This survey focused on determining the top attributes that employers were looking for when they reviewed a résumé. Notice from the list that eight of the Top 10 are soft skills. Technical skills, or "do you know your stuff?" skills, were actually number ten. This doesn't mean your technical skills aren't important, but it indicates that employers view them as a "given." All applicants should have the technical skills necessary for the position. It is your soft skills that will set you apart and hopefully land you the job and lead to your future success.

Top 10 Attributes

1. Leadership
2. Ability to work in a team
3. Written communication skills
4. Problem-solving skills

5. Verbal communication skills
6. Strong work ethic
7. Initiative

8. *Analytical/quantitative skills
9. Flexibility/adaptability
10. *Technical skills

*Denotes a hard skill

Source: Adapted from "Job Outlook 2016", National Association of Colleges and Employers. Retrieved at http://www.naceweb.org/career-development/trends-and-predictions/job-outlook-2016-attributes-employers-want-to-see-on-new-college-graduates-resumes.

Exercise 9-3 How Can You Develop Your Skills?

For each of the SCANS areas listed, fill out the table as instructed.

In Class: What curricular opportunities (i.e., classes) does your school offer to help you develop each skill? What classes are you taking, or do you plan to take (as electives or requirements), that will address each area?

On Campus: What activities (organizations, clubs) does your campus offer that will help you develop this skill?

Off Campus: What off-campus opportunities are available that will help you develop this skill?

The first row is filled out as an example, although you should feel free to add your own ideas. Complete the rest of the chart on your own or with a classmate.

SCANS Skills	In Class	On Campus	Off Campus
Using Resources	Courses that involve research, such as writing and library science.	Holding an office in a club or organization.	A part-time job. A volunteer project in the community.
Interpersonal Skills			
Using Information			
Using Systems			
Using Technology			
Basic Skills:			
Reading			
Writing			
Mathematics			
Speaking and Listening			

(continues)

Exercise 9-3　How Can You Develop Your Skills? (cont.)

SCANS Skills	In Class	On Campus	Off Campus
Thinking Skills:			
Learning and Reasoning			
Creativity			
Decision-Making and Problem-Solving			
Personal Qualities:			
Responsibility			
Self-Esteem and Self-Management			
Sociability			
Integrity			

You now have an idea of how your skill set will develop as you continue your education. Did you have any areas that were difficult to fill in? These might require additional attention.

Although grades are certainly important, they are just one ingredient in the mix. Things you do while in school (campus activities) will tell a potential employer a great deal about who you are and what you can do. These experiences will also show the employer how well you work with others, a major consideration in hiring. Consider these two students who are about to begin a job search upon graduation. Both are seeking entry-level jobs in business management.

Jane is a psychology major with a 2.8 grade point average. She struggled during her first year, but her grades have averaged B or higher during the last three years of college. To help pay for her education, she has to maintain a work-study position in the campus library. In addition to her job, she is involved in some campus organizations, particularly Enactus, her residence hall governing council, and Circle K, a community service organization. She became a president of Circle K during her junior year, and in each organization she has joined, she has attended personal and professional development programs alongside participating in community service projects. Given the demands of her coursework and keeping a job, Jane has to be careful not to overcommit to these campus activities, so she makes the most of every organization she joins.

Food for Thought

Students who work on campus rather than off campus report greater satisfaction with their school experience.

Bill is a business administration major, and a successful one at that. Except for his first year, he has earned dean's list honors each term by achieving a minimum grade point average of 3.3. He always maintains a part-time job, usually working in food service or retail. He has declined invitations to join organizations such as the math club, Habitat for Humanity, and student government, citing his need to study and to maintain his strong grades. His efforts have paid off with his grades, which include an A+ in marketing research, human resource management, and business information systems.

Answer the following questions:

1. Which student has the stronger academic record? _____

2. Which student is more marketable in terms of employment? _____

3. Each student has identifiable strengths. What are they? _____

    _____

4. Each student has identifiable weaknesses. What are they? _____

    _____

Both students will enter the job market with strengths and weaknesses, just like anyone searching for a job. Good arguments could be made for either student having an advantage in the job market, but the edge ultimately goes to Jane. Her grades are not quite as good as Bill's, it's true. However, she has done something Bill has not: She has learned from every facet of the college experience, in and out of the classroom. Refer back to the *SCANS* report. Jane has more relevant experiences in each of these areas than Bill.

Soon you will see sample résumés for Jane and Bill. Both can structure their résumés and cover letters to highlight their strengths, which is what you will need to do. Exercises 9-4 and 9-5 will help you get started.

Exercise 9-4   Develop a Plan

Juanita is about to begin an eighteen-month program to become a respiratory therapist. She has one child and wants to apply for a position at a local hospital after graduation so her parents can continue to help her raise her child. However, the local hospital typically has only one or two openings a year, and the class size averages fifteen to twenty students, with many wanting to stay in the area. What can Juanita do, beyond getting good grades, to maximize her chances of being chosen for the coveted position? List one specific on-campus and one specific off-campus activity that will help her. In addition, describe how she can demonstrate her soft skills to faculty and potential employers to maximize her chances of landing her dream job after graduation.

On-campus activity: _____

_____

_____

Off-campus activity: _____

_____

_____

Demonstrating her soft skills: _____

_____

_____

Exercise 9-5   Opportunities on Your Campus

For information on your curriculum, you can refer to your student catalog, which lists course descriptions, academic policies, and academic program requirements. For other on-campus opportunities, you should check in your student handbook and on your school's website.

Identify the names of courses, clubs, and organizations that are relevant to your major or career interests:

_____

_____

_____

Identify the names of courses, clubs, and organizations that are relevant to your personal interests:

_____

_____

_____

(continues)

9.2f   Internships or Service Learning Experiences

In his *Thoughts on Art and Life*, Leonardo da Vinci wrote, "... experience is a truer guide than the words of others." You learn from your experiences, both good and bad. Some of the best ways to gain experience are internships, service learning, and clinical experience. In these situations, you learn by doing and get a taste of the working world while still in school. The benefits of these kinds of experiences include:

- Applying classroom learning
- Experiencing challenging assignments and duties
- Getting an edge in the job market by networking and branding yourself as a potentially great employee
- Improving communication skills
- Establishing a work routine
- Enhancing critical and creative thinking
- Improving teamwork and time management skills
- Clarifying your career direction

These hands-on learning opportunities can prepare you to enter the work world. You will sharpen your skills and ensure that when you officially begin your career, the first impression you make will be a positive and lasting one.

9.2g   Creating Your Personal Brand

Personal branding is about showcasing what is unique about you. The first step is really getting to know yourself so you can develop an accurate brand. Each experience adds or subtracts from your brand. For example, building a powerful résumé or career portfolio, doing well academically, networking at career fairs, establishing positive faculty connections, and community service all will enhance your brand.

Food for Thought

Internet and newspaper advertisements are one way to learn about job openings, but most people find jobs through networking and word of mouth. Begin developing your network by meeting people through campus events in addition to part-time work.

Today, your *personal brand* is also affected by the information available about you online and on social media. Be certain this information is positive and professional because it can influence whether you're hired for a position or whether you get that promotion. Always keep in mind that negative or harmful information can prevent you from getting the job and can even get you fired. Consider joining websites like LinkedIn® professional networking services or even developing your own website.

Exercise 9-6   The Elevator Speech

In today's fast-paced society, you must be ready to make a quick, concise, and powerful impression to be noticed. One exercise to sharpen your brand is to develop an *elevator speech*. This is what you would tell someone about yourself to catch their attention if you met on an elevator and must finish your story before it reaches your floor. In other words, if you had only a minute and a half to "promote your brand," what would you say? Write and rehearse your elevator speech within the ninety-second limit, and make sure you don't sound rushed.

_____

_____

_____

_____

9.3   Beginning the Job Search: Your Résumé

It should be clear by now that your résumé is a work in progress that should continue to change and grow as you do. It is best to write a résumé when you start college and to update it as you progress through your program.

Your résumé is the first thing an employer will evaluate. It must convince them that you are qualified for the position. Beyond that, it should demonstrate competent writing and word processing skills. Interviewing is very important, but you will not get to an interview if your written presentation isn't appealing to a potential employer.

A résumé details your skills and experience. Because it is often the first screening tool for potential applicants, your résumé should be complete, neat, and free of errors. This shows you have taken pride in preparing the résumé and, therefore, are likely to take pride in your future work.

You can use many formats, but the most commonly used are chronological and functional résumés. *Chronological résumés*, the most frequently used, provide a listing of your experiences in order, with the most recent listed first. *Functional résumés* focus on skill sets and qualifications more than actual work experience, which can be beneficial for job applicants with limited experience.

Before deciding on a format, gather the following information, which you will use to write your résumé.

9.3a   Education Level

Start with your most recent education experience and list your degree, field, and graduation date along with the school you attended. Here's an example:

Bachelor of Science in Nursing, Superior University

Anticipated Graduation Date: May 2019

Associate Degree in Forensic Sciences, Superior Community College,

Graduated May 2010

Write your own here: _____

_____

9.3b   Work Experience

List your jobs in chronological order, the most recent first. Include your job title, the organization that employed you, start and end dates, and responsibilities. Here's an example:

Cashier, JCPenney, 2012–present. Greeted customers, balanced cash register, and assisted with annual inventory.

Note: Use action verbs to begin each description of your responsibilities. Examples include "facilitate," "manage," "assist," "help," and "coordinate." It is also important to keep all verbs in a consistent tense, usually past tense.

List your work experiences here, using action verbs to describe your responsibilities:

_____

_____

_____

_____

9.3c   Skills

List any knowledge, skills, and abilities you have that would be useful to an employer. Many students include their knowledge of computer software programs. Here's an example:

Proficient with Microsoft® Word and Microsoft Excel; skilled in basic web design.

List your own here: _____

9.3d   References

Most résumés end with the references section. It is perfectly appropriate to write "available upon request," as you will see on the examples. Before your job search, though, be sure to ask current and past employers for permission to use their names as references and make sure you have accurate contact information for each. It is polite to let them know in advance about jobs you are applying for so they can anticipate being called.

Take a look at the chronological résumés of our two students from the beginning of this chapter. See Figure 9-2 for the chronological résumé of Jane Smith. Because Jane's on-campus experiences are more extensive than her work experience, she puts these experiences in different sections.

Figure 9-2   Jane Smith's chronological résumé

Jane E. Smith

Grove University
Campus Box #0001
Pittsburgh, PA 16901

Phone: (412) 555-1111
Cell: (412) 555-0000
Email: jsmith@email.com

Education
Grove University
Bachelor of Arts in Psychology
Anticipated Graduation Date: May 2019

Work Experience
Grove University Library
Circulation Assistant (2015–present)
Responsibilities: Assisted students, faculty, and staff with library requests. Maintained records for interlibrary loan requests. Mailed correspondence regarding overdue materials. Organized and shelved returned materials.

Jo's Diner
Table Server (2012–2013)
Responsibilities: Served customers during dinner. Helped greeters during peak hours.

Leadership Experience
Circle K International
President (2015–present)
Achievements: Inaugurated annual fundraising drive for Juvenile Diabetes Association. Increased membership by 20 percent. Increased programming budget. Participated in monthly service projects, including delivering gifts to the local senior center and raising funds for charity clothing drive.

Enactus
Member (2015–present)
Achievements: Developed marketing plan for locally owned drugstore. Presented plan at the annual Enactus conference.

Grove University Residence Hall Council
Representative (2015)
Responsibilities: Attended monthly hall council meetings. Reported on building programs and events. Discussed maintenance and facility issues. Met weekly with residence hall director to discuss residents' complaints and suggestions.

Skills
Fluent in Spanish
Computer skills: Microsoft Word and Microsoft Excel, web design

References
Available upon request

Now let's take a look at Bill Jones's chronological résumé in Figure 9-3. Even though Bill has more work experience than Jane, his résumé is less detailed because Jane has so much more leadership experience to highlight. Bill might benefit from writing a functional rather than chronological résumé, which would highlight his knowledge and downplay his lack of experience. See Figure 9-4 for an example of Bill's functional résumé:

Figure 9-3   Bill Jones's chronological résumé

Bill A. Jones

Grove University
Campus Box 999
Pittsburgh, PA 41290

Phone: (412) 555-1234
Cell: (412) 555-8989
Email: bajones@email.com

Education
Grove University
Bachelor of Science in Business Administration
Anticipated Graduation Date: May 2019

Work Experience
Ward Clothing and Retail
Sales Clerk (2016–present)
Responsibilities: Waited on customers in menswear department. Balanced cash register at the end of each shift.
Assisted with annual inventory.

Pizza Place
Waiter (2015–2016)
Responsibilities: Waited on customers during evening shift. Assisted with cleaning tables and closing restaurant. Responsible for night deposits for evening earnings.

Burger Palace
Customer Service (2013–2015)
Responsibilities: Waited on customers. Supervised drive-through station. Coordinated staff schedule on weekends.

Skills
Computer: Microsoft Word and Microsoft Excel, Visual Basic, web design

References
Available upon request

Note that although both students were creative in their organization, they do not exaggerate their accomplishments. Their résumés share the following traits:

- Both are professionally written.

- Both highlight strengths and downplay weaknesses.

- Both use action verbs to describe accomplishments.

- Both are free of errors in grammar and punctuation.

Figure 9-4   Bill Jones's functional résumé

Bill A. Jones

Grove University
Campus Box 999
Pittsburgh, PA 41290

Phone: (412) 555-1234
Cell: (412) 555-8989
Email: bajones@email.com

Objective: To obtain an entry-level position in business management.

Education
Grove University
Bachelor of Science in Business Administration
Anticipated Graduation Date: May 2019

Coursework Highlights
Microcomputer Applications
Marketing Research
Human Resource Management
Current Issues in Management
Business Law

Skills and Abilities

Presentation and Communication Skills
• Participated in group presentations on many issues, including diversity in the workplace, technology, and education.
• Led presentation on marketing plan for a local company as part of marketing research methods course.
• Interviewed applicants for positions at local restaurant.
• Addressed customer complaints professionally and punctually.

Technology
• Proficient in Microsoft Word, Microsoft Excel, and Microsoft PowerPoint™.
• Experience in developing and maintaining Excel databases.

Research
• Assisted management professor in gathering articles for research.
• Conducted focus groups for faculty member's research project, "Millennials' Perceptions of the Management Landscape."

Work History
Ward Clothing and Retail
Sales Clerk (2016 to present)

Pizza Place
Waiter (2015–2016)

Burger Palace
Customer Service (2013–2015)

References
Available upon request

Exercise 9-7   Writing Your Résumé

Using the information in this section, create your own résumé. Give it to two trusted people to read and evaluate. Then revise your finished copy and update it as you go through your program.

9.3e   Portfolios and Digital Résumés

A portfolio showcases your work. An electronic portfolio can store and organize your information so potential employers can easily find things like your:

• Biographical and contact information

• Career objectives

• Electronic résumé and cover letter

- Academic achievements
- Samples of work
- Honors and awards
- References and testimonials

You can creatively enhance your electronic portfolio with pictures, graphics, videos, and sound to make your brand stand out. Video résumés are gaining in popularity; your elevator speech from Exercise 9-6 can serve as a ninety-second video résumé to grab a potential employer's attention.

Food for Thought

A number of websites provide templates for entry-level résumés. You can use one of those templates to design your résumé, which may save you time with formatting and organizing. If you use Microsoft Office, see www. office.microsoft.com for examples, including both chronological and functional formats.

9.4   Writing Cover Letters

Your résumé is a critical document in your job search. To get an employer to read your résumé, however, you must also write a good cover letter. One of the secrets to a good cover letter is to focus less on why you want the job and more on why the company should want to hire you. With that in mind, *avoid* statements like the following:

I would really like to work for your organization because I think it would be a great move for my career.

Even the most caring employer will be more interested in what you bring to the table rather than what you hope to get out of the position. Instead, try a statement like this:

My education and experience provide the qualifications your company needs in its next accounts manager.

9.4a   Tips for Writing a Cover Letter

Professionalism   Create a letterhead to make the letter attractive and professional looking.

Organization   Remember what we discussed in the chapter on communication about thesis statements and topic sentences. Your introduction should include a thesis that explains why you are qualified for this position. For example:

I am writing in regard to the second-grade teacher vacancy in the Cornfield School District (as advertised in the New York Times *on 7 September 2018). My work experience and educational background have given me the skills needed for this position.*

Topic Sentences   Each paragraph should provide a different reason persuading your reader to give you an interview. For example, introduce yourself in the first paragraph. In the second paragraph, explain how your work experience provides you with the right qualifications. If your work experience is limited, focus on your achievements on campus. In the third paragraph, perhaps you can highlight your educational achievements and how some of your coursework applies to the position.

I earned my undergraduate degree and teaching certificate at Grove University, where I majored in secondary education/English with additional certification in elementary literacy and reading. In my coursework, I learned the history of, and most recent theory about, whole-language and phonetic approaches. Using this knowledge, I developed my own philosophy of language arts education.

My experience in the classroom was very much influenced by my work and volunteer experience in the local school system. I applied my learning to practical situations as a classroom assistant at Grove City Elementary School before beginning my practicum and student teaching assignments at the same school. Although most of my classroom experience was with third-grade students, I have been working since then as an after-school tutor for students in all grades. This breadth of experience has prepared me to work with students at a number of grade levels.

Note that each paragraph focuses on a different part of the student's qualifications: first academic background, then experience.

Your closing paragraph is very important. Here, you want to thank the reader for considering your application, express your availability for an interview, and remind the reader how to contact you.

My academic transcript and résumé (both enclosed for your review) attest to my qualifications for the second-grade teacher vacancy in your school district. I would be happy to discuss my qualifications in person at any time. If you would like additional information about my application, feel free to contact me at (555) 555-1111. Thank you for considering my application.

Conciseness   When applying for an entry-level position, your cover letter should be no more than one page long. Get right to the point.

Focus on the Reader   It's not all about you. Focus on the employer's needs rather than your own, using the pronoun "you" over "I" whenever possible. For example, "If you would like additional information…," "Thank you for considering my application…," "You will find my credentials to be worthy of review…," etc.

Of course, the cover letter should be neat, error-free, positive, and professional looking. The cover letter and your résumé will get you to the next step: the interview. You may also be asked to fill out an application. Have a copy of your résumé handy to help you provide accurate and complete information. In addition, having your résumé on hand will show how organized and responsible you are.

9.4b   The Employment Application

In addition to a résumé and cover letter, often an employer will ask that you fill out an application. You might be required to fill out the application first, or you might be asked to fill it out just prior to the interview. If you are scheduled for an interview, it is a good idea to arrive fifteen to twenty minutes early to not only show your professionalism but to give yourself time to fill out an application if required. Make sure to bring a pen, your résumé, and any other required documentation.

Fill out your application neatly and carefully. Be sure to read all instructions and address any gaps in your employment history. It's a good idea to put "negotiable" under your desired wage or salary. Proofread your application before handing it in to make sure you have followed the instructions and that it's free of any errors!

Complete Exercise 9-8 to create a *personal information sheet*. This sheet contains information commonly requested on job applications and will give you a head start when it comes time to fill out an employment application.

Exercise 9-8   Personal Information Sheet

Fill in the employment form categories with your current information.

Name _____

Address _____

Telephone Number _____

Email Address _____

Position Desired _____

Salary Desired _____

Education/Degrees/Certifications (include school[s] and dates)

_____

_____

_____

Honors and Awards

_____

_____

Professional Associations

_____

_____

Work Experience (include names and addresses of employers, positions held, and dates)

_____

_____

_____

Computer Skills

_____

_____

Military Service/Training

_____

_____

Any Physical Disabilities or Significant Medical History

_____

_____

_____

Any Felony Convictions

_____

_____

Names and Contact Information of References

_____

_____

_____

_____

_____

9.5   The Interview

Your cover letter, résumé, and application are all designed to get you an interview. Now you will be evaluated face to face on your interpersonal skills and professionalism. The following qualities are critical.

9.5a   The Three P's: Punctuality, Professionalism, and Preparation

You've heard the saying, "You never get a second chance to make a great first impression." If you are late for your interview, the interviewer will notice. Anticipate any obstacles, such as traffic or childcare arrangements, and make sure you have a backup plan.

"Interview fact from a contributing author: Be yourself, be confident, and remember you are the competition."

Doug Reed

Your personal appearance is also important in making that first impression. Make sure you are dressed in appropriate business attire. Avoid cologne or perfume in case someone on the search committee has allergies. If you carry a cell phone, make sure it is off during your interview.

Research the company and organization. You should at least be familiar with their webpage. If the company has a mission statement, be prepared to discuss how you fit in with their philosophy. Make sure you are aware of the organizational structure and how you might fit into it.

9.5b   Interview Questions

The following are typical interview questions you should be prepared to answer:

- Tell us about yourself.
- What assets would you bring to this position if we were to hire you?
- What are your strengths?
- What are your weaknesses?
- Where do you see yourself five years from now? Ten years from now?
- What types of work situations do you enjoy?
- What types of work situations do you find frustrating? How do you handle them?

These are just a few of the questions you might be asked. Remember, most schools have a career services office with staff that can help you prepare by doing mock (practice) interviews.

Your Own Interview Questions for the Interviewer:

- What opportunities does your organization provide for professional development?
- What qualities are you looking for in the next (name of position)?
- What is the best thing about working for this organization?
- Does your organization provide any type of tuition assistance for further education?
- How do you measure and reward high-quality and excellent performance?

- Would it be possible to talk with some of your employees currently working in this or a similar position?

Other Interview Tips:

- Treat everyone with respect and courtesy during the interview process. Others, such as the receptionist in the waiting area, may be asked their opinion.

- Be friendly and open. Greet everyone you meet with good eye contact, a firm handshake, and a positive facial expression.

- Do not criticize past employers.

- Follow up after the interview with a brief thank you letter for their time and consideration.

- Go on many interviews to get practice. Try Exercise 9-9, a mock interview.

Exercise 9-9   Mock Interview: *Position Announcement*

Imagine that the information desk on your campus has an opening for a student worker. The position requires a working knowledge of campus office functions and locations, the ability to multitask, and strong customer service skills. Résumés and cover letters can be submitted to the Student Life Office, and interviews will be scheduled within the next two weeks.

With another student, conduct a mock interview with each of you taking turns as the interviewer and the applicant. Prepare a list of questions or use the ones listed earlier. Evaluate each other on the following:

Quality of answers:_____

_____

Quality of appearance: _____

_____

Communication skills:_____

_____

Job knowledge:_____

_____

Suggestions for improvement: _____

_____

Strong Interest Inventory®   This is an assessment that may be available online or through your campus career services or counseling center. The assessment asks questions about your coursework preferences, work preferences, and personality traits to determine possible career paths you may wish to explore. This is one of the most frequently used career planning tools.

The Keirsey Temperament Sorter®-II (KTS®-II)   This assessment can be taken at keirsey.com. It measures personality traits, which can be helpful before beginning a job search. A mini KTS-II assessment is available free with registration.

The Occupational Outlook Handbook   Published annually by the U.S. Department of Labor, this resource provides an overview of many careers, including median pay, typical entry-level education, work experience required, and job outlook (whether it's a growing field). The handbook can be accessed online. Many libraries carry print copies as well.

9.6   Developing Your Leadership Potential

It's likely that your academic journey is just beginning. The topics within this book are designed to set you on the right path. However, the goal of this book is not just to help you succeed in school—it's also to help you succeed in your future career. Before you know it, your academic journey will end, and you will have the opportunity to emerge as a leader. Increasingly, employers are looking for leadership potential in the people they hire. The first step in leadership development is learning more about yourself—something this book has already helped you do. Now do Exercise 9-10, a simple internet activity designed to show you the vastness of what's been said about leadership.

Exercise 9-10   Searching for Leaders

Choose your favorite search engine and enter the word *leadership*.

How many results did you find? _____

The author got 366 million sites—wow!

Now search for "Leadership Development + Books."

How many results did you get? _____

9.6a   Identifying Leaders and Their Characteristics

Interestingly, just about everyone has written something about leadership, as you learned in Exercise 9-10. Now it's time to formulate *your own* understanding of leadership. What are your thoughts on leadership? What has your experience been as a leader? What about the leaders you've interacted with? Once you've explored these questions, we will consider a basic definition or description and ask the most important question: *Do you have what it takes to be a leader?*

One of the best methods to learn about any subject is to study examples. Leaders serve as excellent examples for us to investigate. Start by naming an effective leader. Then ask yourself what characteristics or traits make this person successful in their leadership. Let's see what you think by completing Exercise 9-11.

Exercise 9-11   What Makes a Leader?

Complete the chart by:

1. Listing people you believe are outstanding leaders in their respective fields. (You may select two or three from each area.)

2. Listing the specific characteristics each leader possesses that make them successful.

Names of Leaders within This Field or Profession	Characteristics		
Sports			
1.	1.	2.	3.
2.	1.	2.	3.
3.	1.	2.	3.
Business			
1.	1.	2.	3.
2.	1.	2.	3.
3.	1.	2.	3.
Government			
1.	1.	2.	3.
2.	1.	2.	3.
3.	1.	2.	3.
Historical Figure			
1.	1.	2.	3.
2.	1.	2.	3.
3.	1.	2.	3.

(continues)

Names of Leaders within This Field or Profession	Characteristics		
Entertainment			
1.	1.	2.	3.
2.	1.	2.	3.
3.	1.	2.	3.
Religion			
1.	1.	2.	3.
2.	1.	2.	3.
3.	1.	2.	3.
Family			
1.	1.	2.	3.
2.	1.	2.	3.
3.	1.	2.	3.
Education			
1.	1.	2.	3.
2.	1.	2.	3.
3.	1.	2.	3.
Field or Profession of Your Choice			
1.	1.	2.	3.
2.	1.	2.	3.
3.	1.	2.	3.

With a group of friends or as an entire class, prepare a list of the most frequently selected leaders. Generate a chart of the top choices. Discuss among your team or class what makes these leaders special. Make a list of the common characteristics shared by your top choices. Perhaps a Top 10 list would be appropriate.

Now create your own list of leadership traits in Exercise 9-12.

Exercise 9-12   Leadership Traits

Based on the results of Exercise 9-11, create a short list of the most important characteristics of a leader.

1. _____

2. _____

3. _____

4. _____

5. _____

Now you have created your own definition of a leader!

9.6b   Key Ingredients of Effective Leadership

Remember our metaphor for teamwork where the magnifying glass focused and intensified the rays of sunlight (the efforts of each team member) to ignite a fire (achieve their goal)? A leader is that individual who can unite us and ignite us. Some people see leaders as superheroes: the most valuable player on a team, the award winning director of a movie, the gold medal winner, and so on.

But think about the fact that each person is a leader in his or her own life. You must *lead yourself* through personal growth and your professional career through your daily actions, the goals you strive to achieve, the teams you join, and the results of your choices and decisions. Look at your list from Exercise 9-12. These characteristics can serve as a guide to becoming a successful leader both professionally and in your personal life. Look to those leaders you respect and let them serve as your guides, role models, and coaches. Remember, you're already a leader in your own life—now it's just a matter of becoming the *best* leader you can be at home, at school, and at work.

9.6c   What Makes Someone a Leader?

People often think leaders are born that way. They might say things like, "Who, me?" and "No! I just don't *have what it takes* to be a leader."

This *negative attitude* can become a *self-fulfilling prophecy*, preventing that person from ever reaching their full leadership potential. You *all* have what it takes to become leaders if you invest the time and energy to develop your leadership skills. Let's look at four primary ingredients to developing individual leadership potential. What special things do leaders *H.A.V.E.*? Leaders have **H**eart, **A**ttitude, **V**ision, and **E**nergy!

Heart   One thing we all share is the desire to be recognized and appreciated when we do something well. This sense of accomplishment, along with recognition, helps keep us motivated. As leaders, we need to build relationships and demonstrate that we care and want others to succeed. Sincerity, recognition of a job well done, and encouraging, heartfelt feedback are all part of successful leadership.

All leaders must earn the respect and trust of the people following them. People can tell when someone is leading from the heart. These leaders are the ones who bring hope and possibility.

One obstacle to becoming a caring leader is low self-esteem. After all, how can you become a compassionate leader if you aren't first compassionate toward yourself? Leadership is as *intrapersonal* as it is *interpersonal*—meaning as much as it is about working with others, it is also about self-development.

In Exercise 9-13, you will look at your self-confidence and accountability. Like self-esteem, these are important components of leadership.

Exercise 9-13   Analyzing Your Self-Confidence and Accountability

To answer the following questions, identify the last time you were part of a team at home, work, or school:

_____

1. Were you fully involved and energized in your activities with others? _____

2. Did you frequently review your own actions and work? _____

3. Did you develop a plan for how to improve?_____

4. Did you accept responsibility for your actions and choices?_____

5. Did you speak up for yourself and your beliefs?_____

6. Did you set goals and monitor your progress? _____

7. Did you do what you said you were going to do? _____

If you said "no" to any of these questions, then you have identified some areas for improvement. Effective leaders always strive for improvement. Reframe each "problem" area as an opportunity for positive change (remember the integrated thinking process from the chapter on creative thinking and decision-making). What and how can you improve? Perhaps someone you respect and admire can offer some suggestions.

Attitude   What attitude do you project? Simply put, attitudes really come in two types: positive and negative. We pretty much pick an attitude and run with it each day. (An interesting question: Because each of us has two attitude choices, why would anyone want to pick the negative one?)

One characteristic of attitudes, both positive and negative, is their *contagious* nature—they spread from one person to another. A negative attitude can tear down a team, and a positive attitude can lift them up. A leader must embrace a positive attitude, providing hope and promise to his or her followers. We all know individuals who exude a positive attitude and possess a bright outlook on life. They are much more fun to be around, in both work and play, and help contribute to a more productive work environment.

Leaders must set the tone for the task at hand. They must light the way with a positive attitude. Embracing a can-do attitude gives the team hope and helps the team reach its potential. Explore the power of attitude in Exercise 9-14.

Exercise 9-14   Power of a Positive Attitude

Write down an experience in which keeping a positive attitude helped you achieve a positive result:

_____

_____

_____

_____

_____

_____

Vision   When you think of vision, you might think of your ability to see. But when we say *leaders have vision*, we are referring to a special mindset. In this context, vision can be defined as a combination of goals that together create a grand picture of the future. As we'll discuss in a moment, it takes *energy* to make that vision a reality.

One description of a leader is *a person you would follow to a place you wouldn't get to by yourself.* To reinforce this description, let's look at Martin Luther King Jr.'s famous 1963 speech, which painted a picture of his dream for the future.

> I say to you today, my friends, that in spite of the difficulties and frustrations of the moment, I still have a dream. It is a dream deeply rooted in the American dream … Free at last!

Dr. King's speech that afternoon painted a vivid image, or vision, of a destination, and he inspired others to want to arrive at that destination. Write about your personal vision in Exercise 9-15.

Exercise 9-15   What Is Your Vision?

What is your personal vision for your life during the next five years? You can include details from all areas of your life, including family, career, education, spirituality, finances, and your personal life—anything and everything you can think of:

_____

_____

_____

_____

Map some SMART goals for your vision. What actions must you take between now and then to accomplish your vision?

1. _____

2. _____

3. _____

Remember: Vision with action can change the world—and your future, as well.

Energy   Once a leader has won over their team by leading with heart, has established a can-do attitude, and has come up with and communicated a vision for the future, that leader must be able to motivate their team to fulfill objectives, reach goals, achieve purposes, and, ultimately, realize that vision. A leader must be energized and be able to energize others. The engine that drives the team forward requires fuel. That fuel is enthusiasm. Ralph Waldo Emerson put it perfectly, "Nothing great was ever achieved without enthusiasm."

In Exercise 9-16, describe where you get *your* energy.

Exercise 9-16   Where Do You Get Your Energy?

Think of a time when you had to complete a major project (at school, home, or work) and needed a lot of energy to do it. Describe how you came up with the energy to get it done.

_____

_____

_____

_____

Exercise 9-17   Chapter Summation

This final exercise gets right to the heart of leadership (and maybe even life). Explain in your own words what the following saying means to you: "The best way to lead is by example."

_____

_____

_____

_____

_____

Remember, getting hired for that great job is just the beginning. It is important to make a lasting positive impression by demonstrating that you are committed to your work. In addition, you need to show dependability, interpersonal skills, leadership, and team skills, along with a desire for continuous improvement.

Healthy Decision-Making

Robert's résumé and cover letter have gotten him an interview with a company he knows little about other than its reputation for being a great place to work. The position seems like it is a perfect fit. He knows the competition is tough, but he feels that if he presents himself well at his interview, he has a good chance of getting the job. What steps can Robert take to ensure he does his best during the interview?

_____

_____

_____

_____

_____

_____

_____

_____

_____

Enhancing Your Personal Health

Taking Care of Yourself Along the Journey

Objectives

By the end of this chapter, you will be able to:

- Develop a personal fitness plan for your body, mind, and spirit

- Develop healthy eating and sleeping habits

- Understand disease prevention (or "how not to be sick for that big test!")

- Understand depression

- Understand and prevent addiction

- Make healthy lifestyle choices

Why Learn This Skill?

The journey through this book began with a focus on you; then we discussed your interactions with others; now we will end this journey by bringing the focus back to you. The three things you will carry with you throughout your journey in life, no matter where you go, are your body, mind, and spirit. This chapter discusses these areas.

Messages about health and wellness are everywhere—you hear them in television commercials, social media posts, and by word of mouth. Worse, these messages often offer completely different advice, and that advice seems to change weekly. Eat carbohydrates and avoid fats! No, wait—carbs are out, fats are in! Which is more important, strength training or aerobic exercise?

One of the most important personal choices you will ever make will be the decision about what kind of lifestyle you want to live. Choices you make now will have a big effect on your future health and quality of life. Will you eat properly and exercise? Will you get enough sleep to recharge your body? Will you avoid doing illegal drugs, smoking, and drinking alcohol in excess? Will you avoid risky behaviors that can have serious consequences? These are *your* choices, and what you choose will greatly impact your health, wealth, and success in life.

Let's begin with the effects of peer pressure. We often talk about peer pressure as a negative influence, but what about peers and role models who promote good, healthy lifestyles? Think about it. Do you think it's a coincidence that people who make healthy choices tend to hang out in groups (or that people who make unhealthy choices do the same)? Making a *conscious choice* to surround yourself with people who make good choices can go a long way to helping you stay on track.

Taking individual responsibility and *making informed choices* are two key skills for living a healthy life. To make good choices, you need to be well-informed. This chapter provides a foundation of information concerning your overall health. Over your lifetime, you will be flooded with health information from many sources. Just look at the number of "miracle diets" and "miracle pills" on TV and the internet. Read—and analyze what you read—about health products and routines, and check out their safety and usefulness using multiple *reliable* sources before deciding to try them. Even though the internet is a wonderful source of information, it includes a lot of junk science that is more opinion than fact. Also, be very skeptical of those jazzy TV commercials with fine print you can never read. Trusting the wrong product or advice can have extremely negative consequences for your health.

(Please note: None of the information in this chapter is meant to substitute for medical advice. Consult with your physician or health-care provider about any personal changes you plan to make.)

10.1   Introduction

If you have ever been seriously ill, you know that without your health, nothing seems to matter except getting better. When you hear the word *health*, you may think about it in terms of being sick or well. However, there is so much more to it. The term *wellness* refers to how you are doing in every way—physically and mentally. To achieve overall wellness, you need to maintain *balance* and *moderation* in life.

Benjamin Franklin believed that these two things were the key to a happy, successful life.

This chapter is going to cut through any conflicting or confusing information you may have heard about health with a back to basics approach. While these recommendations can in no way replace advice from your doctor, they are concepts that have stood the test of time and that really work. In this chapter, you will read some background information for each topic, which is followed by key points to take home and to use in the future. With each topic, we will ask you to commit to *one* change that will help you to create a healthier life, no matter where you stand right now. Let's get started by informing ourselves about some basic health issues so we can make the best possible choices.

10.2   Physical Health and Mental Wellness

Several lifestyle factors affect our physical and mental wellness. These include what we eat, whether we exercise, our quality of sleep, what steps we take to prevent disease, and the behaviors we choose. We will explore each of these areas separately, but they are all connected.

10.2a   Nutrition

What and how much you eat plays a critical role in your overall health. First, assess your nutritional habits in Exercise 10-1.

Exercise 10-1   Evaluate Your Current Eating Habits

Answer the questions using the following scale:

3 points = I do this daily
2 points = I do this three to five days per week
1 point = I do this one to two days a week
0 points = I do this less than once a week

_____ I eat several servings of fresh fruits and vegetables.

_____ I drink six to eight glasses water.

_____ I eat a variety of foods.

_____ I avoid most sweets and junk food.

_____ I make sure my diet includes essential vitamins and minerals.

_____ I eat a diet low in saturated fats and _cholesterol_ (a kind of fat that is thought to contribute to

obesity and heart disease).

_____ I eat only when I'm hungry, _not_ when I feel an emotional "need" to eat.

_____ I eat to maintain a healthy weight.

_____ Point total

Where did you score?

24 points:	You have excellent nutrition habits.
20–23 points:	You have good habits but could improve.
16–19 points:	You are doing okay but could improve.
Below 15 points:	You have poor eating habits that are greatly affecting your health.

10.2b   Basic Nutritional Concepts

The only thing you put in your car's tank is fuel. If you filled it up with anything else, your car would run poorly or break down. The same can be said for our bodies. Healthy food provides the fuel our bodies need, but junk food can slow you down or even cause major health problems.

The three basic types of food are proteins, carbohydrates, and fats. _Protein_, found in meat, fish, eggs, nuts, dairy products, beans, and even vegetables, is needed for energy and so our bodies can grow and repair themselves. _Carbohydrates_, found in bread, rice, fruits, and vegetables, are our main source of energy. Some carbohydrates also contain _fiber_, which helps digestion. _Fats_, found in meat, nuts, oils, and dairy products, are often thought of as "bad for you," but a _moderate_ amount of _some_ fats is actually an important part of a healthy diet. Fats are either _saturated_ (solid at room temperature, like butter) or _unsaturated_ (liquid at room temperature, like olive oil). Generally speaking, you should avoid saturated fats and eat only a moderate amount of unsaturated fat.

The foods we eat have traditionally been broken down into the five food groups shown in Table 10-1.

Table 10-1   The Five Basic Food Groups

Food Group	Example of Foods	Nutritional Note
Grains	Whole grain bread, cereals, rice, pasta	Be careful of sweetened cereals and doughnuts, which contain grains but also a lot of sugar. A little sugar is all right—after all, fresh fruit contains sugar—but too much is very bad for your health.
Vegetables	Broccoli, carrots, corn, peas, spinach, lettuce	Fresh vegetables are better than canned vegetables, which lose most of their nutritional value and often have sugar, salt, or other things added; however, all vegetables are good for you. You should wash fresh vegetables and fruits before eating them to get rid of any harmful residue.
Fruits	Apples, peaches, pears, oranges	Like with vegetables, fresh fruit is best because many canned fruits contain added sugar and much lower nutrient values.
Dairy	Milk, ice cream, cheese, yogurt	Skim milk and nonfat yogurt have the least fat. Whole milk, ice cream, and cheese have higher fat content and should be eaten in small amounts.
Meat, poultry, fish, eggs, beans, and nuts	Turkey, beef, tuna, salmon, peanuts, walnuts, black beans, hummus	This group is high in protein and fat. However, you can cut down on fat by making smart choices. For example, buy canned tuna packed in water instead of oil, and use lean ground beef instead of the fatty kind.

Food for Thought

It is a common misconception that fat is bad for you. This is not true. Our bodies need all three food types: carbohydrates, proteins, *and* fats. Again, the key is maintaining the proper balance, eating the right types of food and the right types of fat.

- Avoid trans fats
- Limit saturated fats
- Consume unsaturated and Omega-3 fatty acids moderately

The U.S. Department of Agriculture (USDA) uses the MyPlate model to show you what a healthy plate of food should look like. These portion sizes give you an idea of how to balance your diet. For example, it shows you that fruits and vegetables should cover half of your plate, with slightly more veggies than fruits. However, because not everyone is the same sex, height, shape, age, or fitness level, remember to be flexible in what you eat. The MyPlate model is a good starting point, but you should also *listen to your body* when determining your diet. Some of us may have adverse reactions to foods, ranging from allergies to certain nuts or intolerance to gluten or dairy to finding out that certain foods "just don't agree with you." Only you know how you react to certain foods, so pay attention to how you feel after you eat and adjust your diet accordingly.

More information about MyPlate and resources for a more personalized approach to nutrition can be found at ChooseMyPlate.gov, a site maintained by the USDA. In the meantime, here are a few key concepts to remember:

- Eat a balanced diet with a variety of foods.

- Eat several servings of produce (especially fresh, raw fruits and vegetables) per day. Cooking vegetables makes them less nutritious, but it's all right to lightly sauté or steam them.

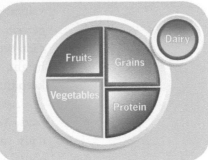

- Eat fats *in moderation only*. Although your body needs some fats, high levels of saturated fats can lead to higher levels of bad cholesterol, which can contribute to obesity and heart disease. Fats found in olive oil, avocados, and nuts (also called poly- and monounsaturated fats) can be good for you in balanced amounts.

- Limit sweets in your diet. Sweets (sugar, jellies, candy, soft drinks) contain sugar that has a lot of empty calories and can lead to obesity and diabetes. If you must use a sweetener, try substituting honey for sugar and avoid high-fructose corn syrup. (It's thought that eating local honey may actually help with seasonal allergies.) Consider this: A teaspoon of sugar weighs roughly 4 grams. Most 20-ounce bottles of soda contain 60–70 grams of sugar (usually in the form of high-fructose corn syrup). That's almost a third of a cup! Would you sit there and eat a third of a cup of sugar straight? I hope not! But that's essentially what you're doing when you drink a bottle of soda.

- Avoid or limit alcohol.

- Cut down on portion sizes. Many restaurants give us way more food than is healthy to eat in one sitting, so don't be afraid to take home leftovers. Try counting your calories. You'll find it's more difficult than you think to stay under 2,000 calories, which is the standard recommendation. In addition, give yourself time to digest your meal. It takes around ten to twenty minutes for our brains to realize that we are full, so it can be easy to overeat. Remember: You should *eat to live*, not *live to eat*.

- Drink six to eight glasses of water every day. Staying hydrated is an important part of nutrition!

10.2c   Read the Label

You should always read the "Nutrition Facts" label on packaged food and drinks, and it's also smart to check the ingredients. Did you know that the ingredients on packaged foods and drinks are listed in order from the highest to the lowest amount? If the first ingredient is sugar or high-fructose corn syrup, that means the food or drink has more sugar than any other ingredient. Try looking for a healthier alternative. *Trans fats* (found in *hydrogenated* and *partially hydrogenated* oils) are thought to be very bad for you, so avoid them as much as possible. Look for foods labeled "no preservatives," and if you see an ingredient on the list that you've never heard of (or can't even pronounce), don't be afraid to look it up! You wouldn't pick up a strange item from the ground and eat it (I hope), so make sure you know what you're putting in your mouth when you purchase packaged food!

A product's nutrition facts tell you how much fat (including different kinds of fat), sodium (salt), carbohydrates (including sugar), and protein are in the product. This information is expressed using two

Nutrition Facts

8 servings per container

Serving size 2/3 cup (55g)

Amount per serving

Calories **230**

	% Daily Value*
Total Fat 8g	10%
Saturated Fat 1g	5%
Trans Fat 0g	
Cholesterol 0mg	0%
Sodium 160mg	7%
Total Carbohydrate 37g	13%
Dietary Fiber 4g	14%
Total Sugars 12g	
Includes 10g Added Sugars	20%
Protein 3g	
Vitamin D 2mcg	10%
Calcium 260mg	20%
Iron 8mg	45%
Potassium 235mg	6%

* The % Daily Value (DV) tells you how much a nutrient in a serving of food contributes to a daily diet. 2,000 calories a day is used for general nutrition advice.

Source: https://www.fda.gov/Food/GuidanceRegulation/ GuidanceDocumentsRegulatoryInformation/ LabelingNutrition/ucm385663.htm

values: *weight*, usually listed in grams (g) or milligrams (mg), and the amount as a *percent of your daily value*. This percentage is based on the recommended amount of each type of food an average adult should eat in a day. Depending on your age, sex, height, weight, and special dietary needs, you may need more or less than average, so keep that in mind.

Also remember to check the number of servings when you read the nutrition facts. You might think a product is healthy because it only has 25 percent of your daily value of saturated fat. Look a little closer, however, and you might realize the container has five servings. If you eat it all, you will have eaten more than the amount of saturated fat you're supposed to eat in an entire day! The same goes for other ingredients, such as sugar or salt, as well as the calories listed. To figure out how many calories are in the entire container, you have to multiply the calorie amount per serving by the number of servings per container. If the nutrition facts say a product contains 230 calories per serving, and there are 8 servings per container, that's 1,840 calories for the entire container. An average adult should eat 2,000 calories a day. If you ate that whole container of food, you would have eaten almost all the calories you need that day! The same multiplication can be done for any item on the nutrition facts label.

Reading and understanding food labels is one of the most important things you can do for your health. Becoming more *knowledgeable* and *aware* of what you are putting in your body is Step 1. Step 2 is *changing* what you put in your body. Avoid ingredients that are bad for you and focus on finding healthy alternatives. Beyond fats, carbohydrates, and protein, vitamins and minerals are also listed on the nutrition facts label. By paying attention to these labels, you can make sure you're getting all the necessary nutrients for a healthy body and a good life.

Food for Thought

Proper diet and hydration are important for healthy skin. This is another reason to drink *at least* six to eight glasses of water a day. Other beverages, like alcohol and caffeinated drinks, are not hydrating like water is. In fact, they can lead to dehydration. Another factor that contributes to healthy skin is sun exposure. While sunlight is important for the production of vitamin D in your body, you should limit your sun exposure to prevent skin cancer. Some forms of skin cancer are treatable; others can kill you. The effect of the sun adds up over time, and severe sunburns in childhood can have awful consequences in adulthood. There are several ways to prevent excessive sun exposure. First, minimize your time in the sun between 10 a.m. and 4 p.m. because this is when the sun's rays are most intense. Wear long-sleeved shirts when possible as well as brimmed hats and sunglasses (polarized for UV protection, and consider wraparounds for blocking all angles). Finally, use sunscreen properly. See Figure 10-1, which shows a skin cancer patient. Lastly, your skin can be affected by smoking, which causes premature aging.

10.2d Vitamins and Minerals

Vitamins have specific jobs in your body (see Table 10-2). Minerals like calcium are needed for strong bones and teeth. However, be careful and informed about taking nutritional supplements. Taking too much (especially of vitamins A, D, E, and K) can actually harm the body because these substances can build up to toxic levels that damage your liver and kidneys. Try to get vitamins and minerals from the foods you eat instead of a pill.

So, what are the key points about vitamins and minerals?

- Although vitamin and mineral supplements can play an important role in your health, most experts agree that it is best to get these important nutrients from eating a healthy, well-balanced diet.

- Stay informed, and consult your physician concerning nutritional supplements.

Now that you are informed on nutrition, what changes would you make? Set a goal in Exercise 10-2.

Chapter 10: Enhancing Your Personal Health

Table 10-2 Vitamins: Functions and Sources

Vitamin	Needed for	Examples of Food Containing This Vitamin
Vitamin A	Vision, development of bones and teeth, infection resistance, healthy skin	Meat, eggs, dairy, dark green and yellow vegetables, carrots and fruits (tomatoes)
Vitamin B (several types)	Healthy nervous system, energy, normal digestion	Whole-grain products, meats, poultry, dark leafy vegetables
Vitamin C	Infection resistance, development of bones and teeth, wound healing	Citrus fruits, many raw fruits and vegetables such as green bell peppers, brussels sprouts
Vitamin D	Development of bones and teeth	Dairy products (also produced when your skin is exposed sunlight)
Vitamin E	Muscle growth, wound healing (may help fertility and prevent certain cancers)	Wheat germ, vegetables such as swiss chard, spinach, kale, and broccoli
Vitamin K	Needed for proper blood clotting	Green leafy vegetables

10.2e Exercise and Wellness

Proper exercise gives us energy, tones our body, improves our heart health, and is a vital component to our overall wellness. First, assess your exercise habits in Exercise 10-3.

Figure 10-1   Skin cancer

Knowing that skin cancer can be prevented, come up with two to three steps you will take to protect your skin.

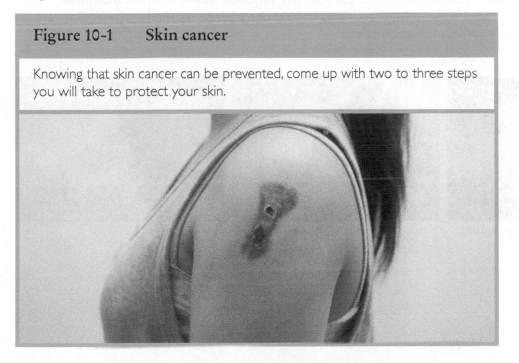

Exercise 10-2 Your Nutrition Plan

Changing your diet is difficult because much of it has become habit. From what you have read so far, pick *one* strategy to improve your diet and write a specific goal regarding the change. Remember to include a target date for when you plan to reach your goal. Many behavioral psychologists feel you need to practice a new habit for at least thirty days for it to become a permanent change. When this *one* positive diet change becomes a way of life, pick another.

Positive diet change goal: _____

_____

_____

_____

Exercise 10-3 What Is Your Current Level of Physical Activity?

Place a checkmark beside any description that fits your life:

_____ I exercise at least three days a week so my heart gets pumping and I sweat.

_____ I walk and take stairs whenever I can.

_____ I do strength training exercises at least two times per week (weight lifting, push-ups, etc.).

_____ I stretch my muscles at least two times per week.

_____ I'm involved in a sport or recreational activity (such as hiking or bicycling) that requires physical activity.

Ideally, all these descriptions should fit your life (unless you have a medical reason to limit any of these activities). If any items are not checked, make it your goal to have one of them checked by the end of next month. Then tackle another until they're all checked. Remember to work on just one at a time.

Exercise is a key ingredient to health.

Although a proper diet is important, it is just one factor in your overall wellness. Diet and exercise go hand in hand. Benefits of exercise and a healthy diet include:

- **Growth and protection of your bones**   A diet rich in calcium and vitamins helps maintain good bone growth and development. In addition to diet, weight-bearing exercise is also beneficial in maintaining healthy bones over a lifetime.

- **Percentage of muscle versus fat**   A higher percentage of muscle makes you stronger, more energetic, and releases *endorphins* ("feel-good" chemicals in the brain).

- **Aging**   Some studies show that exercise increases your number of brain cells, prevents Alzheimer's disease, and slows the aging process. (See, exercise can help your grades!)

Of course, always check with your physician before beginning any exercise program. There are two basic types of exercise: *aerobic* (also known as cardiopulmonary) and *nonaerobic* (things like strength and flexibility training). You should do both kinds regularly. Aerobic exercise gets your pulse pumping and sweat pouring. Examples include running and basketball. Aerobic exercise is best for heart and lung health and in turning body fat to muscle. Nonaerobic exercise involves working to improve muscle strength, endurance, and flexibility, and includes activities like weight lifting, yoga, and stretching. (See Table 10-3.) Like with any dietary supplements, be wary of muscle enhancement drugs. Many are dangerous and have serious side effects. Again, careful, critical investigation is the best rule to follow when considering supplements and changes to your routine.

Food for Thought

A diet low in saturated fats (remember, we all need some fat, but not all fats are healthy), high in fiber, and rich in fruit and vegetables will help keep your heart healthy. However, diet alone is not enough for a healthy heart. Regular exercise—even something as simple as brisk walking for thirty minutes a day, three to four times a week—also helps keep your heart strong. Of course, the right length and intensity for your exercise routine depends on many factors.

Table 10-3 Types of Exercise		
Exercise Type*	**Benefits**	**Examples**
Aerobic (or cardiopulmonary)	Strengthens your heart and lungs	Dance, running, swimming, and active sports such as basketball
Strength (nonaerobic)	Strengthens and develops different muscle groups	Weight training, push-ups, and sit-ups
Flexibility (nonaerobic)	Helps prevent injuries	Stretching and yoga

*Note: Some exercises combine multiple types. For example, using light weights with many repetitions can help you include aerobic exercise in your weight training.

Now, take a minute to view the Activity Pyramid shown in Figure 10-2. Assess your level of activity in Exercise 10-4.

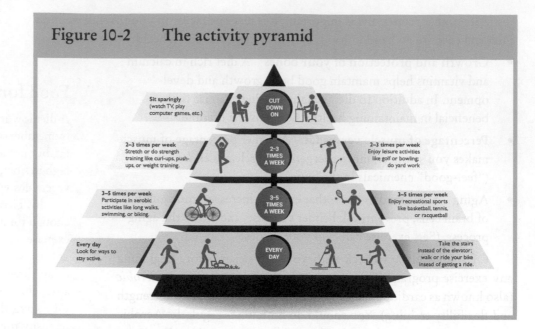

Figure 10-2   The activity pyramid

Exercise 10-4   How Active Are You?

Circle the number that best describes you.

I do exercises that...

1. don't make me sweat or raise my pulse.
2. raise my pulse a little.
3. raise my pulse somewhat.
4. make me sweat, breathe heavily, and raise my pulse a lot.
5. push me to the limit.

I exercise _____ times week.

1. 0–1
2. 2
3. 3
4. 4
5. 5 or more

I exercise for _____ minutes per session.

1. 0–5 minutes
2. 5–15 minutes
3. 16–30 minutes
4. 31–45 minutes
5. More than 45 minutes

Total score _____

3	Inactive—couch potato
4–6	Mildly active
7–9	Moderately active—satisfactory but could improve
10–12	Active—very good
13–15	Very active—you must be an athlete in training!

Regardless of your score, you can find a way to challenge yourself to the next level. If your score is 9 or below, however, we strongly encourage you to make *one* change that will improve your activity level. Come up with a SMART goal for that change:

_____

_____

_____

Here are some main points to keep in mind concerning exercise:

- Avoid being a couch potato. Make exercise a part of your daily life.

- Walk as much as possible; even short bursts of activity can add up. For example, don't spend time and gas looking for that one parking place that's just a little closer to the store. Take an evening stroll and enjoy the scenery. Take the stairs whenever you can.

- Enjoy physical activity, such as shoveling snow or mowing the grass.

- Find a recreational sport or activity (skiing, hiking, dancing) that requires movement and is fun for you. Variety will help you to stay with an exercise program, so mix it up.

- Try to socialize while exercising. Choose a partner who will help you stick with a program. Sign a contract so you both stick with it. Use goal-setting principles, such as writing down specific goals and rewarding yourself when you reach them.

- Always consult your physician about an appropriate and safe exercise program.

10.2f   Maintaining a Healthy Weight

For a long time, your *body mass index* (BMI) has been the main method used to figure out if you are a healthy weight. Your BMI uses both your height and your current weight to determine if you are underweight, a healthy weight, or overweight. You can also use it to figure out your "ideal" weight based on your height. However, this method doesn't take into account things like muscle mass and the *distribution* of fat (where your body stores the most fat), which can also affect your health. Another method that is gaining in popularity is taking a waist measurement. Too much "belly" fat is thought to put you at greater risk for things like type 2 diabetes and heart disease (see Figure 10-3).

You should have an idea of your ideal weight and make it your goal to reach and stay close to that weight. Being too overweight increases your risk of high blood pressure, heart disease, stroke, and diabetes. Being too far underweight increases your chance of osteoporosis (weak, brittle bones) and, on average, will shorten your life in comparison to healthy-weight people.

If you are overweight, you need to lose pounds by burning more calories than you eat. This can be done by eating less and exercising more. If you need to gain weight, you need to increase how much you eat (calories)—but you should still exercise to stay strong and to improve the health of your heart and lungs. Let's explore these two situations in more depth, beginning with being overweight.

Figure 10-3   Finding your BMI and waist measurement

Height	Weight (in pounds)																
4'10"	91	96	100	105	110	115	119	124	129	134	138	143	148	153	158	162	67
4'11"	94	99	104	109	114	119	124	128	133	138	143	148	153	158	163	168	173
5'0"	97	102	107	112	118	123	128	133	138	143	148	153	158	163	168	174	179
5'1"	100	106	111	116	122	127	132	137	143	148	153	158	164	169	174	180	185
5'2"	104	109	115	120	126	131	136	142	147	153	158	164	169	175	180	186	191
5'3"	107	113	118	124	130	135	141	146	152	158	163	169	175	180	186	191	197
5'4"	110	116	122	128	134	140	145	151	157	163	169	174	180	186	192	197	204
5'5"	114	120	126	132	138	144	150	156	162	168	174	180	186	192	198	204	210
5'6"	118	124	130	136	142	148	155	161	167	173	179	186	192	198	204	210	216
5'7"	121	127	134	140	146	153	159	166	172	178	185	191	198	204	211	217	223
5'8"	125	131	138	144	151	158	164	171	177	184	190	197	203	210	216	223	230
5'9"	128	135	142	149	155	162	169	176	182	189	196	203	209	216	223	230	236
5'10"	132	139	146	153	160	167	174	181	188	195	202	209	216	222	229	236	243
5'11"	136	143	150	157	165	172	179	186	193	200	208	215	222	229	236	243	250
6'0"	140	147	154	162	169	177	184	191	199	206	213	221	228	235	242	250	258
6'1"	144	151	159	166	174	182	189	197	204	212	219	227	235	242	250	257	265
6'2"	148	155	163	171	179	186	194	202	210	218	225	233	241	249	256	264	272
6'3"	152	160	168	176	184	192	200	208	216	224	232	240	248	256	264	272	279
6'4"	156	164	172	180	189	197	205	213	221	230	238	246	254	253	271	279	287
BMI	19	20	21	22	23	24	25	26	27	28	29	30	31	32	33	34	35
	Healthy Weight					**Overweight**					**Obese**						

Step 1: Find your height in the left column.

Step 2: Follow the row across until you come to your weight.

Step 3: Your BMI is at the bottom of the column under your height.

How to Take a Waist Measurement
Wrap a flexible tape measure around your bare waist, just above your hip bones.
The tape measure should be pulled tight, but it shouldn't dig into your skin.
Make sure it is level all the way around.
Breathe out and check the measurement.
Write it down here _____

For men, a waist size bigger than 40 inches is thought to put you at greater risk for weight-related illnesses like type 2 diabetes and heart disease.

For women, a waist size bigger than 35 inches is thought to put you at a greater risk for weight-related illnesses like type 2 diabetes and heart disease.

Source: Adapted from "Parent Tips: Knowing What Your Weight Means," by the National Heart, Lung, and Blood Institute; National Institutes of Health; U.S. Department of Health and Human Services. Retrieved at https://www.nhlbi.nih.gov/health/educational/wecan/downloads/yourweight.pdf.

Have you heard the not-too-flattering term "Freshman 15"? This refers to the fact that some students gain weight (around fifteen pounds) during their first year of school.

This weight gain might be due to stress eating and eating fast food (which we do not recommend). It doesn't happen to everyone, but even a five-pound gain can be the beginning of a lifelong problem. Here are some basic but effective ways to avoid the Freshman 15:

- Make good nutrition a permanent part of your lifestyle.
- Be careful of fad diets. These diets can be dangerous because many don't include necessary nutrients and vitamins, they can stress your kidneys, and they can cause heart disease. Always consult your doctor before beginning a diet.
- Drink more water. It is healthy, helps with digestion, and will take away some of your hunger.
- Eat more slowly. Remember, the brain takes ten to twenty minutes to register you are full. Give it time so you don't overeat. In addition, chewing your food thoroughly breaks down the foods and allows your digestive system to process it with more ease. It also allows you to enjoy the tastes longer!
- Eat at regular times, and don't skip breakfast. Eating breakfast is a good idea, especially if you eat foods such as fruit, whole-grain cereal or bread, low-fat or skim milk, and an occasional egg. It is also a good idea to eat smaller portions more often, spread out throughout the day, as opposed to shocking our system with large meals two to three times a day.
- Avoid emotional eating. Find healthy substitutes.
- Keep away from vending machines.
- Avoid eating late at night, especially right before bed, when your body will not have the opportunity to burn the calories.
- As we've already said, maintain a diet that is low in fat and cholesterol, contains plenty of fresh fruits and vegetables, and uses sweets and salt sparingly.
- If you drink alcohol, do so in moderation.

There is also the other extreme of being too far underweight. A starving or malnourished body can't grow, repair itself, or function. People who are excessively underweight often have contributing mental health issues, which may include eating disorders. Eating disorders involve out-of-control eating habits.

Anorexia nervosa is an eating disorder where individuals starve themselves out of fear that they look fat. Even when they are dangerously underweight, these individuals still see a fat person when they look in the mirror, so they continue to starve themselves to reach an impossible "ideal body." *Bulimia*, often called the binge-and-purge disease, is a condition in which an individual consumes a large amount of food and then deliberately vomits (or engages in other behavior to purge the food from the body). This disorder can cause serious digestive system problems. People with bulimia are usually aware that what they are doing is abnormal, whereas many with anorexia nervosa are not. Both conditions require both psychological and medical help.

10.2g Quality Sleep

Sleep is needed for the body to repair and recharge. Poor sleep leads to less energy, lack of focus, illness, irritability, forgetfulness, and decreased reaction time. It also means you are most likely wasting precious study time, not reading effectively, and making more mistakes. Naturally, your academic and personal life will suffer.

In ancient times, sleep was based on the natural cycle of light and darkness, day and night. The invention of light bulbs, TVs, and computers has changed this cycle. Most studies still show we need between seven and eight hours of *quality sleep* each night. Quality sleep is when our bodies go through natural cycles of uninterrupted sleep. During this time, we cycle through periods of light and deep sleep. When you reach deep sleep, your body goes into repair mode and your brain quiets down. Rapid eye movement (REM) sleep is when your brain is very active, but your body is still. During REM sleep, we dream. It's thought that dreams allow us to sort through our emotions and engage in creativity. These cycles flow naturally from one to the other and are necessary each night. Having your sleep frequently interrupted throws off these essential cycles and prevents the body and brain from properly recharging. Both the quantity (seven to eight hours) and the quality (complete cycles for brain and body) of sleep are important for your health.

Here are some tips to help ensure healthy sleep:

- The first step is to figure out if you are getting enough quality sleep. If you nod off or yawn excessively during class, you are sleep deprived.

- Keep a regular schedule. This trains your body to sleep and wake at certain times. Makes sure this schedule allows for enough sleep and follow it even on weekends.

- Reduce noise. If you can't get rid of the noise entirely, a white noise machine can help cover it up to prevent it from disrupting your sleep.

- Avoid naps because they may disrupt your normal sleep cycle.

- Sleep in a dark room. Light can keep you in the lighter stages of sleep.

- Avoid all-night study sessions.

- Wind down, not up, before bedtime. Listen to soothing music, meditate, or take a hot bath. Don't drink alcohol or caffeine (coffee, tea, chocolate, and cola) close to bedtime because they will prevent you from reaching deep sleep.

- Exercise regularly (but not within three hours of when you go to sleep).

- Make sure your sleeping area is comfortable.

- Don't lie in bed and worry about not sleeping. If you can't sleep, get up and do something boring until you get tired.

Do Exercise 10-5, and then improve the quality of your sleep by making one positive change. Happy dreams!

Food for Thought

Sleep deprivation contributes to thousands of car accidents each year. If you have any of the following symptoms while driving—excessive yawning, head nodding, inability to remember the last few miles, or drifting between lanes—you need to pull over immediately and get some rest. It is always best to have a driving partner on long or late trips.

Exercise 10-5   Improving the Quality of Your Sleep

Map out a plan: From what you have learned about getting quality sleep, choose *one* positive change you will make to improve your sleeping habits. Be specific, write down a SMART goal, and place it by your bed. Once you are successful in making this positive change, work on a new goal.

_____

_____

_____

10.2h   Preventing Illness

A healthy diet, exercise, and plenty of quality sleep are all needed for your *immune system* to work. Your immune system is what protects you from getting sick and what helps you heal if you do. Other factors can also assist your immune system.

- Wash your hands often to simply and effectively stop the spread of disease.

- Keep your *immunizations* (vaccinations) up to date. These important shots help prepare your immune system to fight off known diseases. The Centers for Disease Control and Prevention (CDC) website has information on what immunizations you should get and when. Many schools recommend meningitis vaccines because outbreaks are related to living in close quarters, such as dormitories. Some people think shots are needed only in childhood—but this is incorrect. Flu shots are just one example of an immunization that is important for adults and the elderly.

- If you ever need to take antibiotics, make sure you follow the directions for the prescription, and don't stop taking them until the entire prescription has been used. Do not stop taking the antibiotics because you've started to feel better. If you stop short of finishing the prescription, you will still have harmful bacteria in your system. Worse, these bacteria may be stronger and resistant to the antibiotics you were taking. *Drug-resistant infections* (bacteria that aren't affected by common antibiotics) are a real threat and can cause *epidemics* (when many people get the same infection or disease in a community).

- Prevent the spread of *sexually transmitted diseases* (STDs). STDs can harm your reproductive system or even kill you and can be transmitted through unprotected sex of any kind (including oral sex). See Table 10-4 for a listing of STDs from the CDC. The spread of STDs can be reduced or stopped by using safe sex practices, such as using condoms or practicing *abstinence* (not having sex at all).

Food for Thought

Sex with condoms isn't totally safe—just less risky. You can still get a STD, although the risk is greatly reduced, and condoms are *not* 100 percent effective in preventing pregnancy, even when used properly. Human error (using them incorrectly) can make them even less effective.

Table 10-4   Sexually Transmitted Diseases

Disease	Type	Symptoms
Herpes	Viral (herpes simplex virus type 2); can't be cured, though some medications can help manage it	Male: blisters on penis Female: blisters in and around vagina
Gonorrhea	Bacterial; cured with antibiotics	Discharge of pus, painful and frequent urination; can lead to *sterility* (the inability to have children)
Chlamydia	Bacterial; cured with antibiotics	Discharge, burning, and itching in genital area; can lead to sterility
Syphilis	Bacterial; cured with antibiotics	Early symptoms include painless sores followed by a rash. The symptoms may go away, but the disease has not. If left untreated, the final stage can result in death.
Genital warts	Viral (caused by human papillomavirus, HPV)	Cauliflower-like growths on penis and vagina
AIDS (acquired immune deficiency syndrome)	Viral; the HIV virus cripples the immune system; can't be cured, but drugs can slow the disease	Several symptoms related to weakened immune system

Note: Sexually Transmitted Diseases (STDs) are also known as Sexually Transmitted Infections (STIs)

Even with the best precautions, you can still get sick—maybe even sick enough to need medical help. Sometimes it is difficult to know when to go to a doctor. When in doubt, you should always go because it is better to be safe than sorry. Exercise 10-6 will help you begin a personal record of your health.

Exercise 10-6　Keeping Your Health Records

Complete the following questions and activities to create a personal health profile. File the information in a convenient, easy to reach place so you can access it when necessary.

Health insurance policy numbers and phone numbers:

_____

Immunization record (if you have a written record from your doctor, just include it in your file):

_____

_____

_____

Your personal medical history:

Surgeries (include dates) _____

Hospital stays (dates and reasons) _____

_____

Allergies _____

Diseases _____

Prescribed drugs and dosages _____

Any adverse (bad) drug reactions _____

Family medical history (diseases your parents, grandparents, or brothers and sisters have)

_____

_____

You have a right to copy any of your medical records, blood work, eyeglass prescriptions, and so on. Keep these copies in your file. In addition, keep photocopies of your insurance cards in case you lose them or your wallet or purse is stolen. In fact, it is a good idea to photocopy the front and back of all your credit cards, insurance cards, and licenses so you know what you have to replace and have easy access to phone numbers to cancel cards and order replacements. Keep these copies safe and secure to prevent identity theft.

10.2i   Avoiding Harmful Substances

Medication can play an important role in maintaining health and wellness, particularly when prescribed to treat illness. However, *drug abuse*—using prescription or over-the-counter medication for nonmedical reasons or using illegal drugs—harms the mind, body, and spirit.

People abuse drugs for many reasons: pleasure, peer pressure, or escapism. Continued use leads to *addiction.* Addiction can involve being *physically dependent* (your body needs the drug to function) or *psychologically dependent* (you believe you need it to function). Drug abuse causes harm to the user and their family, friends, coworkers, and employers. Remember, drug abuse not only causes devastating personal health issues but also wreaks havoc in the lives of those close to the abuser. Let's start with tobacco use.

Tobacco   Tobacco contains the addictive substance *nicotine,* which leads to physical and psychological addiction. Smoking is the number-one preventable cause of *respiratory diseases* (diseases related to the lungs and breathing). It can damage your lungs and cause chronic diseases like bronchitis, emphysema, and asthma. In addition, smoking makes it more likely that you'll get lung infections and colds as well as sinus infections. Approximately 80 percent of all lung cancers can be traced to smoking. Smoking also affects the heart and, along with excessive drinking, increases your risk for stomach and mouth cancers.

Smoking hurts not only smokers but also those around them. Mothers who smoke while pregnant tend to have babies with lower birth weights, are at increased risk for giving birth *prematurely* (before the baby's due date), and experience higher rates of SIDS (sudden infant death syndrome). And while we're talking about babies and children, don't forget about the hazards of secondhand smoke in the home. Secondhand smoking is when a nonsmoker is near someone smoking and unintentionally inhales that person's smoke. (At least the smoker has a filter!) According to the CDC, it causes forty-one thousand deaths a year in the United States. It is especially dangerous to children. In homes that have at least one smoking parent, children are more likely to have bronchitis, asthma, and ear infections, and their lungs may develop more slowly than other children.

Smokeless tobacco, or chewing tobacco, is also very dangerous. Chewing increases your risk of getting mouth cancers and can cause digestive problems. (Besides, it's a pretty disgusting habit!)

If you smoke, quit! You must be motivated and truly want to stop harming yourself and those around you. There is plenty of help available. Nicotine patches and gum, available without a prescription, can reduce the craving for cigarettes. The gum and patches still contain nicotine, but not the thousands of other dangerous chemicals contained in the smoke. E-cigarettes are another alternative. They may be safer than traditional cigarettes, but they still contain nicotine—and don't think they're 100 percent safe. They contain other chemicals too. Here are some other hints for quitting smoking:

- Seek out support groups and friends who have quit (or want to)
- Avoid situations that make you want to smoke
- Use healthy substitutes like exercise or walking to get your mind off smoking
- Substitute carrots or celery or other healthy alternatives for cigarettes in your hands
- Set goals and make contracts with trusted friends

Real-Life Application

Success Story

When the author was in college, a good friend of his smoked two packs of cigarettes a day. Every day for one year, the author put aside the same amount of money his friend spent on cigarettes. At that time, cigarettes were 50¢ a pack. At the end of the year, the author was able to buy a large TV. This shocked the author's friend so much that he stopped smoking. With today's prices, consider someone who is spending $6 a day on cigarettes. That is $6 × 365 days—about $2,200 a year. That's enough to buy a *great* TV, not to mention the benefits of being healthier.

Alcohol Although drinking alcohol is legal (if you are over the age limit and don't drive while under the influence), alcohol is actually the most abused drug in the United States. It can cause many physical and mental problems and affects the entire body. Alcohol disrupts the quality of your sleep, makes it harder for the body to take in nutrients, slows your reflexes, causes you to make poor or harmful decisions, and damages your liver. For students, the use of alcohol can cause them to miss class, have unprotected sex, and can cause accidents. Take the quiz in Exercise 10-7 to assess your drinking.

Food for Thought

- Nearly six hundred thousand students are injured each year because of alcohol.
- Approximately 25 percent of students report poor academic performance due to alcohol-related issues.
- Over 2 million students drive under the influence each year.
- Each year, some four hundred thousand students have unprotected sex while under the influence of alcohol.

Exercise 10-7   Do You Have a Problem with Alcohol?

Answer yes or no to the following questions:

_____ Do you drink when you feel depressed?

_____ Do you feel a need to drink at certain times (like before bed or after meals)?

_____ Have you tried to stop drinking but found you couldn't?

_____ Do other people tell you they are concerned about your drinking?

_____ Do you try to hide your drinking?

_____ Do you need larger and larger amounts to get the desired effect?

_____ Do you continue to drink even if it is having an impact on your health?

_____ Do you drink and drive?

_____ Do you drink to escape or become someone else?

_____ Do you drink every day?

_____ Do you drink alone?

_____ Do you feel "shaky" and need to drink to make it stop?

The scoring is pretty simple. You have a problem if you answered yes to any of the questions, and you need to seek professional counseling. In addition, support groups such as Alcoholics Anonymous (AA) can help you with your problem.

Illegal Drugs   Some people abuse medication that you can buy at the store, also known as over-the-counter (OTC) drugs. For example, taking *antihistamines* (found in cold medicine) can cause sleepiness and accidents. Some people choose to use illegal drugs to get a desired feeling or to escape their problems. However, the feeling doesn't last long, and these people need more and more of the drug each time they take it, which leads to addiction. In addition, their problems get worse rather than better after they come down from their high. Often, they behave irresponsibly while high, which creates even more problems in their lives and in the lives of those around them.

Table 10-5 lists some commonly abused drugs and some of their major negative effects.

Table 10-5   Abused Drugs and Their Negative Effects

Drug*	Negative Effects
Heroin	Overdose is deadly; injecting the drug can spread AIDS and hepatitis through infected needle use.
Cocaine (including crack)	Highly addictive stimulant that can cause a deadly overdose and heart damage.
Marijuana	Natural substance that alters the mind and causes lack of concentration, coordination, and slow reflexes. Can lead to car and other accidents because people think they can function properly.
Ecstasy	Causes nausea, vision problems, hallucinations, and depression. Long-term use causes permanent brain damage, depression, and memory loss.
Amphetamines	Can lead to unhealthy weight loss, malnourishment, and pain. Prolonged use can cause violence and aggressive behavior.
Sedatives	Slows or stops breathing.
Inhalants (huffing glue and aerosols)	Damages brain, liver, and kidneys.
Anabolic steroids (muscle enhancers)	Many side effects; women become more masculine in appearance (shrinking of breasts, growth of body hair, baldness, and deepened voice); men get high blood pressure, lowered sperm count, acne, heart problems, and sexual dysfunction. Causes liver and kidney damage in both sexes.

*Note: All illegal drug use violates the law and can lead to a prison sentence.

Most drug abuse happens because the person feels helpless, has low self-esteem, or feels a need to escape. Treatment (through counseling and support groups) can help with these problems. Addiction should be treated with medical care in addition to counseling. *Detoxification centers* provide a controlled environment to help addicts get past the withdrawal period. Of course, the *best* treatment is preventative: Don't start taking drugs in the first place.

If you are using a recreational drug and want to see if you have a problem, go back to Exercise 10-7. Take the same assessment but substitute your drug's name for *alcohol*.

10.3   Healthy Lifestyle Choices

So far, you have read about proper eating, exercise, sleep, and avoiding illness and harmful substances. Some other lifestyle choices can help you have a longer, healthier, and happier life. Here are some basic choices, with examples:

Choose to Keep Safe:

- Statistics prove that one thing you can do to increase your life expectancy is wear your seat belt.

- Don't drink and drive.

- Don't walk alone at night, and keep your car and home locked and secure.

Choose *Preventative* Health:

- While many health problems are treatable, it's always better to avoid a problem than to have to fix it. *Preventative care* focuses on taking good care of yourself so that you stay healthy instead of trying to treat health problems only as they happen (think back to the section on *proactive* and *reactive thinking*).

- Prevent illnesses by maintaining a good diet and exercise program, along with healthy life choices.

- Make regular visits to your doctor, dentist, and eye-care specialist.

- Consult a specialist right away for new conditions, such as hearing loss.

- Cavities and poor oral hygiene can lead to diabetes and heart attacks. In fact, the simple act of flossing will enhance your health and prevent heart disease. That's because bacteria that grows in the mouth can escape into the bloodstream and cause problems throughout the body.

- Know the possible causes and warning signs of cancer. Any number of triggers can make a cell cancerous, including genes, radiation, sunlight exposure, smoking, poor diet, viruses, and chemical exposure. Some of these triggers, like genes or some viruses, are difficult to avoid. However, many types of cancer can be prevented or managed with a healthy diet and exercise.

    See Figure 10-4 for the possible causes and warning signs of cancer.

Choose a Safe Home and Work Environment:

- To avoid hearing loss, wear ear protection to safeguard against loud noise. Damage to the ear is *cumulative* (it adds up over time), so there is no better time to start than right now.

Noise protection will prevent hearing loss in later years.

- Special eyewear should be worn to protect your eyes at certain jobs and during some recreational activities.

- Wear protective clothing and masks if you are going to come in contact with dangerous substances or fumes or if you work in dusty areas.

- *Carpal tunnel syndrome* is related to repetitive motion, such as typing on a keyboard, playing a piano, or hammering. It involves nerve damage and can lead to numbness in the fingers. Making sure your keyboard is at the right height and taking periodic breaks from typing and using your mouse will help prevent this condition.

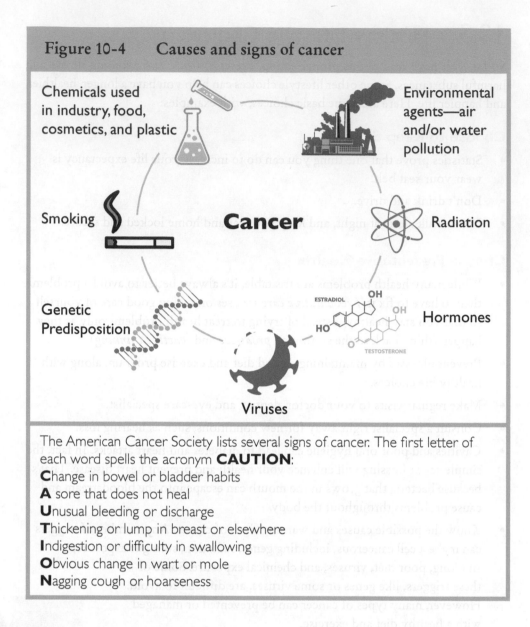

Figure 10-4   Causes and signs of cancer

Chemicals used in industry, food, cosmetics, and plastic

Environmental agents—air and/or water pollution

Smoking

Cancer

Radiation

Genetic Predisposition

Hormones

Viruses

The American Cancer Society lists several signs of cancer. The first letter of each word spells the acronym **CAUTION**:

Change in bowel or bladder habits
A sore that does not heal
Unusual bleeding or discharge
Thickening or lump in breast or elsewhere
Indigestion or difficulty in swallowing
Obvious change in wart or mole
Nagging cough or hoarseness

10.3a   Choose to Understand Important Health Issues

An important wellness issue is mental health. One study shows more than 30 percent of first-year students often feel overwhelmed. We talked about stress and how to manage it, but what if these feelings continue to be overwhelming? Everyone has ups and downs in life, but depression is a feeling that no matter what you do, things will go wrong and never work out.

According to the National Institute of Mental Health, depression affects about 20 million people in the United States each year. It is a widespread illness that is often misunderstood and undiagnosed. Some people wrongly view depression as a personal weakness. These people think the solution is to "toughen up." However, the fact is that there is often a biological and genetic component behind depression.

Being sad following a tragedy or the loss of a loved one is natural, but if that sadness continues for a very long time and affects your daily living and work, it is most likely depression. Sometimes individuals are in a state of depression for so long that they get used to it and can no longer recognize the symptoms. Here are some common symptoms:

- Loss of interest in life
- Frequent crying
- Sleep changes (either sleeping too much or too little)
- Decreased energy and sex drive
- Appetite changes (either eating too much or too little)
- Feelings of worthlessness, helplessness, and "doom and gloom"
- Increased irritability
- Problems with concentration and memory
- Suicidal thoughts
- Decreased academic/work performance
- Isolation from friends and family

Depression is treatable. Medication, psychological therapy, or a combination of the two can help. If you see these signs in a friend, do all you can to get that friend to seek professional help. If you see these signs in yourself, reach out to a trusted friend and seek professional help.

Test Yourself

Depression

State whether the following is true or false:

_____ Teenagers can't "really" be depressed.

_____ Depressed people are just weak.

_____ Talking about depression makes it worse.

_____ People who talk about suicide never go through with it.

These statements are all false. There are many misconceptions about depression—and mental illness, in general, for that matter. Too often, mental health issues have been *stigmatized* (treated as shameful), causing people to hide their conditions. We don't hide the fact that we have the flu or a broken arm, why should we hide the fact that we have been very sad for a long time (depression) and need help?

10.4   Spiritual Wellness

Just what is spiritual wellness? The human spirit is that undefinable thing that makes us question who we are, why we exist, and what our purpose is. Although people don't all agree about religion, everyone can see that human beings are capable of questioning things beyond our day-to-day existence. This questioning nature is what we call *spirit*. It drives us to better ourselves, our communities, and even the world. In Exercise 10-8, you'll have an opportunity to explore your spirit.

Part of spiritual exploration is trying to find out who you are. During the Middle Ages, most people could not read, so symbols and pictures were used for communication. Knights had a *coat of arms* painted on their shields to identify who they were. This visual representation quickly showed what they stood for and what they believed in.

Traditional Coat of Arms Example

Reflect and answer the following questions, and then draw a coat of arms that symbolically represents you. Have fun, and be creative!

Who are the special people in my life?

_____

_____

What is my ethnic background and heritage? _____

_____

What are some traditions and customs that are important to my family and myself?

_____

_____

What do I do best? _____

_____

What kind of books, movies, and music do I like?_____

_____

What are my dreams for my future? _____

_____

(continues)

What activities do I like? _____

_____

What is really important to me? _____

_____

If I had a motto, what would it be? _____

_____

What do I do that improves life for my family, friends, or community? ____

_____

Using inspiration from your answers, draw your personal coat of arms.

Some suggestions to develop your spiritual wellness:

- Always search for a higher meaning to your life.
- Commit to making your community a better place. You can volunteer for organizations such as the American Cancer Society, American Heart Association, Easterseals, or local help centers.
- You can give back by reading books at a children's hospital or donating blood.
- Work with Habitat for Humanity, an organization that builds houses for the poor.
- Volunteer for Special Olympics, where you can make a big difference by simply cheering for someone.

Now that we have come to the end of the chapter, we wish you a happy, safe, and successful journey through life and hope this book serves as a helpful travel guide. Keep this book handy so you can refer to it down the road. One day, you may need to brush up on your résumé writing or time and stress management skills, your team and leadership abilities, or reassess your personal wellness. How easily we forget! The road may get bumpy along the way, so don't be afraid to pull over and take a look at this manual every so often. Continue to maintain your vehicle for success using what you've learned and always remember, you are the driver.

Healthy Decision-Making

Jules's father smoked two packs of cigarettes a day and died of lung cancer. Jules misses his father, especially now that he has become a father himself (he has a two-year-old daughter). Jules has returned to school to better his life, but the added stress has caused him to start smoking again. In addition, he has stopped exercising. He's already feeling less energetic than he used to. He's concerned about doing well in school. This fear is driving him to smoke more. What are some suggestions you can give Jules to help him (and his family)?

_____

_____

_____

_____

_____

_____

_____

_____

_____

_____

Know Your School

Your school has support services to help with wellness, whether you are experiencing a wellness problem or simply want to better your life. Identify school resources that can help you. Examples would include any personal counseling services, the school health center, and any wellness centers or gyms. List the information here, and for quick reference, place the information in a prominent place such as on your refrigerator.

Resource Name: _____

Office Location: _____

Phone Number: _____

Email Address: _____

Resource Name: _____

Office Location: _____

Phone Number: _____

Email Address: _____

Resource Name: _____

Office Location: _____

Phone Number: _____

Email Address: _____

Resource Name: _____

Office Location: _____

Phone Number: _____

Email Address: _____

Resource Name: _____

Office Location: _____

Phone Number: _____

Email Address: _____

Appendix

Answer Key for Exercise 8-6:
Consensus Exercise

1. You would have to light the match first.

2. You can infer that *-cyte* means "cell" and *phag-* means "to swallow." Therefore, a *phagocyte* is a cell that swallows (or digests debris).

3. Seven combinations:

   1 nickel, 1 dime, 1 quarter

   3 nickels, 1 quarter

   4 dimes

   3 dimes, 2 nickels

   8 nickels

   6 nickels, 1 dime

   4 nickels, 2 dimes

4. 2,200 ft. Remember, it has to travel there and back.

5. Zero—roosters do not lay eggs.

6. The squirrel has two ears on its head.

7. Maria.

8. Zero, Moses did not have an ark, Noah did.

Glossary

Acronym
When you take the first letter of each word you want to memorize and put them together to form an abbreviation or new word

Acrostic
Traditionally, when the first letter of each line of a poem or other written work together spell out a word; also when you take the first letter of each word you want to memorize, often in a specific order, and use them to create a sentence where all the words start with those initial letters

Active listening
Paying close attention to both the verbal and nonverbal messages you are receiving and seeking to truly understand them

Asynchronous distance education
Where online bulletin boards, chat rooms, and text dialogues are the main form of interaction

Bad stress
Stress that is overwhelming and counterproductive; also known as *distress*

Conscious mind
The part of the mind we are most aware of and that involves day-to-day thoughts

Creative thinking
Thinking that's designed to *generate* (come up with) *ideas* rather than judge them

Critical thinking
Looking at facts or ideas without emotion or opinion, using logic to make a decision

Deductive reasoning
A form of logical thinking where you reach a *definite* conclusion (or answer) based on facts, called *premises* (If the premises are true, the conclusion *must be* true.)

Emotional intelligence (EQ)
A kind of social intelligence that involves being aware of your own emotions and those of others and using that information to guide your thinking and actions

External locus of control
The belief that someone or something else controls your life

Feedback
In communication, information sent from the receiver back to the transmitter about the message

Filter
In communication, any barriers the message must pass through (like noise, distractions, or a lack of attention on the part of the receiver)

Fixed expenses
Things that cost you the same amount every month, like rent or a mortgage

Good stress
Stress that is necessary to progress and succeed; also known as *eustress*

Grants
Financial aid that does not need to be paid back later; most are based on need

Gross income
The total money you receive from all sources

Group
Two or more people who interact to complete tasks, achieve goals, or fulfill needs

Hard skills
Skills related to one's knowledge and ability to perform a specific task or activity

Inductive reasoning
A form of logical thinking where you reach a *likely* conclusion (or answer) based on facts, called premises (If the premises are true, the conclusion is *probably* true.)

Information literacy
Being able to figure out *what* you need to know, *where* that information can be found, *whether* it is accurate and credible, and *how* to use it

Integrated thinking
A model of the thinking process that breaks it down into five steps: (1) opportunity for positive change, (2) idea generation (creative thinking), (3) decision-making (critical thinking), (4) implementation and evaluation, and 5) feedback, all of which are affected by the environment

Interest
The amount you must pay back in addition to the amount you borrowed

Internal locus of control
The belief that you control your own life

Locus of control
Your belief about who or what controls your life

Mnemonics
Words, rhymes, or other devices that help you remember

Multiple intelligences
A theory by Howard Gardner that we each have many different types of intelligence, some of which are more developed than others

Net income
Your gross income minus things like taxes, social security, and insurance, which are deducted; also known as take-home pay

Objective exam
A test where your answers are either right or wrong, including multiple-choice questions, true or false questions, and other items where your answers are either correct or incorrect

Parliamentary procedure
A set of rules that describe how to run a large group meeting

Plagiarism
Using someone else's work (partially or as a whole) without giving credit, including trying to pretend it's your own; also, reusing your own work without specifying where and how it was used before (sometimes called *self-plagiarism*)

Proactive thinking
When you try to predict what problems might occur in the future and prevent them from happening

Procrastination
When you put off doing something until the last possible minute

Reactive thinking
When you wait for a problem to arise and then try to fix it

Scholarships
Financial aid that does not need to be paid back later; can be based on need, achievement, community service, or other factors

Self-fulfilling prophecy
When you make something true by acting like it's true

Soft skills
Personal attributes that enhance career prospects and performance on the job

Stress reaction
How our minds and bodies react to events, people, and situations in our lives, largely shaped by our perceptions

Subconscious mind
The part of the mind we are mostly unaware of and that is involved with survival

Subjective exam
A test where your answers will be judged on more than whether they're right or wrong, including essay questions, where *how well* you make your point can be as important as whether you are correct

Subsidized student loans
Low-interest loans supported by the federal government; may not need to be paid back until after graduation

Synchronous distance education
Where students and faculty log in at the same time, sometimes with face-to-face interaction over video chat

Team
A group whose members interact *with focused intensity* to complete a shared, specific goal

Transferable skills
Those skills you can carry from one job to another or use in a variety of careers

Value
A standard used to assess oneself and others; a principle that you consider important and by which you live your life

Variable expenses
Things that don't always cost the same amount, like food

Index